# War and Money

# War and Money

The Imperialism of the Dollar

Maurizio Lazzarato

*Translated by Jason Francis Mc Gimsey*

London • New York

This English-language edition first published by Verso 2025
Translation © Jason Francis Mc Gimsey 2025
First published as *Guerra e moneta. Imperialismo del dollaro, neoliberalismo, rotture rivoluzionarie*
© DeriveApprodi 2023

The manufacturer's authorized representative in the EU for product safety (GPSR) is LOGOS EUROPE, 9 rue Nicolas Poussin, 17000, La Rochelle, France
contact@logoseurope.eu

All rights reserved

The moral rights of the author and translator have been asserted

1 3 5 7 9 10 8 6 4 2

**Verso**
UK: 6 Meard Street, London W1F 0EG
US: 207 East 32nd Street, New York, NY 10016
versobooks.com

Verso is the imprint of New Left Books

ISBN-13: 978-1-80429-656-1
ISBN-13: 978-1-80429-657-8 (UK EBK)
ISBN-13: 978-1-80429-658-5 (US EBK)

**British Library Cataloguing in Publication Data**
A catalogue record for this book is available from the British Library

**Library of Congress Cataloging-in-Publication Data**
A catalog record for this book is available from the Library of Congress

Typeset in Minion by Hewer Text UK Ltd, Edinburgh
Printed and bound by CPI Group (UK) Ltd, Croydon CR0 4YY

# Contents

Introduction 1
    Imperialism is money and war 3
    Debunking war 6

Chapter 1
    What is to be done? 13
    From imperialism to superimperialism 14
    Continuity and discontinuity 21
    The dollar and war 24
    The war that was already there! 31
    The consequences of war 35
    On imperialism 38
    'Political error' according to Rosa Luxemburg 42
    Nationalism, an invention of capitalism 45

## Chapter 2

| | |
|---|---:|
| Capitalism is not neoliberalism | 49 |
| Why neoliberalism is not capitalism | 54 |
| Marx and triple centralization | 56 |
| Political and military centralization | 59 |
| Lenin and the new capitalism: Imperialism | 62 |
| The supremacy of monopoly over competition | 65 |
| The counterrevolutionary 1970s | 67 |
| Neoliberalism is maximum centralization | 70 |
| War's totalization | 72 |
| Centralization: Institutional democracy/democracy of capitalism | 74 |
| Towards world civil war? | 83 |
| Democracy or oligarchy? | 89 |

## Chapter 3

| | |
|---|---:|
| War and neoliberalism | 93 |
| War: Prerequisite for the international division of labour and power | 96 |
| The constituent power of revolutionary civil war | 98 |
| Neoliberalism: Prototype for contradictory critical thinking | 103 |
| Rent and human capital | 108 |
| 100 Orders | 116 |
| Return to cyclical theory: The political controls the economic | 118 |
| What is neoliberalism? An ideology? | 120 |
| Rationality and its critique | 123 |
| Foucault 'the Revolutionary' | 125 |

## Chapter 4

| | |
|---|---|
| Theories of money and dollar imperialism | 129 |
| Marx and money | 133 |
| Money flows and power | 139 |
| The state/capital machine | 141 |
| Industrial capital and financial capital | 144 |
| A return to imperialism: The functions of state and capital | 147 |
| Imperialism as analysis of power | 148 |
| Imperialism: Permanent phase of capitalism | 158 |

## Chapter 5

| | |
|---|---|
| Time are a-changin' | 163 |
| How to understand war | 165 |
| Attacker/attacked, or the categories of imperialist ideology | 170 |
| The new political phase | 171 |
| Emancipation and revolution | 175 |
| Emancipatory movements | 180 |
| Identity of production and destruction | 186 |
| The new subject and new knowledge | 189 |
| Many emancipations, one revolution? | 196 |

*Index*     203

# Introduction

The current wars in Ukraine and Gaza oblige us to redefine capitalism and its dynamics, as well as the state and its strategies that have, until today, excluded the very concept of war itself. But, above all, they force us to question the future of class conflict. From the beginning of the twentieth century, civil war was conducted – sometimes clandestinely, sometimes openly – under the political forms of liberalism and democracy but were, for a brief period, possible to transform into revolution. Are we now sliding towards a new form of world civil war?

Ever since the postwar period, capitalism has gone through different types of conflict based on power relations between classes, and according to whether these conflicts developed in the North or in the South, in the centre or in the periphery. Between 1945 and 1970, civil war against fascism in the West created a democracy based on political parties, an updated version of citizen democracy, in which the conflict between capital and labour functioned as a dialectical engine for the development of both democratic institutions and the economy, while, at the same time, socialist or civil wars of national liberation raged in the South. After the demise of the world revolution in the 1970s, after the civil wars in Latin America, after the political victories of Thatcher and Reagan over the working class in the North, and after the victory of the right wing of the Cultural Revolution in China, the uneasy truce between postwar capital and labour was unilaterally repudiated, both by the state and capital. Counterrevolution completely neutralized party democracy, marginalizing and criminalizing the forms of conflict that had been based on the capital-labour compromise, and dictated a logic of confrontation that would become direct after 2008. The great financial crisis opened a third phase where class polarizations and tensions between states further deepened. Conflict, once repressed and rejected as a fundamental element for balancing of the entire system, re-emerged as war and civil war. The most advanced struggles in the North (labour strikes in Europe in 2022 and 2023), as well as the insurgencies that have been bubbling throughout the South since 2011 (for example, in Egypt, Chile, Iran), both show that there is no room for negotiation, nor compromise, in the dialectics of conflict. The extraordinary sequence of the French struggles (the *gilets jaunes* [yellow vests], the massive mobilizations against pension reform, the simultaneous environmental struggles in the same period, and revolt of the *banlieues* soon thereafter) exemplifies a total blockade imposed by a power structure that responds only in warlike and legal ways, via the police and the courts respectively.

With the ecological war, we have the necessary conditions to intensify a world civil war. It is as if ruling classes are aware that the conditions – neither Keynesian (public policies), nor Schumpeterian (great innovations), nor ecological, nor geopolitical (the South now rejects its secular despoliation for new accumulation) – no longer exist for a further transformation of capitalism. Hence the need for austerity, servile and precarious work, the destruction of welfare, and the imperative need to nullify, neutralize, and criminalize all conflict, because the system has no margin for any compromise. Only a revolution will be able to civilize the future, now looming with destruction and death. Only a radical rupture will be able to curb the unleashing of all kinds of violence, misery, fascism, racism, and sexism that already abound – provided, however, we do not deceive ourselves and we remember that revolution and rupture, inherently, cannot be peaceful.

War, in all its variations – class war, race war, sex war, neocolonial war – is capitalism's regime of truth. In a single century (1914–2022), capitalism has brought humanity to the edge of the abyss four times: the First

World War, the Second World War, the Cold War, and the present wars. Whether it is competitive or monopoly capitalism, Fordism or financialization; whether a new capitalism has been invented every day, as since the 1980s (immaterial capitalism, cognitive capitalism, biopolitical capitalism, neuronal capitalism, platform capitalism, reproduction capitalism, ITC capitalism, logistical capitalism); whether the rule of liberalism, Keynesianism, or neoliberalism is imposed – war still arrives, like clockwork, with astonishing regularity.

Before the war in Ukraine, did Europe really enjoy seventy years of peace? Throughout the Cold War, a third position between peace and war settled in ('improbable war, impossible peace,' said Raymond Aron). With the collapse of the Soviet Union, a relatively frozen world civil war – partly controlled (in the North), partly active (in the global South) – has become the only possible, and now current, reality.

Capitalism has, since the late nineteenth century, become imperialist. Samir Amin would instead say that it has *always* been imperialist. A problematic category, rejected by Antonio Negri and Michael Hardt, and ignored by Gilles Deleuze and Michel Foucault. This is not the same imperialism experienced by Lenin or Rosa Luxemburg, because it is no longer territorial, but rather monetary and financial. It is an even more sophisticated, predatory imperialism – an imperialism that, like others, I call 'dollar imperialism', in which profit and rent tend to blur. Its action is not limited to what Marx calls 'capital', but is directly integrated into the war machine: the state, both its bureaucratic-administrative and military functions. Of the four main features of Lenin's imperialism that are acutely accentuated in contemporary capitalism – financialization, colonization, monopoly, and war – the latter seems to me the most significant, because it constitutes a novelty that Marx's *Capital* did not yet contemplate as an indispensable condition of capitalist accumulation.

## Imperialism is money and war

The formation of imperialism has radically altered both economics and politics. Capital and the state political system (including administrative and military bureaucracy) complement each other, constituting a machine that does not, however, completely annul their specificities: capital pursues an infinite accumulation of profit and the state an equally infinite accumulation of force. Together, they function in a complementary manner, constructing a new concept of sovereignty and state. Carl von Clausewitz's famous statement, 'war is the continuation of politics by other means,' should be supplemented with the following: war is the continuation of economics by other means. More precisely, politics and economics are the terrain of class struggles, and war and civil war are a continuation of them. What remains of social movements fails to see politics, economics, or class struggle in war. They do not realize it is a structural and strategic condition of capitalism. If they cannot see this, why should they care about a war between imperialisms? For today's social movements, the coming world civil war seems like something from another galaxy.

Imperialism is the right of life and death over the populations of the entire planet. The power to 'make die or let live' (the sovereign's right, in Foucault's vocabulary) has not been replaced by the power to make live or reject in death – or governmentality, which, instead of repressing, preventing, and blocking, would act positively on life, favouring and increasing its development. War, imperialism, but also, in a different way, monopolies (the 'sovereigns' in economics) remind us that this opposition is either false or ideological.

US imperialism, through its trade deficit, inaugurates not only the hegemony of the dollar, but also a debt economy that is the foundation of accumulation in globalization: the colossal US debt ensures an outlet for Chinese goods, and the Chinese reinvest the astronomical sums of dollars accumulated in financing the debt itself (investing in finance and real estate). This globalization is challenged by war because, while, in the short term, it has safeguarded American hegemony and the so-called American way of life, in the long run, it has economically and politically reinforced the global South, which must instead remain radically subordinate to the dollar. In attacking this complementarity between the US and China, the South condemns globalization to failure. The value chains and exchange in globalization become political and are only possible between allies.

Under no circumstances can capitalism be identified with neoliberalism. The latter is but a series of devices for – temporarily and partially – managing capital, while capitalism surpasses and dominates it. Michel Foucault was the first to make the mistake of conflating the two, creating a catastrophic theoretical and political confusion in critical thought that has only worsened over time. Capitalism has got rid of neoliberal governmentality, as it had with classical liberalism a century earlier, moving to new forms of populism, fascism, civil war, and ultimately war, in order to defend the interests of the owning classes.

The principles and rules of dollar imperialism are different from, and indeed contrary to, the principles and rules of neoliberalism. Imperialism is built at the intersection of a threefold centralization of power in the hands of a very few: economic centralization (industrial monopolies and oligopolies, but especially currency); political centralization (the executive usurping the legislative); and military centralization (professional armies). Together, they eliminate or reduce the market, competition, and free enterprise – the alpha and omega of neoliberalism – to insignificant phenomena. These centralizations are not *automatic*, but the work of *political strategies*. Normal competitive market forces, which are supposed to ensure balance and prevent war, are being replaced by the strategies of investment groups, multinational corporations, pension funds, and, above all, large states. These actors dictate power relations through economics, politics, and military action; in combining economic, technological, and monetary warfare they lead us eventually to armed confrontation. This so-called competition is not strictly economic; it is a struggle between great economic-political powers that is regulated not by the market, but rather by direct power relations and war.

Capitalism has always imposed a precise hierarchy, still active today: government is subordinate to the infinite accumulation of profit and the infinite accumulation of power. Imperialist policies include financialization, privatization, wage freezes, the precarization of the workforce, neocolonialism, the transformation of redistributive policies (welfare) into a source of finance for corporations and the wealthy, postponement of retirement, racism, and sexism. Neoliberalism can only maintain such policies over short periods: they are the conditions for capturing globally produced value through the dollar, credit currency, and finance. Neoliberalism merely governs the interests of US monetary financial imperialism before it is set aside. It must neutralize any conflict that threatens its naturalization. This is the first task of 'governmentality'! And it is also its greatest failure: removing class struggle, conflict, and direct confrontation results in open warfare between states, and in low-intensity civil war.

## Debunking war

War debunks, beyond any doubt, both the proponents of the identity of neoliberalism and capitalism, as well as the critics of the concept of imperialism.

Contemporary war is a clash between imperialisms for a new division of power in the world market: a global imperialism (the US) and a regional imperialism (Russia), where reach is still limited. What China lacks – according to the Chinese themselves – is not a large army, but a currency that functions at both a national and an international level. This is one of the main reasons why the rise of Chinese hegemony at the expense of the Americans, as predicted by Giovanni Arrighi, does not appear to be realistic in the short to medium term. It is also one of the reasons for an emerging period of conflict, instability, unpredictability, and chaos that is likely to last for quite a while.

The main cause of war is the gradual weakening of Western economies (from 80 per cent of world production down to 40 per cent) and their technological and scientific monopolies, which, once absolute, have become relative.[1] The only great supremacy of the West (which calls itself

---

1 Biden says: 'As a nation, years ago – 35 years ago, we invested 2 percent of our entire GDP in research and development. We do half of that now. We do half of that. We used to be number one in the world. Now we're number 13 in the world. My administration – we're changing that. The United States used to own the innovation field. In fact, it was a Department [of Defense] research program that established DARPA. It was the first development of an anti-tank missile with advanced infrared guidance systems that culminated in today's Javelin. The Bipartisan Innovation Act is

an international community, in spite of the fact that it comprises only one-third of the world's population) is its military and arms production. Exporting Western values – first and foremost, so-called democracy – has slammed up against the global South because, for these countries, the 'democracy' of the West is merely the imposition of imperialist interests. But at the heart of the current clash is the monetary and financial system built on the dollar. Bringing the South out of dependence on the dollar and US finance is the fundamental reason for building (regional) monetary and financial regimes disengaged from the tyranny of US currency and finance. Every step in this direction is a declaration of war against the US because it weakens the mechanism that guarantees US hegemony and thereby endangers the American way of life, the colossal waste paid for by the rest of the world. Through the dollar and finance, the US is using a new form of colonization to which its allies (Europe, Japan, England) are also subjected.

Europe – a docile US colony – is in the forefront of the war against Russia. But it is, above all, at war with itself, because it is serving American interests whose goal is to reduce the European (essentially the German) economy to the same condition as the Japanese economy – that is, permanent stagnation. Politically, the war has already replaced the Franco-German axis with the US–UK–East-European-countries axis, with Poland at its centre. Italy's neofascist prime minister, Giorgia Meloni, told the truth about the kind of Europe the US is preparing for us with the war: Poland, the most right-wing, most reactionary, most sexist, most homophobic, most anti-European country, 'is the moral and material border of the West'. Until recently, the Polish state led the European constitution of nationalisms and neofascisms imposed by the Americans, under the dumbfounded gaze of Germany and France, while the Italian government aligned itself with its eastern brothers under the cover of a so-called war of democracy against autocracy. Europeans are

---

going to help reverse decades-long decline in federal research and development investment. And it should create [jobs] and support entire families, and expand U.S. manufacturing and strengthen our national security. Where in God's name is it written that the United States can no longer be a leading manufacturer in the world?' 'Remarks by President Biden on the Security Assistance to Ukraine', 3 May 2022, whitehouse.gov.

reacting to this homegrown war with indifference, as they do with every war fought by Westerners in the South.

The political regime of dollar imperialism, the rentier economy, and financialization is not democracy, but oligarchy. The three oligarchies that dominate the American economy and politics are already turning out to be the big winners in the current war. The extractive oligarchy, having achieved the sabotage of Nord Stream 2, is cashing in on record benefits with the energy crisis triggered by the war. The armament oligarchy is at the centre of today's politics, because its production (at the limit of capacity) stimulates US growth, revealing – as if there were any need – the identity of production and destruction. The financial oligarchy, saved by government intervention immediately after 2008, is now becoming richer than ever. The naive who believe that the West is fighting to save democracy from the oligarchy are deaf and blind. They are the ideal subjects for the disaster that is brewing.[2]

Why revolution? The limit of sovereign power is not the political economy (Foucault), just as the limit of capitalism is not schizophrenia (Deleuze and Guattari's decoding acceleration). The economy in no way establishes a limit: instead, it represents imbalance, crisis, the inordinate concentration of wealth, and the production of increasing polarizations between North and South, between social classes, between states. Together with sovereign power, which amplifies both imbalance and polarization, it leads to war. Accelerating the forces of capitalism does not lead, as Deleuze, Guattari, and their accelerationist followers believe, to overcoming capital, but rather creates the conditions for war.

The only real limitation of capitalism is *revolution*; we know of no others. Only the revolution managed (temporarily) to limit capitalism/

---

2 According to Biden, trade representative of Western ideology: 'Things are changing so rapidly that we need to keep control of them. There is a battle going on in the world between autocracy and democracy. Xi Jinping, the leader of China, who I talked to . . . clearly says that democracies are not sustainable in the 21st century . . . because things are changing very rapidly and democracies require consensus . . . But that will not be the case. If that happened, the whole world would change. And thanks to you – in this first battle [in Ukraine], if you will – it is determined whether that will happen.' Ibid.

imperialism, neutralizing its greatest weapon, finance (via Keynes's 'euthanasia of the rentier') and, at the same time, gaining not only power in many colonies in the global South, but also social, economic, and political rights for the whole world (albeit differentially). With revolution out of the picture, social and political gains in wages and income have evaporated. After fifty years of counterrevolution, we have returned to a distribution of income and property that predates the Russian – and even the French – revolutions. Revolution is the only chance we have to civilize the violence of war and civil war.

Dollar imperialism not only sparked the 2008 financial crisis that sparked armed confrontation between imperialisms and low-intensity civil wars (US, Brazil, Peru), but also the many uprisings and veritable insurrections that have erupted since 2011, especially in the global South. The political and theoretical disappearance of revolution puts these social movements in serious difficulty because socialist critique has produced nothing else that is effectively able to establish favourable power relations for the oppressed. While states are aware of what is at stake, social movements have been thrown into war without realizing that this political phase has changed radically. They seem to want to continue peacetime politics, when, in fact, war shrinks or nullifies the political spaces that made these conditions possible.

Twentieth-century revolutions have always been associated with war, because capitalism, by pushing globalization to the limit and failing to achieve it, opens breaches in its ability to control and reproduce the system. Continuous and linear development has come to an end, and we are now in an epoch that has been derailed: an open, unpredictable era where the collapse of capitalism and the future of the world are at stake.

France, more than others, has shown the great political strength of the variegated and dispersed contemporary class composition. These groups have expressed themselves in radical and protracted forms of struggle: the *gilets jaunes*, or the new labour realities not represented by the trade union and leftist parties; the traditional wage earners at the origin of the French '*mars*' (March) revolt against pension reform; the ecological struggles that took place in the same period and immediately after; and the fight in the *banlieues* of the internally colonized against state racism.[3] All these struggles came up against a total blockade of power, with the refusal of any compromise. The state, from a dominant position, made no concessions. The only responses to such social movements have been violent police repression and gradually harsher and more vindictive class justice: governmentality exercised through frontal confrontation without mediation. This formidable sequence of struggles has already given us an accurate picture of the world civil war to come (actually already under way). Governmentality has been reduced to the management of a wholly negative power that has integrated the laws of the state of emergency into ordinary law by making the exception the rule.

The uprisings and insurrections taking place in both the North and the South pose the problem of revolution and civil war under these new conditions. Survivors from these social movements have neither the theoretical nor the practical tools to deal with this new political phase; they have dropped revolution, war, and civil war from their vocabulary and political agenda. Revolutions are always civil wars, while civil wars are not always revolutions. What is looming is a new world civil war, because, for the time being, no subjective forces capable of transforming it – of civilizing it – into revolution, have emerged.

Neoliberal governmentality is the entirely ideological project of a process that has also been adopted by critical thinking, *making the negative – the actions introduced by capitalism and the state, branded as a tool of dialectics – positive*. In this vision, power is not prohibitive, but rather inciting, urging, fostering; neoliberalism is neither domination nor repression, but rather production, or something that increases the capacity of forces to act. The negative (exploitation, racism, sexism, wars of all kinds) – which had never disappeared – stubbornly deploys all its destructive power in the war between imperialisms, and shows that it has little to do with dialectics. War is the impossibility of synthesis, conciliation, compromise. Instead, it must determine the victor and the vanquished, and only from the subordination and subjection of the latter to the former can it create synthesis, conciliation, pacts, and a kind of peace.

---

3   Translator's note: *mars* as in the month of March 2020.

The critical thought that excluded the negative in the 1960s is late to the war – not this war, but the First World War. During a previous cycle of globalization, production and destruction already tended to coincide. The Great War was an intense socialization of production and labour, aimed at destruction. Today, after a century, production and destruction correspond perfectly, and not only in war. The rejection of the negative is one of the major contradictions produced by the theories of the 1960s and 1970s, because history still continues to advance through its negative side. It is the reason why we did not see war coming and merely take note of ecological disaster; the latter is simply a by-product of the identity of production and destruction, something ecologists fail to integrate into their politics.

'There is no longer an outside. Thus the ultimate stage of globalization appears . . . Static and compact immanence: neither caesuras, nor voids, nor lines of escape, nor any way out,' writes Donatella Di Cesare.[4] There is no longer an outside, Negri and Hardt announced even earlier, in *Empire*. Nevertheless, imperialism creaks on all sides, conspicuous breaches open in its domination/control. Caesuras of all kinds manifest themselves: insurrections, revolts, civil wars, wars between states. The outside is not inevitable, but it happens, it survives. It is the 'inactual' that brings division, that imposes rupture. It comes with war, it is updated with revolts, it is embodied in insurrections. Immanence does not mean the impossibility of caesura or that there is a viable way out. Immanence means that the way out must be created, that the path out of capitalism is not already marked, but is made by walking, by organizing.

The oft-quoted statement 'it is easier to imagine the end of the world than the end of capitalism' is either false or irresponsible, a sign of ignorance of the laws of history. The state-capital machine is not destined to collapse but leads us, sooner or later, to a borderline situation, war and civil war. Capitalism regularly arrives not at its collapse but at the end of its world (of its accumulation regime). These ends have been regularly repeated since the beginning of the twentieth century. Today we are

---

4  See: Donatella Di Cesare, 'It Is Time for Philosophy to Return to the City', *Journal of Continental Philosophy* 1, no. 2 (2020), pp. 201–16.

immersed in the end of the world that was born with dollar imperialism in 1971. What worked in that world no longer works today and forces us to rethink – from a partisan point of view – a new world. This is precisely what that unfortunate statement – 'it is easier to imagine the end of the world than the end of capitalism' – invites us *not* to do, a symptom of the deep theoretical and political bewilderment of contemporary critical thought.

# Chapter 1

*Two centuries ago, a former European colony decided to catch up with Europe. It succeeded so well that the United States of America became a monster, in which the taints, the sickness and the inhumanity of Europe have grown to appalling dimensions.*

Frantz Fanon

## What is to be done?

What is to be done in the face of war? 'War is the continuation of politics by other means. Every war is inextricably connected with the political regime from which it derives.' This is the statement the revolutionaries of the twentieth century started with, to cite Clausewitz again. The first thing they did – and that we must do as well – was to define politics, social classes, the state, and the tensions of yesteryear, which all continue in today's armed clash. As we shall soon see, this is not a matter that can be taken for granted: in order to define the nature of contemporary capitalism, it is necessary to dispose of the neoliberal/biopolitical narrative (both the regime's narrative and the critical narrative) because it grossly misrepresents today's capitalism.

The actual exercise of economic and political power cannot be ascribed to the neoliberal categories of market, competition, freedom, governance, individual initiative, human capital, or entrepreneurship. Much of this narrative – accepted by critical theories as corresponding to the workings of capitalism – is power's storytelling; it constitutes ideology, because neoliberalism gives us a partial, reductive, false, and pacified image of capitalism.

The concepts that define contemporary capitalism (monopoly, finance, rent, currency, state, racism, sexism, centralization, imperialism, oligarchies, war) are radically opposed to the categories elaborated by neoliberalism and even more so to *ordoliberalism*. We will see later the absolutely subordinate and ancillary function to the American capital-state machine of what is defined as governance (or 'governmentality', in Foucault's terms).

The political movements that developed post-'68 (feminist, ecological, decolonized, and trade union movements) have, albeit from another point of view, a similarly limited and partial view of capitalism, one that makes their 'what is to be done' problematic. We will address this issue later, after defining the nature and action of the contemporary state-capital machine.

In response to the crisis of the 1960s, which was fundamentally a political crisis with world revolution as the main actor, the US state-capital machine was not inspired by post–Second World War capitalism, which produced high productivity and very high profits, but instead aimed for financial hegemony: a rent economy, colonialism, monopolies, and war – the same kind of war that had led to the First World War and fascism.

Capital has a natural tendency to financialize itself, that is, to become rent and especially to make war a structural and strategic element of its policies. Neoliberalism has the function of telling another story, with concepts supposedly different and distant from the real exercise of power on which it depends: dollar imperialism.

## From imperialism to superimperialism

In order to grasp the reasons for the ongoing war in Ukraine, let us follow Lenin's suggestions – much more useful than the misery of contemporary political analyses (Étienne Balibar, Pierre Dardot, Christian Laval, Slavoj Žižek, and Western media pundits).

'We must not take this or that example, this or that particular case [Ukraine and Russia, the reasons of the former and those of the latter]. We must take the whole policy of the entire system of European states in their economic and political interrelations if we are to understand how the present war steadily and inevitably grew out of this system.'[1]

In order not to limit ourselves to the Russia–Ukraine conflict, we must start our analysis from class relations and relations between states, as well as – an important distinction – from these relations exercised on the world market.

During Marx's and Lenin's times, the possibility of rupturing and overcoming capitalism began from the world market, but in two different ways that manifest a profound change between their two eras. For Marx, *crisis*, with its destructive violence, emerged in the world market and this renewed the possibility for rupture. Instead, for Lenin, *war* emerged in the world market, in all its destructive violence, and thus opened up the possibility of revolution.

Within the transition from the former to the latter, the strategic conflict that took place in the space of the world market was called *imperialism*.

Is 'imperialism' still the name of the struggle around which world hegemony (and within it, possibly revolutionary rupture) is played out? And is the space of the world market still the starting point from which we might understand the current war? Many theories that emerged during the development of contemporary capitalism strongly doubt this. These doubts are not about the centrality of the world economy, but rather about the relevance of the category of imperialism, considered to be tied to a bygone, and therefore theoretically useless, era.

Instead, I will focus precisely on what has been called 'American dollar imperialism', analysing the continuities and discontinuities with late-nineteenth-century and early-twentieth-century imperialism, because the

---

1  V. I. Lenin, *Collected Works*, vol. 24, Moscow: Progress Publishers, 1964, pp. 398–421.

main cause behind the unleashing of conflict between state powers is found in the crisis of hegemony that guaranteed American political supremacy over the planet until about a decade ago. In other words, the dollar and American finance guaranteed the capture of the wealth produced in the rest of the world, a prerequisite for the reproduction of the American way of life.

Imperialism, as defined by Lenin, Luxemburg, and all the revolutionaries of the first half of the twentieth century, no longer exists, but not because it has been replaced by non-sovereign and transnational devices managing neoliberal governmentality on a world scale (empire), but rather because it has become a *superimperialism*. *Super Imperialism* is the title of a book published in 1972 by a young economist, Michael Hudson. The title is the publisher's; the author would have preferred 'monetary imperialism' or 'dollar imperialism'.

So, the new imperialism I will discuss is financial and monetary in nature: an imperialism even more radical and fierce in its centralization of economic, political, and military power, which, like the imperialism that preceded it, inevitably lead to war. Thus, it is both very different and very similar from the imperialism that came before.

The most succinct definition of this imperialism can be understood through the duo of money (currency) and war, the elements which constitute its most fearsome weapons. Imperialism is the form that capitalism has taken since Lenin's time and, since then, it has only perfected, intensified, and generalized the use of both money and war. Using the term imperialism to define capitalism can function as a discriminator: critical theories developed in the North by white thinkers have virtually excluded it from their vocabulary, while it remains very much present in the South and in decolonial thought. The same thing can be seen in feminism: it is practically absent in white feminism but, on the other hand, often used in Black feminism.

Dollar imperialism's current hegemony is rooted – like everything else in the twentieth and twenty-first century – in the First World War. At the end of the war, the US was in a financially dominant position because all the victorious powers were heavily indebted to it. The US cancelled only a portion of the allied debts (those related to weapons and other equipment supplied during the period of US participation in the war). Debts incurred before the US entered the war had to be repaid. This would later be one of the main causes of the financial crisis of 1929 and the outbreak of the Second World War, because England and France were forced to demand war reparations from Germany in order to repay their huge debts to the US.

The imperial will of the economy, already dominant, was immediately manifest.

The Second World War decreed the final handover of world leadership from England to the US. During Bretton Woods, the US imposed its dollar as the currency of international trade, rejecting Keynes's proposal for an international bank, and thereby inaugurating the disproportionate power of US currency, which, functioning as both national and international currency, would become the main feature of dollar imperialism.

During negotiations with England, the US imposed a so-called free market on the perfidious Albion's trade with its colonies, abolishing all the special tariffs and protections that the British Empire had imposed in the Commonwealth. The US made clear that free markets must be the rule for all, except for those on whom it could impose duties, tariffs, and taxes at will. The British lords were astonished: 'They are treating us like Germany, as if we had lost the war.' The US' relationship with the Allies, reduced to economically and militarily dependent vassals, was immediately understood. There was no doubt who commanded and who obeyed, and what liberalism really was: a mere function of imperialism with variable geometries.

After the war, the dollar had become the hegemonic currency, but, from the American perspective, there was still a flaw in the monetary system because it was pegged to gold. Any deficit in the balance of payments would turn into an outflow of gold from the US, which, at the end of the war and in the years immediately following, held three-quarters of the world's supply.

From 1951 on, the balance of payments was always in deficit (except for a very brief period under Clinton, and evidently now, thanks to war) because of expenditures incurred to finance the Korea and Vietnam wars. Trade was at par throughout the 1950s, 1960s, and 1970s. The deficit came only from military expenditures for the wars the US waged against the 'Third World' (against the world revolution led by Communist parties). Gold kept flowing from the US reserves because France, which still had colonies in South Asia where a lot of dollars circulated due to regional conflicts, demanded (as did Germany) the conversion of its dollars into gold, even to the point of upping the percentage that the US had to guarantee (to 25 per cent), according to the agreements set in Bretton Woods.

As early as 1968, the convertibility of the dollar into gold was suspended. In 1971 Nixon officially declared inconvertibility.

The dollar's inconvertibility was an opportunity to reassert its world supremacy, already threatened in the late 1960s. Thirty years after the end of the war, Germany and Japan had, year after year, gnawed away at the economic power of the US, which in 1945 had been unchallenged. The dollar imperialism arising from inconvertibility would be immediately directed against the US' allies, Europe and Japan. The latter quickly yielded while Europe (with Germany as the main target) would cede in a gradual, humiliating manner by the time of the Ukraine war.

Let us now look at how the mechanisms of this imperialism were constructed and how they work.

Hudson's book is interesting because it came out at a time when the US was hesitating over what strategy to adopt. Hudson showed that managing world leadership from a position of debtor, rather than creditor (as had been the case until then), could bring many advantages to the US. The relationship between states is always between creditors and debtors, but the dominant power has to base its supremacy, its being a world bank, on debt and not credit.

Keeping the US balance of payments in deficit meant flooding the world with dollars (globalization is equivalent to dollarization) corresponding to US expenditure (imports, but mainly military expenditure and investment). Trade is done using the dollar, the international currency.

Since the dollar was rendered inconvertible, total US holdings and credits to the rest of the world advanced by 15 per cent a year, and thus dollarization increased by just as much.

The central banks of other countries were beginning to accumulate dollars as reserve currency. What could they do with these dollars that could no longer be converted into gold? They could only buy US Treasury bonds, that is, US government debt to other countries, a debt that has now been declared as never to be repaid.

US attention was focused on the fact that the value of every commodity is expressed in dollars, and every transaction was made using its own currency. When OPEC increased the price of oil by as much as four times, US officials flew to Riyadh. They told their OPEC allies that they could raise prices as much as they wanted, as long as these prices were expressed in dollars and thus recycled the huge amount of dollars from the increase in crude within the US (hence closing in on the petrodollar circuit, something that would be repeated later with other currencies – euro, yen, rouble, and especially Chinese currency).

The negotiation was not only economic; the Pentagon's strength also played a direct or indirect role. The oil sellers accumulated dollars with which they could not buy companies or whole pieces of the American economy (purchases that would be considered by the US as an act of war) but only minority stakes, while the bulk of these dollars had to be invested in buying US Treasury bonds (in recognition of a debt that could not be repaid and whose interest rate was less than 1 per cent).

Creditor countries could not even freely buy technology and innovation, even if their financing had made a direct contribution, because the sale was strictly controlled by the Pentagon (which practised free market trading according to cases and circumstances: a variable-dimension liberalism that no longer depended on statecraft but rather on US national security).

In this way, from its position as a universal debtor, the US could increase its debt, theoretically, indefinitely, simply by printing money. Creditor countries financed the balance of payments deficit and the federal deficit. Tax cuts to the rich were paid for by the rest of the world, just as the rest of the world paid for military spending, with nearly eight hundred US bases around the world keeping creditors under pressure and control. It is easy to demonstrate both a continuity and a discontinuity with classical (British) imperialism. The British colony India guaranteed an army, fully paid for by India itself, that England used mainly for the wars it waged in the South. Today, all countries – allied and non-allied alike – are all caught up in the monetary system of international payments and world financialization, and bear the insane expenses of the US military, which also commands and manages research and innovation for all US businesses.

The monetary system works on a *double standard that is a double power regime*. Deficit countries cannot continue to go into debt and must imperatively submit to the so-called economic laws of debt reduction and repayment: raise interest rates, stop economic development (recession and austerity), and sell the most productive enterprises to repay creditors; for the same reasons, they must privatize state monopolies, making them private monopolies – the first consequence of which is an explosion in the price of services, which are transformed into rent-producing services for private individuals.

On the other hand, the universal debtor (US) is not subject to any of the rules that the market imposes on others, since it enjoys 'sovereign' privilege. As is usually the case, creditors cannot intervene in the behaviour of debtors because the universal debtor is treated as an exceptional nation, guided by the hand of God – that is, it has the strongest economy and army on the planet and can impose its rules. The market, free competition, and economic laws apply primarily to subordinate countries, to the losers of the economic-military confrontation, and certainly not to the universal debtor.

Every country that applies for IMF funding must submit to certain principles (austerity, privatization), while the US receives continuous and automatic aid from the workings of the dollar.

As Lenin sharply points out, the capitalism that emerged in his time associates financialization and colonization. Dollar imperialism inaugurates a new domination of the centre (US) over the peripheries (which include all the rest of the world). The typical colonial extortion of the nineteenth and twentieth centuries that affected so-called developing or underdeveloped countries continues and worsens. In the postwar period, US food imperialism forced such countries to buy US agricultural products and develop agriculture only for export, thus undermining their food autonomy and deepening their dependence on industrialized and hyper-productive US agriculture.

Added to this historical plundering – which has lasted for four centuries – is our new imperialism's pillage that affects every country, including 'central' countries (especially Europe and Japan) that are considered by the US as allies to be milked even more than others because they are richer. New imperialism's colonization is further enhanced and pervasive compared to historical colonization because it extends over the whole planet, including the North.

Capitalism is not satisfied with only money, technology, and science, just as it is not satisfied with wage labour to produce profit; it must continually impose a pillage of free or underpaid labour and resources. Colonialism may change, but it remains a structural necessity.[2] This is another confirmation of the relevance of the category of imperialism.

## Continuity and discontinuity

There are many continuities from classical imperialism to dollar imperialism, but there are also many significant differences.

Gérard Duménil and Dominique Lévy, confirming my analysis thus far, point out the novelties that the US introduced in respect to the capitalism of Lenin and Luxemburg. Classical imperialism was based on an overproduction of goods and capital that necessarily had to be exported to places that had not yet been hit by capitalist development. Contemporary US imperialism, on the other hand, while exporting goods and capital just like classical imperialism, must also import more goods than it exports (deficit balance sheet) and bring in more capital than it exports (surplus capital account).

---

2   For a more in-depth discussion of this issue, see Maurizio Lazzarato, *The Intolerable Present, the Urgency of Revolution*, trans. Ames Hodges, Los Angeles: Semiotext(e), 2023.

The US imposes 'the export of its goods and capital on the world, simultaneously importing masses of goods greater than its exports, and letting the inflow of foreign capital finance its expenditures'.[3] This new phenomenon was not observable in classical imperialism, because it is only with the supremacy of the dollar that its operation happens, starting from a deficit balance of payments that sets into motion another novelty that has characterized our situation for the last fifty years: the debt economy.

Paul Sweezy, who acknowledges his debt to Michal Kalecki (and thus to Luxemburg), grasped the new possibilities of accumulating surplus value now open to capital – solutions beyond colonization and the 'external markets' of classical imperialism.[4] New possibilities that require even stronger state intervention. Imperialism and monopolies are still involved but, unlike Lenin's time, *consumption* and *public spending* in countries of the centre can function as the 'external markets' and represent very effective counter-trends to the stagnation (and fall in the rate of profit) that monopolies inevitably produce. In a 'society of opulence', these expenditures have a 'colossal capacity to generate private and public waste', with enormous negative consequences for the inhabitability of the planet.[5] Sweezy went even further, anticipating a new function of finance/credit it did not possess in the era of classical imperialism: in the mid-1960s, the great indebtedness of the state and corporations – and especially, starting in the mid-1970s, *the indebtedness of families, workers and even the poor* – made it possible to realize surplus value by freezing wages without cutting consumption.

---

3 Gérard Duménil and Dominique Lévy, *Capital Resurgent: Roots of the Neoliberal Revolution*, Cambridge, MA: Harvard University Press, 2004.

4 Luxemburg's 'external markets' (colonies) and Kalecki's 'internal exports' (deficit-financed government spending, private consumption, also defined by Sweezy as 'internal colonization'), along with investment in armaments, support effective demand and thus the realization of surplus value and its accretion. These allow profits to rise above the level determined by private investment and consumption by capitalists (incapable by themselves of realizing the surplus value produced).

5 Paul M. Sweezy, *Modern Capitalism and Other Essays*, New York: Monthly Review Press, 1972, 3.

*Interest* now intervenes in the capital–labour struggle (the interest produced by money), displacing both, but destroying only the latter because the former is itself but a higher and more abstract form of interest (credit). The policy of mass indebtedness (and therefore also of the poor) saw its fulfilment in the subprime crisis, the cause of the breakdown of the financial system at the origin of the current war. The effectiveness of the countertrends to stagnation (central banks flooding economies with liquidity) generated, in turn, a radicalization of class polarizations.

Military spending constitutes a resource in the hands of the state to prevent the economic collapse of capital, both in Lenin's and Kalecki's time as well as today. Indeed, the Pentagon's latest budget is the highest ever: $885 billion.[6]

Wars also have a fundamental economic function because they are, along with revolutionary innovations (steam engine, railroads, automobile), fundamental external stimuli against the stagnation inherent in monopoly-dominated economies.

> From the standpoint of their economic consequences, wars must be divided into two phases, the combat phase and the aftermath phase. Both involve a shaking up of the economy, the more radical, the more total the war and the longer it lasts. It is for this reason that great wars like those of 1914–1918 and 1939–1945 are, economically, similar to epoch-making innovations.[7]

The strategic weapon of dollar imperialism is not the so-called enterprise society (ordoliberals) or even 'the entrepreneur himself' (Becker/

---

[6] In *Guerra o rivoluzione: Perché la pace non è un'alternativa* (Rome: DeriveApprodi, 2022), I briefly discuss Kalecki's positions to which I refer.

[7] 'During the combat military demand of course shoots up ... and civilian demand is curtailed ... In the case of durable goods for civilian use (both producer and consumer goods), production may even be halted altogether ... Existing plants are ... converted to war production, and most new investment is similarly channeled.' The consequences? 'In this way, investment outlets are created which can absorb large amounts of surplus for several years to come.' Paul A. Baran and Paul M. Sweezy, *Monopoly Capital: An Essay on the American Economic and Social Order*, New York: Modern Reader Paperbacks, 1966.

Foucault), but the credit that allows one to do (and have) *now* what, without it, one would have to do (and have) later. Debt allows everyone to acquire time by reversing the before and after: 'Consumer credit (intended for the buyer) allows one to anticipate the time of enjoyment; circulating credit (intended for the merchant) to anticipate the time of payment (of suppliers); investment credit (intended for the entrepreneur) to anticipate the time of production; creditor's credit (intended for the banker) to anticipate the time of the debtor's amortizing the debt.'[8]

The state (central bank, welfare) and finance anticipate this time – which is activated throughout society and has nothing to do with Marxian labour time – to delay the explosion of contradictions, to defer the catastrophe and the war that, despite and because of credit, will nevertheless come. Through credit, everyone gains time, as does the state-capital machine, which thus seeks to delay class conflict and clashes between states, to procrastinate its ever possible implosion.

Lenin's imperialism was already not limited to territory, because finance played a central role in it as well. In contemporary imperialism, currency and finance push a further deterritorialization.

It is credit that is the real instrument of control over labour (wage and non-wage labour) and rent in the world market, just as Sweezy, uniquely among the Marxists, already understood in the early 1970s.

## The dollar and war

Dollar superimperialism does not function on the basis of the rules enunciated by neoliberalism and ordoliberalism, market and free competition, but from the economic-political power relations of which the use of armed force and war are part. Economists never introduce war into their theories, so it remains an exogenous phenomenon.

'Prior to the 1914–1918 world conflict, the habit of economists to regard wars as mere perturbations' of the economy 'may have been fully

---

8   Jean-François Lyotard, *Libidinal Economy*, trans. Iain Hamilton Grant, Bloomington: Indiana University Press, 1993.

justified'. But, in the course of the twentieth century, they completely changed in role and function. In Sweezy's words, wars are no longer mere accidents in an otherwise peaceful economic process: 'No person in possession of his full mental faculties would claim that without wars the economic history of the 20th century would have been what it actually was.'[9]

We are in a situation where the tendency enunciated by Lenin has become a reality: it is no longer possible to distinguish economics from politics from militarism, as one could in Marx's time.

In order to investigate the relationship of dollar imperialism to war, I will refer to the work of the Chinese general Qiao Liang, one of the two authors of *Unrestricted Warfare*, who, after the success of the book, set out to study finance in order to understand the mechanism that allows the US to impose its supremacy over the world. Although the result – *Empire Arc – America and China at the Ends of Parabola* – is a bit deterministic and in thrall to the power of the dollar system, its simplified approach is useful for its grasp of the nature and techniques of new imperialism, with its unprecedented colonization.

Perhaps in tune with the sentiment of the military spheres of the People's Liberation Army and the Communist Party of China, Qiao Liang expresses the crux of China's strategic problem as follows: 'What China faces is not so much military hegemony as financial hegemony. For nearly four decades, the US has used its monetary scepter to create a Dollar cycle that can swallow up global wealth by periodically increasing and reducing the flow of monetary liquidity.'[10]

*Why does the US wage wars all the time?* asks the Chinese general. Not primarily for oil, not fundamentally to appropriate raw materials or cheap labour, but to impose and safeguard the dollar that allows them to procure material and human resources through more 'abstract' devices (finance and money) but whose operation necessarily involves war.

---

9   Baran and Sweezy, *Monopoly Capital*.
10  See Liang Qiao and Xiangsui Wang, *Unrestricted Warfare: China's Master Plan to Destroy America*, Panama City: Pan American Publishing Company, 2002.

The general points out that, in dollar imperialism, if the balance of payments must be continually in deficit, the capital account, on the other hand, must be always in surplus. For the system of 'financial exploitation' (Lenin) and world colonization to be imposed, it is necessary for the debtor country continually to export dollars by importing products from other countries, investing abroad, developing military expenditures, and so on. But these dollars and capital (the debt issued by the US Treasury and investments abroad) must return to the US and be invested in its three markets: Treasury bills (debt), futures, and securities. The US needs $700 billion a year that it does not produce itself in order to reproduce its power and a way of life that President George W. Bush called 'untouchable' during the Second Gulf War.

Qiao Liang gives very clear examples to explain the mechanism of capturing globally produced wealth and expropriating it through dollar imperialism. He calculates that, over the past four decades, the Federal Reserve has raised interest rates five times and cut them five times, with the result that the rest of the world has undergone development and recession/austerity the same number of times.

US imperialism opens and closes the cycle of capital, by manoeuvring the cost of money, alternately providing the necessary liquidity or, conversely, reducing the supply of money. This flow and reflux of dollars and investment causes growth or recession in the world market, controlling the development of the world economy and allowing the US to appropriate a large share of world production (through imperial pillage and rent). Through opening and closing liquidity, through sending out and repatriating capital, the US reaps extraordinary harvests, while frightening financial crises proliferate (everywhere, but especially in Latin America and South-East Asia) in which war plays a key role. Latin American countries were the first that, in the 1970s and 1980s, were seemingly able to profit from this availability of liquidity and investment created by dollarization, to develop their economies. 'A nation like Argentina for a time even touched the threshold of the most developed countries.'[11]

---

11 Qiao Liang, *L'arco dell'impero. Con la Cina e gli Stati Uniti alle estremità*, ed. Fabio Mini, trans. Rachele Faggiani, Gorizia: LEG, 2021.

But when inflation rose in the US and threatened to become hyperinflation, the Fed decided to raise interest rates, implementing what some economists call the Fed's blow or the Volcker blow: a drastic increase in the target rate from 11 per cent in 1979 to 20 per cent two years later, with dramatic consequences – recession, unemployment, wage freezes – but above all, the worldwide launch of the debt economy. The dollar began to strengthen, and capital began to flow out of Latin America and into US financial markets.

But this first return of capital was not yet significant. This would come with the Malvinas War (1982) between Argentina and England. A general rule became evident: a political upheaval, an apparent financial accident, and then a military conflict, pushing investors out of deteriorating economies and into the safer and more profitable American markets.

As it leaves, *capital takes with it the wealth produced during development*, now crystallized in dollars that return to the US. Another layer of financial capture is added: with this influx of capital, *Americans buy whole chunks of the economies of countries that the withdrawal of investment has put into serious crisis*. Enormous wealth was thus doubly appropriated and transferred to the US, as Latin America plunged into crisis. Countries such as Argentina rapidly moved from being considered developed to developing countries, or even declining ones.

According to different calculations, between October 1978 and February 1985, the dollar appreciated by between 50 per cent and 100 per cent, leading to a debt crisis caused by the rise of the dollar throughout the continent.

The reason for the liberalization of capital – achieved in Europe by the policies of centre-left governments and in the US by the Democrats – can be wholly explained by the need for this exit and entry of capital into the US, itself necessary in order to capture global wealth. The same mechanism was activated in South-East Asia, although the crisis and the consequent flight of capital was caused not by war but by George Soros's attack on the Philippine currency. In 1987, the US stock market collapsed, with the Fed forced to make an 'emergency rate cut' and open dollar reserves. This time, investments were directed towards South-East Asia.

The development of the four so-called Asian tigers was lightning fast but, by 1994, the Fed raised rates from 3 per cent to 8 per cent while Soros forced the Philippine currency to devalue, sparking a debt crisis in the region.

The tigers' economic boom was converted into capital that went to the US, while the Americans tried to buy up the broken economies of South-East Asia with this repatriated capital. They bought their most profitable enterprises with the labour and production of these countries, embedded in the capital that had fled to the US. Our Chinese general is fascinated by this technique, even as he writes: 'The world will certainly remember the Korean mothers who took off their gold rings, bracelets and necklaces and gave them to the Korean government so as to get more foreign exchange and prevent famous Korean companies from being bought and turned American.'[12]

In this crisis, the Americans intervened directly without any mediation from the IMF.

It is, above all, this cutting away that passes indifferently over tangible or intangible, cognitive or biopolitical production, over the industrial economy or service economy, over the development or underdevelopment that justifies the decentralization of production out of the global North, and not only over the importation of cheap goods – even though the latter generate enormous profits. Importing goods from the global South is yet another dollar-capturing device (the fourth, after the free financing of US deficits, the return of capital inflated by economic booms, and the purchase of businesses in crisis-ridden countries) that appropriates immense fortunes without ever lifting a finger (other than the one that inputs transactions to a computer): 'In 2011, for example, the United States spent 433.4 billion on imports from China. These were largely low-end products, such as T-shirts or toys, which never cost more than two dollars. But when Americans put them on the shelves they would multiply the price "generating" trillions that would then add up to the US GDP.' The Chinese general asks: 'While the world envied America's wealth, was anyone doing the math? . . . Some might say this is

---

12  Ibid.

not looting or exploitation, but just market economy.' Actually, it is pillage under cover of a market economy that does not require a 'blatant subjugation of other peoples to enjoy their material wealth'.[13] The currency supported and defended by the US military is enough. Currency and war are the uniform of American imperialism, as I have said.

The same predatory treatment has been applied not only to the global South, but also to supposedly allied countries such as Japan and those of Europe. Indeed, the richer they are, the more abundant the raids will be. The method used is extra-economic: negotiations on the basis of power relations in which armed force plays a central role.

On 22 September 1985, the US convened the G5 to decide on the appreciation of the yen because Japan was becoming too dangerous an economic competitor. The Americans obliged Japan, England, Germany, and France to buy the expanding US debt and imposed an appreciation of the yen on Japan: from 250 to 82 yen per dollar. The Japanese economy would never recover from this shock – it has been stagnant ever since. The Japanese could buy a part of the US with that yen appreciation, but the latter would consider such behaviour an act of war. This was the second defeat inflicted by the Americans against Japan, after Hiroshima.

Assuming that war is the most important cause in bringing about a worsening investment climate, the US also used the war in Yugoslavia to attack the euro, which risked becoming a serious competitor to the dollar. Only a few months after the introduction of the euro, the Americans, through NATO and the suicidal tendencies of the European ruling classes, pushed for war in Yugoslavia. The bombing of Belgrade definitively convinced the markets that there was no favourable investment climate in Europe. About $400 billion was withdrawn from European investments, but only half returned to the US – the other half went to China. The Americans then *accidentally* bombed the Chinese Embassy in Belgrade.

China is evidently the country that contributed most to the establishment of this dollar tool, producing colossal trade surpluses for years that were then reinvested in US Treasury bonds. China constituted the

---

13  Ibid.

factory that the US needed to run its perpetually deficit-ridden monetary imperialism and to supply the cheap goods needed for the US wage freeze that has been going on since the 1970s (via Walmart).

After the 2008 crisis, the Chinese Communist Party (which, unlike the European vassals, never accepted the liberalization of capital movements, making American plunder impossible) – realizing that US finance could destroy trillions of dollars in a single day, and noting China's perilous dependence and subordination to Fed/Wall Street decisions – began the process of de-dollarization and the much more difficult project of creating a financial and monetary system external to the dollar. This was effectively a declaration of war on the US, or at least that is how the Americans took it.

Military action is the other necessary and unavoidable face of dollar imperialism. The state and the military are strategic players in world markets. Economic action without armed action – in a global framework where confrontation is not only with other capitals and other economies but also with other states – is ineffective.

Instead of inaugurating an era of peace and prosperity, the end of the Soviet Union and the victory of liberalism and democracy have produced a resurgence of American military activity. The Pentagon and the US military have engaged in an impressive series of wars: Panama, 1989; Iraq, 1991; Kuwait, 1991; Somalia, 1993; Bosnia, 1994–5; Sudan, 1998; Afghanistan, 1999; Yemen, 2002; Iraq, 1991–2003; Iraq, 2003–11; Afghanistan, 2001–15/21; Pakistan, 2007–15; Somalia, 2007–8, 2011; Yemen, 2009–11; Libya, 2011, 2015; Syria, 2014–15.

Congressional Research Service reports list 100 overseas military operations between 1945 and 1999, and as many as 184 between 1999 and 2021 – virtually double in half the time. Not to mention the hundreds of covert operations carried out by the CIA with non-military personnel and funds.

Italian general Fabio Mini writes: 'Being the empire that it is, America has overseas colonies; from them it carries out wars all over the world, openly plunders resources, imposes its policies and enslaves the subjugated peoples.' It distinguishes between new colonies (so-called territories such as Samoa, Guam, the Northern Mariana Islands, Puerto Rico, and the US Virgin Islands) and old-style colonies – that is, countries dominated by old colonialism. The new colonies include the more than 700 'military bases abroad. Inside, American authority prevails, outside they politically and economically influence the "host" states that have always been "vassals", and the forces and weapons with which to maintain and strengthen the empire depart from them.'[14]

## The war that was already there!

The current war in Ukraine contains many wars. No less important is the one that the Americans, for years, have been fighting against Europe and that, dazzled by the titanic clash between democracy and autocracy, most do not see.

Once again under cannon fire, Europe has become an unpropitious ground for investment, which, in effect, flees, and allows the US to complete what it had begun with the war in Yugoslavia and the outbreak of hostilities in Ukraine in 2008. The start of the war in Donbas and the annexation of Crimea was another opportunity to push capital to flee the investment-unfriendly European climate, but, with China still enjoying the highest rate of development in the world, capital headed to Hong Kong. When the Americans saw where this capital (not peanuts, but $1 trillion) was going, they realized that war against China was inevitable and had to accelerate its implementation. Which would come, right on time.

With the current war in Ukraine, Europe's suicide is now complete. It will be forced to pay for this war in full with another economic downgrade. This undeclared war with the Americans is transforming Europe's economy (not that of the US) into a war economy. Europe will pay for energy at seven to nine times the prices paid by the US; it will be forced to raise interest rates again (0.75 is the highest interest rate since the euro has existed, following a previous increase of 0.50 a few months earlier); and meanwhile its currency continues to lose value – the euro has already

---

14  See Fabio Mini, *L'Europa in guerra*, Orléans: PaperFIRST, 2023.

reached 0.99 to the dollar. It will have to manage the recession (since the beginning of 2023 the most affected country is, incidentally, Germany), and cope with an inflation that is caused not mainly by the war, but by the impact of monopolies (as always, reinforced by years of battles against them conducted by neoliberal policies for supposedly free competition). Europe can no longer export to Russia and will find it increasingly difficult to sell to China (for, the moment it buys Russian oil, at inflated prices, from China and India), which should be its natural outlets for trade. This is a full-blown suicide on the altar of imperialism that will bleed it dry and block it for decades, as has already happened with the Japanese economy.

From the US point of view, an ally must be an obedient vassal, one that panders to its every will, at the cost of decreeing its own demise, as is happening now to Europe. What is Europe today? It is a collection of eastern countries, with Poland – the most reactionary, conservative, sexist, and pro-Atlantic – at the centre, plus the US and England (Brexit seems to have been planned – in any case, it came at precisely the right time). The Franco-German axis has been completely undermined; it must manage the consequences of yet another defeat of Europe, which is becoming one big American colony.

Germany is already the great loser of the current war: the axis that it had been building for decades with China, via Russia and Central Asia, which, in recent years, had become quite consolidated (demonstrated by increasingly significant economic and technological exchanges), is forever blocked (the Americans think) by the war in Ukraine, the real objective of which is to challenge these relationships. This economic and political bloc with the East risked seriously endangering American hegemony and shaking its already battered monetary imperialism.

European ruling classes are not only suicidal because they have accepted, without hesitation, the sabotage of their economies, but because they are channelling the violence they suffer from American imperialism – and against which they do not know how to rebel – to their subordinate population. In this way, the mechanism of dispossession through debt is applied by European vassals to their subordinates. This is exactly what the Germans and French did during the Greek debt crisis, although the relationship between European states and the Greek state has typically been a relationship between creditors and debtors.

James Galbraith, an adviser to Greek Finance Minister Varoufakis, when asked if European institutions (IMF, European Commission, and European Central Bank) would have to bail out Greece indefinitely, replied:

> There is no 'bailout,' there is no 'reform' going on. I really need to insist on this, because these words creep into our discourse. They are placed there by the creditors in order for unwary people to use them, but there is nothing of the kind taking place. What is going on is a seizure of the assets owned by the Greek state, by Greek businesses and by Greek households.[15]

In fact, the drastic measures imposed on the Greek 'parasites' has failed miserably: Greece's public deficit has skyrocketed to 200 per cent. This goes unmentioned because it illustrates the obvious failure of austerity policies.

The use of feudal vocabulary – in describing the fleecing that the US sovereign regularly practises on the rest of the world and that European valvassors pass on to their vassals – is not just metaphorical. The rent economy has much to do with the levy that the aristocracy imposed on feudal society. The night of the abolition of privileges (4 August 1789) is still on the political agenda, and is the measure of how far back capital has pushed us.

In October 2022, *Le Monde* published this assessment of the American currency:

> If the American dollar only confirms its hegemony, it is simply because there is nothing that can replace it. What to buy in its place: the euro, when the Old Continent is suffering the lash of the war in Ukraine and an energy crisis? British pounds, which are not so much better off, and

---

15 Luis Martín and James Galbraith, 'The Poisoned Chalice', Open Democracy, 1 September 2015, opendemocracy.net.

even less attractive after Brexit? Yen, in free fall, even as Japan keeps its rates at zero? The Chinese currency, while the country is mired in a real estate crisis and poses a greater geo-economic risk, under the neo-Maoist leadership of President Xi Jinping? Bitcoin, whose value is as volatile as a tech start-up on Nasdaq?[16]

The balance sheet seems to describe a strong position of the dollar and the US. In reality, both suffer from great internal and external weaknesses. The US was in a very difficult situation precisely because the dollar imperialism it had imposed since 1971 began to show cracks and its dominance had been rejected by Russia and the nations of the South. World supremacy based on financial plunder had already begun to reach its limits when Russia disposed of the US oligarchies and created its own; the international division of labour necessary for the functioning of the US deficit (the US factory South) was reversed through the empowerment of countries such as China and India, which started to seek spaces of autonomy and independence from the one-sidedness of US imperialism. But it is war that demonstrates the impotence of the US, because it is virtually the only option left to try to oppose the obvious signs of the decline of American hegemony. War means that domination comes through the direct use of weapons; it means political fragmentation of globalization. The US thought it would dominate after the fall of the USSR, but war forces it to plunder allied economies (to continue milking Japan, and finish off deconstructing Europe).

But the most obvious symptom of the checkmate of dollar imperialism is the internal civil war that manifests its loss of control, not only over the world, but also over its own people. Financial raids and plundering have also directly affected the US proletariat (in 2007, real wages adjusted for inflation were a bit lower than in 1973 in the US). Vigorous polarization has split the population along class lines and could spill over into civil war at any moment.

---

16  Pierre-Antoine Dusoulier, 'L'hégémonie du dollar est à la fois cause et symptôme de la perte d'attractivité du continent européen', *Le Monde*, 29 October 2022, lemonde.fr.

## The consequences of war

War will only accelerate processes that have been ongoing for years. The Shanghai Cooperation Organisation (SCO), founded by the Chinese in 2001, met on 15–16 September 2022 in Samarkand, Uzbekistan. This included the 'group of five' (China, Russia, Kazakhstan, Tajikistan, Kyrgyzstan), Uzbekistan (which held the rotating presidency), Pakistan, India, Iran, and Afghanistan; Mongolia and Belarus were present as 'observers'. In addition, there were several 'dialogue partners': Sri Lanka, Turkey, Cambodia, Nepal, Azerbaijan, Armenia, Egypt, and Qatar. These were joined by Bahrain, the Maldives, Kuwait, United Arab Emirates, and Myanmar for the first time. Together, they account for 45 per cent of the global population and 30 per cent of the world's GDP. They discussed trade and economic cooperation, but the conversation is really about how to build a world organization that can put an end to dollar hegemony.

The payment system not expressed in dollars that these countries are trying to build will be very difficult to implement, but the fact that it is already being considered and that, after the outbreak of war in Ukraine, the process has accelerated, is already significant. This is the greatest danger to the US. Democracy, like autocracy, has nothing to do with it.

After Lula da Silva's victory, negotiations were started with the Argentine president to begin building a common currency for South America that would not replace national currencies like the euro did but would be used only for trade and financial exchanges. The stated purpose is always the same, common throughout the South: how to reduce dependence on the dollar.

It seems quite clear what policies are at work, what the power relations are in the world market, what forces are fighting economically, politically, and militarily, either to safeguard hegemony over the rest of the world (US) or to defend themselves against this supremacy that has enormous political and economic costs. War is a continuation of these policies.

After only a few months into the Ukraine war, its real causes were clearly emerging: the role that the West has reserved for itself for centuries – deciding and controlling the destinies of the world – finds growing resistance in its former colonies, parts of the globe where dollar colonialism continues to rage.

While OPEC is certainly at the root of the monetary and political order of US imperialism, through an agreed recycling of petrodollars with the Americans, today, with the war in Ukraine, we are witnessing a spectacular reversal of the alliances on which the US has based its power. OPEC, in October 2022, decided to cut production heavily, against the advice of the US, whose president, Joe Biden, had flown to Riyadh to ask for Saudi Arabia's cooperation against Russia. Instead, Saudi Arabia reduced production drastically, exacerbating the chances of recession, especially for an already dismal Europe, the first victim of this war. The price of oil drives the speculation that fuels inflation, and in turn an interest rate hike is imposed on the entire world by the Fed.

Saudi Arabia's agreement that trade with Russia will not be conducted in dollars is symbolically significant because it breaks from the fifty-year-old understanding, established at the beginning of the imperial dollar system, to realize all oil production in US currency.

OPEC cannot and will not accept that the global North decides the price of oil by setting a ceiling to sanction Russia. This is another important sign of the West's isolation, of its material weakness, of the fact that it does not hold all the cards – neither economic nor political – necessary for managing global power. Its relative decline, its inability to impose itself unilaterally, will only become clearer and clearer. The global South, which has not sided with the West during this war, is likely to come out strengthened from the ongoing global confrontation.

The identity of the Americans' main enemy is also clear in the strategic documents of US imperialism.

Beginning with global NATO, the armed hand of imperialism on a planetary scale, the Pentagon is redesigning value chains for the postwar period. Capital is subordinated to the needs of the military economic strategy of the confrontation between the West and China. Value chains will be redesigned politically.

On 7 October 2022, just before the Chinese Communist Party Congress, the balkanization of globalization crossed another threshold.

The 135 pages of products that the United States now prohibits from being exported to China herald worsening relations between the two countries. All companies – not just US companies – have been banned from selling semiconductors, crucial for technological development, a ban accompanied by threats of economic retaliation against the slightest infringement.

Thomas Friedman, a journalist specializing in foreign affairs at the *New York Times*, says: 'In case you haven't noticed, let me alert you to a bracing turn of events: The U.S. is now in conflict with Russia and China.'[17]

'There is no possibility of reconciliation,' says an anonymous Chinese source quoted by Bloomberg business television.[18]

Samir Amin spoke of the reorganization of imperialism after the Second World War, which he defined as a 'collective imperialism' – that is, an alliance between the US, Europe, and Japan, which, under US command, was to share global income/production. This alliance especially profited the Americans, who, although no longer winning in the global South, scored one victory after another against their own allies.

Between the 1970s and today, there has been a change in the Americans' strategic, economic, and political enemy. Its identity has changed during the rise of globalization: it is clearly not terrorism, as was naively believed, but rather the growth of the global South, with China at the forefront.

In October, the US Department of Defense released its '2022 National Defense Strategy', which states: 'The most comprehensive and serious challenge to U.S. national security is the [People's Republic of China's] coercive and increasingly aggressive endeavor to refashion the Indo-Pacific region and international system to suit its interests and authoritarian preferences.'[19]

---

17 Thomas L. Friedman, 'We Are Suddenly Taking On China and Russia at the Same Time', *New York Times*, 12 October 2022.
18 '"No Possibility of Reconciliation" as US Slams China Chips', Bloomberg, 10 October 2022.
19 See '2022 National Defense Strategy of the United States of America', Department of Defense, 2022, defense.gov.

While China tries to avoid confrontation, conscious of its military inferiority, the US is actively seeking it by all means, aware that it cannot delay it too long, lest it find itself in an unfavourable situation.

Imperialism is not only monetary and financial; it is also a cultural, linguistic imperialism, imposing fashions and lifestyles that are taken up and reproduced throughout the world. Consumer standards are imposed from the centre of the empire, even though they are experienced only through television and advertising images for a large part of humanity. Communication patterns are equally created and spread by the imperial centre. But without the dollar, without its supremacy, without the financial availability it makes available, none of this would be possible.

## On imperialism

At the turn of the nineteenth and twentieth centuries, globalization radically changed capitalism because, among other things, a new relationship of the state to capital was established. The concept of imperialism perfectly captures this shift: sovereign, administrative, and military actions are absolutely necessary to the life and development of capital (as they are indeed to technological and scientific development).

In the 1920s, Carl Schmitt summarized the new role of the state forged during the phase of globalization and colonization at the turn of the twentieth century and later consolidated by the Great War: it intervenes in wages, supports the income of whole sections of the population, guarantees 'enormous subsidies to the different branches of industry', and legislates on every aspect of social and economic life. Even then, this broad spectrum of actions required 53 per cent of the national product to pass through its administration.[20]

The state can no longer exercise its sovereignty independently of the economy, and the latter cannot develop without the intervention of the

---

20  Lars Vinx, *The Guardian of the Constitution: Hans Kelsen and Carl Schmitt on the Limits of Constitutional Law*, Cambridge: Cambridge University Press, 2015.

former. The state no longer intervenes, as Schmitt wished, beyond the classes, but directly within class conflict, by trying to control, subordinate, and neutralize the action of the masses, who are ousting its old sovereignty when they question its monopoly over politics, decision-making, and war.

This is where the state-capital machine is born. Subsequent development will only confirm this alliance, where, depending on the phase, either capital or the state, either accumulation or war prevails, but they always coexist.

Two opposing but specular positions have faced off in recent decades. The first (Negri, Deleuze), which could be defined as 'immanentist', has made the Marxian definition of capital its own: an immanent power that knows no limits, that faces obstacles it continually removes and poses again, ad infinitum. In this definition, the state seems to play a minor and subordinate role, or has no function at all. The second (Mario Tronti, Massimo Cacciari) – which could be called 'transcendent' (quite widespread in Italy) – privileges the action of the state, in the wake of Carl Schmitt's political teleology.[21] The state is considered to exercise a sovereign power that is autonomous from capital. These two theoretical

---

21  Unlike Schmitt, leftist theorists (even Marxist ones) who advocate political theology seem to ignore capitalism and its power to reconfigure the state: 'In the age of rapid industrial development, it is no longer the theological alternatives Catholicism, Lutheranism or Calvinism that present themselves as options. It is now a matter of choosing the political system appropriate to the scientific, technical, industrial development of society . . . Instead of the religious, theological and confessional problem, obsolete today, we have the adage "cuius industria, eius regio"'. Laila Yousef Sandoval, '"Cuius regio, eius oeconomia": La crítica de Carl Schmitt a la economía liberal desde su perspectiva interna e internacional', *Revista europea de historia de las ideas políticas y de las instituciones públicas* 11 (2017), pp. 369–88. This text is from 1978, but already by 1927 the centrality of capitalism had clearly been stated: 'That economic contrasts have become political . . . only indicates that the culmination of the political can be reached starting with the economy.' Today the destiny of humanity is represented by the economy or, more precisely, become something political thanks to the class struggle and proletarian revolutions that have been threatening the state-capital machine since 1848. Replacing the analysis of capitalism with economic theology is yet another impasse in critical thinking. See Carl Schmitt, *The Concept of the Political*, trans. C. J. Miller, Quakertown, PA: Antelope Hill Publishing, 2020.

currents ignore the actual functioning of the state-capital machine in which neither term possesses the independence and autonomy that these authors assign here to capital, there to the state. Imperialism displaces these positions because it redefines the state, capital, and their relationship.

The last two globalizations (the one that led to war in 1914 and the one that is currently fragmenting) were hegemonized by financial capital. During the first, Nikolai Bukharin argued that the hegemony of financial capital necessarily implied imperialism because exporting capital (as well as commodities) – a necessary condition – could only be accomplished under these conditions.

But the definition of financial capital runs the risk of being ambiguous and limited if state action, monopolies, and the use of military force are not associated with it. This is absolutely evident in the US, where extra-economic force is part of every supposedly economic decision concerning the function of the dollar, and is a prerequisite. Instead, we should be speaking about a tool where Wall Street (financial capital proper) is inseparable from the monetary action of the Fed (the US state), industrial monopolies and oligopolies, and the Pentagon (military force and the most important source of financing for techno-scientific research and production). For a complete and accurate picture, financialized enterprises must be added, whose mega-profits are monopoly rents that do not cease to grow. *Instead of being a 'subjectless process', accumulation is the result of a political-military strategy*: the US state and its deployment of armed force across the globe played a key role in changing the modes of accumulation between the 1960s and 1970s.

Rosa Luxemburg had already defined imperialism as the device that holds economic and political-military action together. Can the final stage of capital 'ever really happen'? Luxemburg's question 'is, of course, theoretical fiction, precisely because capital accumulation is not just an economic process but also a political process'.[22] 'Political' in this context means not only the administrative and legal intervention of the state but

---

22   Rosa Luxemburg and Nikolai Bukharin, *Imperialism and the Accumulation of Capital*, London: Penguin, 1972.

also its military and sovereign action, just as Luxemburg points out. 'Political violence is also the instrument and vehicle of the economic process ... capital comes [from birth] dripping from head to foot, from every pore, with blood and dirt.'[23]

While Marx sometimes seems to concede the existence of economic and monetary processes moved by autonomous laws (like the fetishes created by the hands of men, but animated with a life of their own), with imperialism the possibility of a process without political will or the strategy of a collective subject is inconceivable.[24]

Imperialism is the modern form that capitalism assumed immediately after Marx's death, and which it has never abandoned. Rather, it has continually perfected it, resulting in a sophisticated form of monetary and financial imperialism that indiscriminately uses the indirect violence of currency and the direct violence of the use of force.

A 'Third World' vision of imperialism, *according to the logic of unequal development*, has – ever since the emergence of Italian *operaismo* (workerism) – repelled critical thinking and colonizing the whole world – as if this so-called colony were not as modern as the English factories or those in Detroit; as if the domination of dollar imperialism were not a new form of colonialism that perfects the techniques of colonial dispossession (even if they are not territorialized).

---

23   Ibid.
24   Karl Marx, *Capital*, vol. 1, Moscow: Progress Publishers, 1954 (1887), available at marxists.org. All power is exercised through goals and strategies, but these do not necessarily result from the choices and decisions of an individual subject (or a central committee of affairs). Dollar imperialism is defined by the action of a multiplicity of subjects (economic, political, military), who are not necessarily coordinated, and might even have different interests; it is the fruit of a strategy that is fabricated by making itself, through mistakes and successes, defeats and victories, that allow the project to be modified, reconfigured, and calibrated as it is being carried out. But starting from a key objective, from a strong desire: to kill the revolution, to defeat the political enemy that lurks within it. 'Intentional and nonsubjective action' (not of a non-individual subject), in Foucault's terms. That is, what is decisive in dollar imperialism is not the relationship between currency and desire (Keynes, interpreted by Deleuze and Guattari), but between currency and strategy, between the dollar and American political will.

## 'Political error' according to Rosa Luxemburg

Together with Luxemburg, let us call the 'theoretical-political' error of post-'68 thought the inability to elaborate concepts capable of grasping the nature of new imperialism. Imperialism was not only ignored around the turn of the last century – repeating the same error as before – but was even eliminated as a relevant concept (Michael Hardt and Antonio Negri).[25]

Luxemburg was not intimidated by Marx's authority and confronted his concept of capital head on: 'Marx's analysis of accumulation was developed at a time when imperialism had not yet entered on to the world stage. The final and absolute rule of capital over the world – the precondition on which Marx bases his analysis – entails the a priori exclusion of the process of imperialism.'[26]

Luxemburg spoke of Marx's 'error', but stressed the difference between his fruitful errors and the 'vulgar errors of his epigones', among whom we can include many contemporary theorists who assume the 'exclusive and general domination of capital'. Capital as immanent power would subordinate states' sovereignty to a supranational empire (Negri and Hardt), capable of achieving the globalization of capital, and this was deemed impossible by Luxemburg. States would become mere components, subordinated to a world capitalist machine; instead, it is precisely within globalization that capital shows that it cannot exercise 'absolute and exclusive domination'. On the contrary, it needs the state and its administrative and military apparatuses to survive and prosper.

Luxemburg emphasizes the impossibility of accumulation under the conditions indicated by Marx because accumulation requires the exploitation of new 'non-capitalist' regions, an exploitation that it cannot accomplish with economic weapons alone. Imperialism arises from the requirement to create surplus value; it needs the export of goods and

---

25 See the series of books by Michael Hardt and Antonio Negri: *Empire* (Cambridge, MA: Harvard University Press, 2000), *Multitude* (New York: Penguin, 2004), *Commonwealth* (Cambridge, MA: Harvard University Press, 2009), and *Assembly* (New York: Oxford University Press, 2017).

26 Luxemburg and Bukharin, *Imperialism and the Accumulation of Capital*.

capital to countries and regions not yet fully subjected to capitalist production, and must overcome the resistance of the peoples of occupied colonies and the competition of other imperialist machines. This programme requires a massive use of extra-economic force.

Without state action, capital cannot survive, either economically or politically, within its territory or on the world market.

Within its own borders, capital cannot cope with the class struggle that reached soaring heights in twentieth-century revolutions, and which left behind, even when defeated, demands for income, wages, and welfare that capital cannot guarantee without the fiscal and welfare policies established by the state. Externally, in the world market, competition is not only economic, but is also between political and military powers.

The state, for its part, cannot survive alone within its own territory, nor can it hold up externally in the world market without the capitalist competition. Its legitimacy can no longer be derived from the Hobbesian preservation of life, but must instead be assured through employment, wages, income, and welfare. Its military and political power in the world market depends directly on the quantity and quality of *production*. The state does not possess the autonomy and independence that political theology theorists attribute to it. State sovereignty is undermined and conditioned by capital (and, more precisely, by class struggle).

Capitalism is straining under new contradictions, ones Marx could not have foreseen, squeezed between the two poles of state and capital.[27] Both aim at endless accumulation, the former of power, the latter of profit; this is the reason why they cannot identify with each other. They pursue relatively heterogeneous ends, all the while constituting a single war machine.

This is particularly true for large contemporary states such as the US, China, or Russia, which exercise their sovereignty over great spaces. It is only these powers that can practise imperialism; the European statelets

---

27 One could reserve the term 'capital' for the Marxian definition of the production process and the term 'capitalism' for the state/capital/military force machine and the multiplicity of subjects acting on it, again described by Marx in *The Eighteenth Brumaire*.

that invented it are no longer able to do so, because they have neither the demographic, spatial, nor economic numbers to impose it.

Capital is an expression of an absolutely contradictory double dynamic: on the one hand, it tends continuously to globalize, to expand its production and its financialization throughout the world market. It is an uprooting force that seems to attack even borders, the boundaries of states. On the other hand, it cannot carry out this globalization because, in order to hold its own in the world market, to guarantee internal peace and an external shock force for itself, it must be anchored to a state, to a currency that can only be national and to a legitimate monopoly of force that can only have one nationality. By definition, there is no world state that can accompany the worldwide becoming of capital.

Each time, the liquidity of capital must be solidified, petrified in property, reterritorialized in the nation – in racism, in sexism, in the state and its armament. This *liquid society* is power's ideology, narrative, and pure storytelling!

This contradiction is perfectly expressed by the currency of US imperialism, the national currency of the US and, at the same time, the international currency used for exchanges on the world market that must perform in the interests of the country that controls its creation and destruction. The dollar has always been the US currency and, ever since 1971, the Americans have been telling the rest of the world: 'It is our currency and your problem.' For a long time, it looked as though it would be able to perform the function of international currency and also accommodate everyone's interests. The 2008 crisis debunked this happy globalization myth, favourable to all states, and the currency became fiercely American. War also makes production national. The US is desperately trying to repatriate the production it once relocated ($400 billion in concessions through subsidies for companies who return and set up on US soil). For fifty years, US capitalism has tended to globalize, but inevitably from the US base, where it must return when globalization falters.

Imperialism continually lives within this tension between opposite poles. The contradiction cannot be resolved; it cannot be reconciled through synthesis. It can only be managed, regulated, and governed by a military-political strategy, a thousand miles away from Foucault's 'governmentality' and mainstream governance.

Critics of imperialism, in the face of the manifest impossibility of a supranational imperial order, cling desperately to globalization. They believe it is an incontrovertible fact, an outcome from which there is no turning back – as if globalization were not undermined by a multiplicity of globalizations, produced and managed by different state-capital machines, each tending to expand without limits at the expense of, and in competition with, each other. In the upward phase of the cycle, they seem to complement each other harmoniously (above all the US and China). In reality, they have divergent interests and pursue different goals that, at the first major crisis (2008), openly manifest themselves and explode into war (2022).

Globalization is being reconfigured according to political logic (between state-capital machines allied against others, and according to their different alliances, and therefore enemies), just as has always been the case.

War brings out clearly the role of the state in the functioning of the market and the economy. In crisis, and especially in war, the constitutive relationship of the two-headed state-capital machine is unbalanced in favour of the former. The state violently takes over from capital.

The market does not govern and distribute resources according to the laws of economics; rather, the state decides where and how one can produce, what and to whom one can export, how and how much should be spent (prioritizing investment in armaments, reducing expenditures and social rights), all according to the laws of politics and power. So even goods – especially technology and science – turn out to have a homeland.

## Nationalism, an invention of capitalism

Capital is caught inside another terrible political contradiction that becomes fully manifest in imperialism, causing it to oscillate continuously between cosmopolitanism and nationalism.

The concept of *national capitalism*, which, from the point of view of the 'exclusive' and 'general domination of capital' (capital as immanent power) is a contradiction in terms, is instead the reality of capitalism perfectly expressed by the concept of imperialism.[28]

Nationalism does not function outside capitalism; it is not a reaction to its deterritorialization, to its producing displacement. Rather, it is a component of its operation, because the state and its armed force – indispensable to its functioning – are always national.

Marx asserted in the *Communist Manifesto*: 'National differences and antagonisms between peoples are daily more and more vanishing, owing to the development of the bourgeoisie, to freedom of commerce, to the world-market, to uniformity in the mode of production and in the conditions of life corresponding thereto.'[29] This approach has been debunked, because if capital always works in conjunction with the state, it cannot break out of this relationship. Marx is betrayed here by the universalizing and revolutionary task he attributes to capitalism. We have entered another era of imperialism and its two-headed state-capital machine: one where universalization still seems to be the goal, and turns out instead to be an insurmountable problem.

The contradictions of imperialism are thus without solution because it is caught within a double impossibility: the impossibility of becoming worldwide by bringing globalization to completion ('having a tendency to become a world form, breaks itself over its incapacity to actually become this world form of production'), but also the impossibility of becoming national, of keeping production and financialization inside the boundaries of the state, when first crisis, and later war, breaks out.[30]

---

28   Karl Marx, 'The Chapter on Capital', in *Grundrisse*, Hammondsworth: Penguin Books/New Left Review, 1973, available at marxists.org.

29   Karl Marx, 'Manifesto of the Communist Party', in *Karl Marx and Frederick Engels Selected Works*, vol. 1, Moscow: Progress Publishers, 1969 (1848), available at marxists.org.

30   Rosa Luxemburg, cited in Maurizio Lazzarato, *War, Capitalism, Ecology: Why Can't Bruno Latour Understand Anything about Them?*, trans. Eric Aldieri, Ill Will, 3 April 2022, illwill.com.

When the impossibility of globalization manifests itself through class polarizations within the nation, and polarizations between states in the world market, nationalism is the obvious political solution, but one that always proves dangerous. Fascist and Nazi territorialization is the danger that hangs over all nationalisms. Despite these nefarious experiences, the state-capital machine is forced to unravel the globalization it helped build with other imperialisms.

The spillover from the universality of capital, currency, technology, and science, into the territory and identity of a nation, is always the promise of internal and external violence whose governmentality can only be assured not by neoliberalism but by new forms of fascism, authoritarianism, and populism.

The belief in the universality of money, capital, and the market breeds monsters (war). Contradictions and oppositions exist. Hegel did not invent them – on the contrary, he pacified them – and they are not superficial or apparent differences; they are very *real*, and produce wars of all kinds.

Real capitalism holds the power of dollar imperialism at its centre, while dominant political thought has imposed the centrality of neoliberalism on us. Before examining how this imperial policy in the world market space generated the war in Ukraine, and before we understand how contemporary social movements are disarmed in the face of this new political phase, I will analyse the relationship between new imperialism and neoliberalism, and the confusion, misunderstandings, and limitations of critical thought that have developed through focusing on the latter, while practically ignoring the former.

# Chapter 2

*The few were always ministers of the few and the most powerful.*
                                                    Niccolo Machiavelli

*It is evident that accumulation . . . is but a slow process compared to that of centralization.*
                                                    Karl Marx

## Capitalism is not neoliberalism

How anyone could have believed that there was ever a possibility of the establishment of a supranational and non-sovereign empire capable of replacing unilateral dollar imperialism is hard to imagine (see Negri and Hardt). The Americans must destroy, through force of finance or arms, any attempt to break free of this unilaterally constituted and conducted financial system, without which US decline would no longer be relative, but absolute. Instead, they can threaten anyone with exclusion from the monetary and financial system: *If you do not agree to finance us for free, you will end up like Cuba, Venezuela, Iran – or, worse, Saddam Hussein and Gaddafi.*

Starting with dollar imperialism, we can also wonder what neoliberalism really is, because there is a huge discrepancy between the functioning of the economic-political imperialist machine centred on the dollar regime and the categories of ordoliberalism and neoliberalism obsessively celebrated by intellectuals, the media, and politicians focused on competition and the market. One might even say that they act in exactly opposite ways.[1]

Contemporary critical thought has unhesitatingly followed Foucault, whose lectures on ordoliberalism and neoliberalism contain a highly problematic definition of contemporary capitalism. The limitations of the philosophical-political thought of the 1960s, and especially the 1970s, which had a great influence on later theoretical development, are contained in his concepts of capital and capitalism and have all been debunked over the last fifty years because they expunge the concept of imperialism, war, and civil war.

This particular revision of the Foucauldian concept of capitalism is significant because it has been adopted as a critical point of view, when in fact it is subordinate to the political-ideological initiative of the state-capital machine of the 1970s and 1980s. Foucault's views on biopolitics and neoliberalism, meanwhile, demonstrate the challenges, if not the failure, of critical thinking, unable to grasp the emergence of counter-revolutionary, imperialist capitalism and its relation to the state, to war and, more generally, to class struggle.

Foucault's judgement of capitalism, which is also shared by many Marxists, fails to grasp the profound transformation wrought in the late nineteenth and early twentieth centuries, which is still the matrix of our present day. The resulting confusion, particularly around biopolitics and neoliberalism, has had a great impact on what is considered to be critical or revolutionary thought.

---

1  At this point, we must also ask ourselves about the meaning of *biopolitics*, an overblown concept in critical theory. 'To study liberalism as the general framework of biopolitics,' Foucault suggests. If we follow this indication, it becomes clear that the limitations of the concept of neoliberalism are all found, none excluded, in biopolitics, whatever version is adopted (Foucault, Agamben, Esposito, Negri).

In *Lectures on the Will to Know*, Foucault declares that the aristocracy's appropriation of wealth at the time of feudalism, which he sees as the exercise of *negative power*, is no longer operative. In feudal society, 'power was exercised essentially as a levy, a mechanism of subtraction, a right to appropriate a part of the wealth, extortion of the product, goods and services, labor and blood of the subjects'.[2] This can be understood as the right to take things, time, and life. With the advent of capitalism, these *negative* devices of capture became marginal because they were replaced by *positive* power relations that 'incite, reinforce, control, monitor, optimize and organize the forces under it'. Instead of preventing, forbidding, or blocking forces, capitalism makes them grow, strengthens them, and produces them.

This conception was shared by some classical economists, who fought a hard fight against rent and rentiers. It also owes much to Marx, and his insistence on capitalism as a revolution of production against the forces of the *Ancien Régime*. Contemporary capitalism, though, is not only or even principally a capitalism of production, because it is the oligarchies, for whom rent and profit are blurred, who actually direct it. In Foucault's own words, dollar imperialism functions precisely as 'levy, mechanism of subtraction, right to appropriate a part of the wealth, extortion of the products, goods and services, labor and blood of the subjects'.[3]

Foucault considered Lenin as little more than a politician. Yet it is through him (and through Luxemburg and other revolutionaries of the first half of the twentieth century) that one must read capitalism. This is because the radical change in the mode of production that occurred during his epoch manifested all its novelties in the First World War. The Bolsheviks understood this perfectly, but Foucault totally ignores it.

The change can be expressed very simply: the Marxian formula of capitalism as *production for production* becomes *production for rent*, in which profit and rent overlap.

---

2  Michel Foucault, 'The Mesh of Power', trans. Christopher Chitty, *Viewpoint Magazine*, 12 September 2012, viewpointmag.com.
3  Ibid.

Foucault makes the function of power (including economic power) absolutely positive, precisely when the hegemony of rent is a symptom that the 'revolutionary' (Marx), productive function of capital (if there ever was one) is running out – although not in the sense that production is disappearing. On the contrary, the increase in production and productivity is vertiginous; but equally vertiginous is the destruction that accompanies this growth (in the postwar period, ecologists call this *the great acceleration* – the destruction resulting from the reconstruction of economies annihilated by war). With the reversibility of rent and profit, production and destruction also become reversible. The more production increases, the more destruction increases; leaps forward in productivity are leaps forward in destruction. As early as 1915, Lenin announced: 'Formerly progressive, capitalism has become reactionary.'[4]

So, instead of disappearing, the *negative* role of power grows in proportion to its positive, productive function. The first victims of this *positive* conception of a power that, in reality, works against itself, are the wars and class struggles, the latter being considered expressions of a now outdated negative process. Instead, the negative, both of class struggle and the destruction wrought by capital, continuously and stubbornly erodes the positive from within, a process that will end in war.

The ascendant phase of capital's cycle, where production and destruction go hand in hand, quickly runs out, and it is the latter that eventually overwhelms the former: the destruction of war; the destruction of societies where low-intensity civil war prevails; and the ecological destruction of the planet. The negative pattern enhances internal differences, bringing destruction to unknown heights.

Ordoliberalism and neoliberalism will interpret everything through a positive conception of power while ignoring the negative functions – of rent, finance, monopoly, and war – that are embodied in dollar imperialism. The contradiction will be resolved by a failure of accounting: either consciously, by masking the functioning of the imperialist machine through

---

4  V. I. Lenin, *Collected Works*, vol. 21, Beijing: Foreign Languages Press, 1970, pp. 295–338.

the market and competition; or unconsciously, by simply ignoring it (as with Foucault and all the leftist critics of neoliberalism, including Dardot, Laval, Wendy Brown, Colin Gordon, and Barbara Stiegler).

Dollar imperialism covers use of force, arbitrary domination, cynical use of power relations (determined by wars, world and otherwise), conflict for planetary hegemony, and the right to choose life or death over entire populations and nations.

On his inauguration day, Alan Greenspan supposedly uttered something like: 'Gentlemen, I am now the chairman of the Federal Reserve. During my term of office, in this room, you can always talk about anything you want, there is only one issue that I ask you not to talk about, and that is the dollar.' I do not know if this is true, but one thing is certain: all the theories that have criticized neoliberalism have followed his advice to the letter: ignore the dollar completely; talk, gossip, and rant about the market, free competition, human capital, freedom, and free enterprise. This approach started with Foucault and has continued through a seemingly endless list of leftist critics. On the subject of liberalism or ordoliberalism, they have apparently covered everything: they have written about the new forms of relationship between economic, legal, and political structures; the devices of governmentality and its new forms of subjugation; the importance of the legal; the norms and rules of the economic constitution; the concept of human capital – all while scrupulously neglecting the financial side of power that invalidates much of what they write, and without which one can understand little of the counterrevolution in progress since 1971, nor of neoliberalism, nor of the current war.

Foucault introduced the bad habit of basing his criticism upon books written by theorists of neoliberalism, and upon the real exercise of power. It has been clear for some time that these criticisms have become an ideological appendage to the very object of their attacks.

In Foucault's text, which has unfortunately become a school of critical thought, no trait that characterized the capitalism of Lenin's time has continued to characterize, or even become accentuated in, the contemporary state-capital war machine: finance, money, monopoly, pillage, rent, colonization, centralization, sovereignty, or war (class, race, or gender). The aggressiveness and violence of monetary-financial capture and war conducted by imperialism to safeguard the dollar is reduced to the soft power of 'governmentality'!

On the contrary, neoliberalism and biopolitics must be judged in light of the 'regime of truthfulness' of war, civil war and class struggle – the 'real' spaces of power in which neoliberalism is limited to functioning temporarily as a pacifying governmentality.

As early as the nineteenth century, the unbalancing force of capital, which develops by passing from crisis to crisis, constantly destroying and creating new configurations, was woven together with the force of the state which, in turn, expresses its power by passing from war to war, from conquest to conquest, both colonial and continental. This conjunction of powers has, when necessary, swept away classical liberalism with fascism and war. Having been pushed towards increasingly authoritarian governmentality, power is now again replacing these ordoliberal or neoliberal forms with new forms of fascism and new forms of war. This proves – if any proof were needed – that capitalism (imperialist monetary/financial) and neoliberalism *are not the same thing.*

## Why neoliberalism is not capitalism

Neoliberalism presents itself as a new and autonomous form of power when, in fact, it is hierarchically and politically subordinate to imperialism and its institutions (currency, debt, war, finance, globalization, dollarization), which function according to *different, if not opposite, principles.*

Neoliberal and ordoliberal ideologies were built on two basic pillars: the denial of war, violence, and the use of force by economic action; and the dual assertion that competition functions as a peaceful and pacifying substitute, as well as the engine of the market through which equilibrium is achieved. In producing equilibrium, the market and competition prevent the formation of power centres, which are the origin of imbalances, polarizations, differences, and harbingers of conflict.

The actual functioning of capitalism shows us a completely different reality: the market and competition always and necessarily produce monopoly. The market and competition always determine the centralization of economic power in the hands of a few; they build huge centres of unbalancing, polarizing, differentiating power that start conflict, crisis, and war – in that order. The good capitalist flees competition by securing monopoly positions. This has been, from the beginning, the story of capitalism, only – and especially – confirmed in neoliberalism.

To grasp imperialism's entirely different way of acting – which means establishing a clear difference between capitalism and neoliberalism – we will focus first on the concept of *competition*, and later on the concept of *war*. The former plays a fundamental role in liberal and neoliberal theory, as Foucault reminds us. For the latter, the market/competition coupling constitutes a 'regime of truthfulness' because it is capable of producing the 'truth' of the process of price formation and market equilibrium. 'Pure competition . . . is the essence of the market', and not exchange, Foucault assures us. While describing the ordoliberal point of view, he seems to appreciate it, if not actually embrace it. He continues: pure competition is, and must be 'an objective, an objective thus presupposing an infinitely active policy. Competition is therefore an historical objective of governmental art and not a natural given that must be respected.'[5]

I do not know whether Foucault realized while writing *The Birth of Biopolitics* (maybe the more cynical and more political neoliberals did!) that *pure, perfect, undistorted competition means zero profits*, leading to the death of capitalism.

With the usual arrogance of the Silicon Valley venture capitalist, Peter Thiel dismantles in two lines this whole political theoretical framework (or *ideology*) of the market and competition: 'Actually, capitalism and competition are opposites. Capitalism is premised on the accumulation of capital, but under perfect competition, all profits get competed away.

---

5  Michel Foucault, *The Birth of Biopolitics: Lectures at the Collège de France 1978–79*, London: Palgrave Macmillan, 2008.

The lesson for an entrepreneur is clear: competition is for losers.'[6] The losers are the capitalists who cannot secure a monopoly position and escape competition.

The 'infinitely active' intervention of the state to make competition possible, described by Foucault and invoked by ordoliberals and neoliberals, will only foster centralization, the concentration of power in the hands of a few, and a growing imbalance of all economic forms (income, wealth, movable and immovable property). The free market produces not only imbalance, but also the seemingly paradoxical result of suppressing it: competition, instead of regulating itself, crumbles.

## Marx and triple centralization

In analysing capitalism, it is necessary to recognize (dollar) imperialism as its regime of truth because it combines capital, state, and military force. The principles of centralization and monopoly work on all three of these forces. Without the political centralization of the state, both administrative and military, and especially the centralization of executive power, imperialism (but also Marx's *Capital*) would be impossible.

This triple centralization converging on imperialism knows no interruption, no reversal (least of all on the part of neoliberalism); indeed, it only intensified after 1971, resulting in war.

The brief reconstruction of the processes of centralization and monopoly that we propose begins with Marx.

Competition as the main actor in the construction of monopolies was already highlighted by Marx: 'competition . . . always ends in the ruin of many small capitalists, whose capitals partly pass into the hands of their conquerors, partly vanish.' The result is centralization, the absorption of the smaller capitalists by the larger ones or the departure of the former from the market. But the real centralizing force is the credit system,

---

6 Peter Thiel, 'Competition Is for Losers', *Wall Street Journal*, 12 September 2014, wsj.com.

which again according to Marx constitutes 'an enormous social mechanism for the centralisation of capitals', because credit offers the 'absolute control within certain limits over the capital and property of others, and thereby over the labour of others'.[7]

In Volume 3 of *Capital*, Marx identifies two processes of centralization: one industrial; the second, more importantly, financial. In both cases, these centralization processes work through expropriation (and rent).

> Success and failure both lead here to a centralisation of capital, and thus to expropriation . . . [which] extends here from the direct producers to the smaller and the medium-sized capitalists themselves. It is the point of departure for the capitalist mode of production; its accomplishment is the goal of production . . . This expropriation appears within the capitalist system in a contradictory form, as appropriation of social property by a few; and credit lends the latter more and more the aspect of pure adventurers.[8]

The abstract nature of credit permits an even more powerful centralization: an appropriation imposed by an even smaller number of enterprises and an even more pervasive control of the economy. 'Since property here exists in the form of stock, its movement and transfer become purely a result of gambling on the stock exchange, where the little fish are swallowed by the sharks and the lambs by the stock-exchange wolves.'[9]

At the end of the nineteenth century, credit brought about a quantum leap in the construction of banking monopolies, leading to a hegemony of finance capital and rent that Marx could only partially grasp. 'The development of credit and the enormous concentration of money-lending in

---

[7] Karl Marx, *Capital*, vol. 1, trans. Samuel Moore and Edward Aveling, ed. Frederick Engels, Moscow: Progress Publishers, 1954 (1887), chs 25, 27, available at marxists.org.

[8] Karl Marx, *Capital*, vol. 3, ed. Frederick Engels, New York: International Publishers, 1959, ch. 27, available at marxists.org.

[9] Ibid.

the hands of large banks' arises from real accumulation, but, at the same time, differs from it and develops autonomously, with its own laws and behaviour. Gains and losses, 'through price fluctuations of these property titles, as well as their centralization' in the hands of a few, will be 'more and more the result of the game which appears in the place of labor as the original mode of acquisition of capital property and also takes the place of direct violence'.[10]

Marx still holds the illusion (which we can also find among contemporary Marxists, such as Negri and Hardt) that currency can replace the use of force: that direct violence is incorporated by the economy and transformed into the exercise of indirect violence. Imperialism, and especially dollar imperialism, will demonstrate the structural function of force in monetary and fiscal policies. There is no substitution, but complementarity and the chaining of the two forces together (currency and use of force, finance and military power).

Engels lived longer than Marx, and saw a more mature evolution of economic centralization than his comrade. As early as 1894, he stated that competition was not the regulating principle of the market, but what drowns it – its gravedigger.

The 'celebrated freedom of competition' has had its day and must 'confess its evident and scandalous bankruptcy', because 'the great captains of industry of a certain line meet for the joint regulation of production by means of a kartel ... This led in some lines, where the scale of production permitted it, to the concentration of the entire production of this line in one great stock company under one joint management.' British alkali production, 'which forms the basis of the entire chemical industry, has been replaced in England by monopoly, and the future expropriation of this line by the whole of society, the nation, has been well prepared'.[11]

---

10   Ibid.
11   Ibid.

## Political and military centralization

Marx not only analysed economic centralization but, in the *Eighteenth Brumaire*, he perfectly described the mechanisms of political centralization, which *precede* – by far – the process of the concentration of economic power in a few hands. The latter, without the former, would be impossible. The centralization of state power (sovereign, administrative and military) begins with absolute monarchy; it accelerated with the French Revolution and deepened again with the repressions exercised against the proletarian revolutions of the nineteenth century.

> The executive power with its enormous bureaucratic and military organization, with its wide-ranging and ingenious state machinery, with a host of officials numbering half a million, besides an army of another half million – this terrifying parasitic body which enmeshes the body of French society and chokes all its pores sprang up in the time of the absolute monarchy, with the decay of the feudal system which it had helped to hasten.[12]

The French Revolution ('with its task of breaking all separate local, territorial, urban, and provincial powers') is the other vital stage in the construction of this centralizing 'state machinery' that Napoleon 'completed'.

Marx connects a seemingly opposite process to this centralization, a multiplication and diffusion of the devices and techniques of government and control because the 'social groups' directly or indirectly involved in production increase as it expands. The state organizes 'a greater division of labor, increasing at the same rate as the division of labor inside the bourgeois society created new groups of interests, and therefore new material for the state administration'.[13]

---

12   Karl Marx, *The Eighteenth Brumaire of Louis Bonaparte*, Moscow: Progress Publishers, 1937, available at marxists.org.
13   Ibid.

It is important to emphasize Marx's analysis because this double movement of centralization and diffusion, of concentration and decentralization, exists also in neoliberalism. Marx does not fall (as did Foucault and the leftist critics who followed him) into the naïveté of opposing state sovereignty and centralization to the multiplication and diffusion of centres of power, of techniques of control. Power resides in centralization processes that control and decide a diffuse and radically subordinate social and political multiplicity.

Marx also explains that the instruments of the continuous strengthening of executive power, police and army, are required for the state's struggle against revolution.

> The parliamentary republic, in its struggle against the revolution, found itself compelled to strengthen the means and the centralization of governmental power with repressive measures. All revolutions perfected this machine instead of breaking it. The parties, which alternately contended for domination, regarded the possession of this huge state structure as the chief spoils of the victor.[14]

The third centralization regards the use of armed force (widespread, in feudal times, as the centres of power) and leads to the establishment of the 'legitimate monopoly of force'. Generally, the emphasis is on legitimacy, while the starting point, here as in economics, is monopoly. Only those who have a monopoly of force, that is, those who are the strongest, see their force legitimized. It is therefore monopoly that produces legitimacy, and not the other way around.

The monopoly of armed force legitimizes, domestically, only 'public violence' exercised by the state; 'private violence' must be regulated not by arms but by the courts. In neutralizing violence within society, the state pushes it to the borders, where it is exercised against an external enemy. Internal appeasement is embodied in electoral systems, which constitute an exemplary form of 'political game' and thus of limited internal warfare (with winners and losers vying for wages, welfare, and

---

14   Ibid.

power) that can always spill over, however, into real war – civil war – as found throughout the twentieth century. The monopoly of force is then exercised against an internal enemy, of which Bolshevism is a model.

Beginning in the seventeenth century, regular armies were set up for the legitimate exercise of force. The French Revolution transformed these into *popular armies*, which played a decisive role in the massacre of nineteenth-century revolutions, particularly in France, and later in the process of establishing economic monopolies, through colonial conquests and in the two world wars.

In 1933, Simone Weil pointed out that in 1792, during the French Revolution: 'Military technique was still far from having reached the same degree of centralization it has attained today; regardless, since Frederick II, the subordination of those soldiers charged with carrying out military operations to the high command responsible with coordinating those operations had been very strict.'[15]

War, even revolutionary war, gives rise to a centralized command apparatus that will not cease to strengthen. More generally, both war and production follow a parallel path: they merely require 'the arms and lives of the masses to be put increasingly at the disposal of the controlling apparatuses'.[16] Production and war gradually become more and more collective, while the centralization of command and decision-making functions are in the hands of an ever smaller number of people. A further leap in military centralization would be made with the dismantling of conscription (compulsory military service) and the formation of professional armies that avert the danger of 'soldiers' soviets', a constant concern for the bourgeoisie and the state because of the function they have exercised in all revolutions.[17]

---

15  Simone Weil, 'Reflections on War', trans. Chris Fleming, *Journal of Continental Philosophy*, 2021.
16  Ibid.
17  Ibid.

## Lenin and the new capitalism: Imperialism

These processes intensified after Marx's death, because finance capital became hegemonic, because the state and its armed and administrative forces played a decisive role in internal accumulation and external colonial pillage. With globalization and the First World War, which was a direct consequence of globalization, capitalism made a qualitative leap that the revolutionaries of the time called *imperialism*.

The matrix of contemporary capitalism is not to be sought in post–Second World War capitalism, which is a short parenthesis (twenty-five years) in its long history, but instead in the imperialist state-capital machine analysed and criticized by Luxemburg, Rudolf Hilferding, Leon Trotsky, Lenin, and others.

We can only really talk about a *world market* from Lenin onwards: 'Lenin is rightly credited with composing the transition from competition to monopoly, from the export of goods to the export of capital, into a theoretically significant representation' capable of capturing the developmental 'tendency of the world market and the contradictions it creates at the same time'. The criticisms levelled against Lenin's positions by Luciano Ferrari Bravo's *operaismo* did not prevent the latter from recognizing him as the 'last great creative theoretical effort of Marxism' – from which, however, one must pass in order to grasp the nature of 'modern imperialism' or American 'neo-imperialism'. Again, according to Ferrari Bravo, it is only from Lenin onwards that the workers' point of view on the world development of capital is given and fixed 'as a refusal'.[18]

Paul Sweezy also strongly emphasized that Lenin's work on monopoly capitalism 'was really a decisive advance in Marxist theory'.

Marx was aware of the existence of monopolies in the England he had chosen as a model of the workings of capital. However, like the classical economists before him, he did not consider them essential elements

---

18  Luciano Ferrari Bravo, 'Old and New Questions in the Theory of Imperialism' (1975), trans. Andrew Anastasi, Alessandra Guarino, and Dave Mesing, *Viewpoint Magazine*, 1 February 2018, viewpointmag.com.

of capitalism, but rather what remained of feudal and mercantilist economies, from which abstraction must be made in order to grasp the true nature of capital. 'Marx is perfectly familiar with the processes of concentration and centralization inherent in competition among capitalists,' Sweezy further states, but he did not attempt to investigate what a capitalism dominated by monopolies and political and military centralization would have been. Marxian analysis 'still rests on the assumption of a competitive economy', in which the empirical material for developing a theory of monopolies was still insufficient, the American Marxist suggests.[19]

The weak-minded (and there are many!) consider Lenin a dead dog. I, on the other hand, consider him a theorist, not only of the revolution, but also of capitalism, because, with the concept of imperialism, despite all the theoretical weaknesses that can be detected in it, he describes with political certainty four characteristics that are also found in mature dollar imperialism. Lenin, like the revolutionaries of his time, is also to be studied and absorbed for another reason. Contemporary critical thinking is forced, in its poverty, to look to geopolitics as a way of understanding war at world-market level. Geopolitics is an institutional discipline that reduces capitalism to relations between states, stripping them of their nature as a struggle between classes. To escape the limitations of geopolitics and bring back the scaffolding within globalization around class struggle, Lenin is still very useful.

At the end of the nineteenth century, industrial capital lost its supremacy to financial capital. The significance of this must be immediately made explicit: the hegemony of finance capital means economy and rentier classes dominating and controlling profit, to the point of blurring the two categories. For England and France, the two most important states and colonial empires of the time, rent played an essential role. Fundamentally colonial in nature, it is extracted through imperialism, that is, through the combined and coordinated action of state and capital.

---

19   Paul Baran and Paul Sweezy, *Monopoly Capital*, New York: Monthly Review Press, 1968, pp. 3–4.

Quoting a French newspaper of the time, Lenin revealed another reality of capitalism that is still relevant today – that the hegemony of finance, the blurring of rent and profit, is not matched by the political system of democracy but by oligarchy: 'France is a financial monarchy, France is a financial oligarchy, France is the world's money-lender.'[20]

Colonization is, after financialization or rent, the second characteristic of the new capitalism: 'Britain, a country which owns the greater part of the globe, a country which ranks first in wealth . . . has created this wealth not so much by the labor of its workers as by the exploitation of innumerable colonies.'[21] In the colonies, the robbery of resources and the export of goods and capital – without which capital could not reproduce itself – are inseparable from military intervention.

The third characteristic of imperialism comprises the processes of centralization that have grown even more severe since Engels's analysis of competition as the undertaker of competitive capitalism. Imperialism is the coming together of two formidable processes of centralization: the older, political one of the state; and the newer, economic one of capital. These are not identical because one is centred on profit and the other on power.

The 'boundless force' of this capitalism derives from the concentration of economic power in the hands of 'four or five super-banks handling billions of rubles, and handling them in such a way that it can be said without exaggeration that there is not a patch of land in the world today on which this capital has not laid its heavy hand, not a patch of land which British capital has not enmeshed by a thousand threads.'[22]

This potent economic centralization (monopolies) is matched by an equally powerful political centralization (state), which facilitates the first: 'The capitalism of the free-competition age, into the capitalism of giant trusts, syndicates, and cartels . . . [combines] the colossal power of capitalism with the colossal power of the state into a single mechanism.'

---

20  V. I. Lenin, 'War and Revolution', in *Collected Works*, vol. 24, Moscow: Progress Publishers, 1964, available at marxists.org.
21  Ibid.
22  Ibid.

This mechanism – the state-capital machine – does not produce an identification of the state with capital but rather holds the different parts together.[23] The state intervenes directly in the functioning of financial capital, industrial capitalism, society, and competition; its action is decisive in colonial conquests, in wars necessary to control growing parts of the world market, which is itself centralized – that is, it possesses its own centre of power (England), but in continuous imperialistic dispute with established (France) or emerging (Germany) centres of power.

In this capitalism, war – the fourth characteristic of the new capitalism – plays a fundamental role both economically and politically. It does not constitute an extrinsic reality, an accident with which accumulation must occasionally come to terms. The great socialization of production in the countries of the North (a phenomenon that 1960s Italian *operaismo* called the 'social factory') took place during the First World War, which activated all of society (general mobilization) to produce materials for the war, so that *production would be forever marked by war*. The other major change brought about by the socialization of production as a function of war was the identification between, and reversibility of, production and destruction.

The end of imperialism would mean the exclusion of war, monopolies, and the state from the functioning of capitalism. Instead, monopolies and competition between imperialisms, with the resulting arms race, constitute the processes of centralization of command over labour in the world market. Imperialism is, above all, a new phase of class confrontation, the phase of world revolution, in which oppressed peoples (and no longer the working class) play a central role. There is a double leap from Marx: one concerns capitalism, the other revolution.

## The supremacy of monopoly over competition

There is a clear continuity in forms of centralization. At the end of Fordism, a period now economically and nostalgically coveted,

---

23   Ibid.

monopolies and centralization processes were again reinforced in comparison to the first part of the twentieth century. James O'Connor's 1973 book, *The Fiscal Crisis of the State*, reviewed the US economy immediately prior to the advent of self-styled neoliberalism and (the very real) superimperialism. It highlights a relationship between monopoly and competition that provides an excellent example of the coexistence of centralization (monopoly economy) and diffusion, or decentralization (competitive economy), according to a strict and precise hierarchy.

O'Connor describes the US economy as divided into three sectors: state-controlled economy; monopoly economy; and competitive economy – a new version of the non-contradictory process between the concentration of economic power in a few hands and widespread production organized by competition, and rigidly subordinated to the former. Each of these sectors employs about a third of the labour force, but with very different weight and power. The monopoly sector is characterized by high productivity; indeed, it has as its main goal a continual increase. It employs a well-trained and well-organized working class in labour unions that exchange continuous increases in productivity for high wages. It produces relative surplus value, so these are capital-intensive enterprises. The state intervenes by financing and producing, through the Pentagon, the technological innovation necessary for its development. In the second half of the twentieth century, during Fordism, monopolies, instead of shrinking, became even stronger. The process of monopolization of the economy – the integration of state and capital – was not reversed during Fordism; on the contrary, it was deepening and strengthening as early as the 1960s. The only monopoly that was regulated, for a short period, was finance (it had caused too much damage, leading to world wars, fascism, and Nazism); but that quickly resumed its process of concentration, returning to the centre of capitalist strategies soon after the declaration of non-convertibility of the dollar into gold.

The competitive sector, on the other hand, based on the production of absolute surplus value, is characterized by low capital intensity and high exploitation of labour power manifested through longer working days and weak investment in fixed capital. Profits can grow only by keeping wages low, imposing poor working conditions, and overtime. The employed working class in this sector is not well-educated, nor does it have a good level of union organization. In the competitive economy, new firms enter and leave the industry relatively easily because competition is high but productivity low.

The market model in which the law of supply and demand and competition works – which neoliberals and ordoliberals proclaim as the truth regime of the economy – actually consists of a ragged, poor, internationally uncompetitive capitalism that has *never* had a chance to establish itself as the leader of the national American economy.

In the early 1970s, the monopoly sector led and directed the economy, while the competitive sector occupied a secondary and subordinate role to the logic and interests of the former. Even in Fordism, state sovereignty was not undermined by the economy, as Foucault believed, because the latter, in turn, never ceased to sovereignize itself – intensifying, inexorably, monopoly and centralization.

## The counterrevolutionary 1970s

Samir Amin has summarized the waves of centralization that have characterized capital during the second half of the nineteenth century: the first, which began immediately after the Paris Commune in response to the first long structural crisis of capitalism (stagnation), was commercial, industrial, financial, and colonial in nature. Industrial centralization had very real effects on the working class and the economy as a whole, but the subordination of small and medium-sized enterprises was still partial.

'The second wave of the centralization of capital, which took place in the last third of the twentieth century, constituted a second qualitative transformation of the system', which Samir Amin calls 'generalized monopolies' that bring about a new and integral subordination of production, in the sense that they go beyond the separation between monopolistic and competitive economies (as described by O'Connor).

'They also succeeded in imposing their direct control over the whole production system. The small and medium enterprises (and even the large ones outside the monopolies), such as the farmers, were literally dispossessed, reduced to the status of sub-contractors, with their upstream and downstream operations, and subjected to rigid control by the monopolies.'[24] At the same time, the ban on industrialization in the South has been lifted and massive investments have been shifted to a labour market where the workforce is poorly paid or underpaid.

But what is really new is the quantum leap made by the centralizations driven by finance and money, processes grasped very late by Marxist thought, even in its most heterodox forms. Luciano Ferrari Bravo's *Imperialismo e classe operaia multinazionale* (Imperialism and the multinational working class), a collection of essays by Marxist authors who have worked on imperialism (James O'Connor, Martin Nicolaus, Ernest Mandel, Stephen Mayer, Nicos Poulantzas, Ferruccio Gambino), is symptomatic of the limitations of these theories.[25] The texts were written in the first half of the 1970s (Ferrari Bravo's essay dates from 1974). Reading them now, it is striking that no one mentions, even in passing, the strategy that the counterrevolution had been organizing since the late 1960s. The discussion revolves around industrial capitalism, companies (which have become multinational), the world market and its determination of wages and rate of profit, and the transformations of labour and workers. Even the new theories that integrate desire into production (Deleuze and Guattari) or the biological into the political (Foucault) seem oblivious to the form the state-capital machine was already taking.

The counterrevolution, on the other hand, was organizing itself on wholly other bases. At its centre, we find not industry and businesses (even if multinational), but finance capital, money, and consumption – driven not by wages, but by debt. Capitalism shifted its centre of gravity from

---

24 Samir Amin, 'The Trajectory of Historical Capitalism and Marxism's Tricontinental Vocation', *Monthly Review*, 1 February 2011, monthlyreview.org.

25 Luciano Ferrari Bravo, *Imperialismo e classe operaia multinazionale*, Milan: Feltrinelli, 1977.

labour to consumption through debt because wages had to be locked in. This new strategy would have enormous consequences for accumulation, forms of subjugation, the organization of society – and its governance.

At the turn of the 1970s, the only Marxist who grasped the new configuration of global control over labour and society was Paul Sweezy: the 'corporate paradigm' built around the joint stock company, part of a set of monopolies and oligopolies, lost its centrality and became one element of a device commanded by finance, money, and debt. Power, said Sweezy, is not to be sought so much in the boardrooms of corporations as in financial markets. The centre of the economy had shifted from the production of goods and services to the buying and selling of money and the multiplication of financial assets.

The crux of the counterrevolutionary strategy was the 'large indebtedness' affecting businesses, the state, and consumers. Sweezy insisted on the latter: the growth of consumer debt is, at the same time, *cause and effect of the fundamental role of consumption in the process of accumulation*, which it will not abandon from then on.

Sweezy criticized not only his own work (*Monopoly Capital* underestimated the function of finance and debt), but Marx and Marxism more generally, for the tendency to separate industrial accumulation and financial accumulation, real economy and virtual economy, capital that produces and sells commodities and capital that produces and sells money and financial products.

Finance was not defined as parasitic, and could not even be captured by the Marxian concept of *fictitious capital*. We could have spared ourselves many unnecessary debates at the turn of the century if we had adopted this definition of finance and capitalism.

> Does the casino society in fact channel far too much talent and energy into financial shell games. Yes, of course. No sensible person could deny it. Does it do so at the expense of producing real goods and services? Absolutely not. There is no reason whatever to assume that if you could deflate the financial structure, the talent and energy now employed there would move into productive pursuits. They would simply become unemployed and add to the country's already huge

reservoir of idle human and material resources. Is the casino society a significant drag on economic growth? Again, absolutely not. What growth the economy has experienced in recent years, apart from that attributable to an unprecedented peacetime military build-up, has been almost entirely due to the financial explosion.[26]

The centralization, the verticalization of power through finance, currency, and debt, thanks to their nature as commodities and abstract – but terribly effective – devices of control, reaches a peak.

Sweezy identified a further feature of accumulation through finance and consumption that would prove increasingly important: great debt is the origin of great waste, because production comes to see as its engine the opulent American way of life which has at its heart the industries of arms and consumption, and becomes in turn a paradigm exported to Europe and Japan. *Waste* is Sweezy's name for the destructive force of capital's accumulation. He considers stagnation an underlying tendency of capitalism that only waste, wars, armaments, and consumption turning on itself can counteract. Stagnation is intrinsic to capitalism, and expresses it as regression, destruction, and nihilism.

## Neoliberalism is maximum centralization

The new (self-styled neoliberal) configuration of the economy always includes two different monopolies at its centre: the monopoly of the American imperial machine that centralizes and plans command over currency as never before in the history of mankind; and the financial centralization that reaches unthinkable heights. All the while, so-called production is spread throughout the world and subordinates every kind of activity to the logic of profit.

The *monopoly* against which ordoliberals and neoliberals stand has been further strengthened through currency. *Only the Fed decides*, in

---

26   Harry Magdoff and Paul M. Sweezy, *Stagnation and the Financial Explosion*, New York: Monthly Review Press, 1987.

complicity and/or tension with Wall Street and financialized firms (monopolies), on interest rates, availability of liquidity, and the amount of currency issued, which have immediate effects on the world economies.

It is not the *market and competition* that set the prices of strategic goods. The most important ones, those of money and credit – decisive for development or recession – are the prerogatives of big government, Wall Street, and the Pentagon – the oligopolies – that is, the combined state-capital machine of America. The price of money and credit *do not depend on the law of supply and demand*. Instead, they are established on the basis of relations between dominant and dominated forces.

The state, banks, and big business defend themselves in every way against competition because it is the main cause of fall in profits, and instead work hard and in concert to reduce and/or eliminate it.

A handful of Marxist economists (Emiliano Brancaccio, Raffaele Giammetti, Stefano Lucarelli), after some long and commendable research (limited, however, to economics alone), concluded that 80 per cent of stocks are owned by less than 2 per cent of stockholders in the US. Centralization affects every imperial machine, not just the US. Also, according to this study, China surpasses even the US in this centralization process.[27]

The huge derivatives market is controlled by a limited number of banks reminiscent of Lenin's era, only now the value of controlled securities is astronomical. Precisely 95.35 per cent of the derivatives trade is handled by only five investment banks (listed according to the quantity of the amount controlled): JP Morgan Chase; Goldman Sachs; Citibank National Association; Bank of America; and Wells Fargo.

The hint of a questioning of the US oligarchy and its financial monopoly is at the heart of the contemporary Ukraine war.

The centrality of the monetary monopoly is joined by new and mighty industrial monopolies. All new enterprises that are considered strategic (IT, communication, arms production) are monopolies built through

---

27  Emiliano Brancaccio, Raffaele Giammetti, and Stefano Lucarelli, *La guerra capitalista: Competizione, centralizzazione, nuovo conflitto imperialista*, Milan: Mimesis, 2002.

state intervention, measures that immediately transform them into rent-producing devices that widen US sovereignty, which is no longer territorial but is asserted through electronic, digital networks. The body of the sovereign dominates in new ways.

Fifty years of so-called free competition, market, and supply and demand have produced even stronger and more aggressive monopolies. The capitalist economy has certainly not become competitive through neoliberalism (the only great competition conceived, designed, and constructed pits the workers of relocated industry in the global South against the workers of the global North). From this point of view, capitalism always works by concentrating economic and political power in whatever it exploits: labour, life, desire, biology. Inside the shortage caused by the COVID-19 crisis and the winds of war, the monopoly sector is even more comfortable in setting prices, based not in the relationship of supply and demand, but on unilateral power. The term *pricing power* has also been coined to express the balance of power available to large groups, which can impose prices, escaping competitive constraints and driving inflation.

## War's totalization

The current war in Ukraine allows us to complete the *law of centralization decreed by Marx*. Just like globalization, it is impossible for totalization and centralization to reach their completion, and become fully realized. In the world market, all other competitors can never be eradicated through the economy and the administrative action of the state. The state's sovereign power and capital's *sovereignty* (monopoly) can grow, but cannot become absolute.

Capital and the state are centres of power that are always relative, but can become absolute through war. The processes of globalization, centralization, and totalization that cannot be completed economically can be achieved through war. For the past century, economic competition has systematically resulted in warlike power struggles. War is the way in which imperialism – the state-capital machine – tries to overcome its internal contradictions: the impossibility of bringing globalization to fruition, of bringing the economy back within the boundaries of the nation-state. War accomplishes what economic-political force does not. In the theoretical framework outlined by political economy, but also by Marx, monetary/financial power does not have the option of war at its disposal, and thus remains within the limits of economic/political action. On the other hand, when the political-economic machine no longer functions according to expectations (it does not capture the value necessary for its reproduction), and when warlike competition becomes too dangerous for both profit and power, dollar imperialism does not hesitate to unleash, today, yesterday, wars of all kinds and types.

Foucault also believed that totalization was impossible, but his belief was based on the reasons given in the ideology of classical and neoclassical economics. The economic world is 'by nature not totalizable': no one can claim to have a 'comprehensive and totalizing' view because the viewpoint of economic actors never exceeds their immediate interest. 'In the middle of the eighteenth century, political economy denounces the paralogism of political totalization of the economic process.'[28] Economic phenomena are the result of the impersonal action of the market and competition, and never of politics.

In order for 'the greatest good [to be] attained for the greatest number of people, not only is it possible, but it is absolutely necessary that each actor be blind with regard to this totality'. Economics 'is a discipline without totality' which manifests the leitmotif of the theory of governmentality: 'the uselessness, but also the impossibility of the sovereign point of view ... There is no sovereign in economics. There is no economic sovereign.'[29]

On the other hand, there are indeed sovereigns in economics, because monopolies act as such, because the monetary government acts as such, and because the state also exercises its sovereignty through the economy.

---

28  Onur Ulas Ince, *Colonial Capitalism and the Dilemmas of Liberalism*, Oxford: Oxford University Press, 2018.

29  Foucault, *The Birth of Biopolitics*, p. 302.

None of these will ever be able to totalize the process, however. They are not blind; they see quite well, and, depending on what is before their eyes, they adopt strategies to concentrate even more economic and political power by eliminating competition – not only by economic means, but also by extra-economic force. If the process of political totalization fails, it is not due to any purported anti-sovereign ontology of the market and competition, but to the clash of different political strategies.

The actors, both oligopoly and state, are not individuals limited by specific interests, but collectively organized forces that have a global point of view that aims at totalization, because both monopolies and sovereign money power decide on commodity and money prices, and above all *impose* them on other economic actors and other states. Imperialism is precisely this leap, where economic and political forces eschew competition, and impose, as if they were sovereigns, their views on the world market, even using arms to do it.

It is true that they cannot completely totalize the *economy*, and complete globalization, because there is a fierce struggle for hegemony; but then war comes into play as an attempt to finalize the process. At least until now (beyond the ideology of political economy taken up and developed by the theory of governmentality), war has played this role by putting into place, most recently, the imperial power of the United States. That this power exercises sovereign privilege in both economics and politics is demonstrated by the fact that the Americans are exempt from enforcing and obeying laws, provisions, and treaties that they themselves have imposed, and that all others must instead accept and abide by.

## Centralization: Institutional democracy/ democracy of capitalism

That in capitalism we can no longer distinguish politics from economics, and that capitalism forces the political to reconfigure itself, is demonstrated by the evolution of democracy. We also find the double movement that the accumulation of capital has shown us in this evolution. On one hand, we have an apparently democratic process of growing freedom that increasingly coincides with the horizontal spread of consumption (which is always, however, differentiated and hierarchized according to polarizations of income and wealth, but also according to differences between the centre and the periphery), whereby democracy becomes the *social democracy* of the consumer rather than of the citizen. On the other hand, the verticalization of executive power depletes legislative power (and thus also voter power), so that democracy quickly degenerates by integrating new forms of fascism and civil war in its increasingly authoritarian functioning.

With financial capitalism, both consumption and debt (individual, corporate, and state) – the condition and prerequisite of the former – become economic forces that drive accumulation, accelerating (growth) or restraining it. They destroy productive forces (deflation), and the *forces that transform subjectivities*, but also the main *political forces* capable of guaranteeing democratic consensus and stability, or exclusion, repression, and the destruction of entire social classes and institutions.

The political analysis of consumption has always been neglected by critical thought. We begin to find important insights in this regard in the 1970s, however: in Sweezy's work, it becomes a strategic economic weapon to beat the working class thanks to financialization (and Pier Paulo Pasolini or Jean Baudrillard, and even Jacques Lacan, highlight its force of subjugation). Its political function is rarely highlighted though. Here I will attempt to analyse its triple effect: its economic, subjective, and political effects, insisting particularly on the latter.

Dollar imperialism is characterized not only by the export of capital, like the old imperialism, but also by the export of the political forms of American capitalism to the rest of the world. The spread of this so-called democracy succeeds only in Europe and Japan, while it fails miserably in the global South.

This take-away democracy emerged from a republic that was not created democratically, but which resulted from a civil war waged against the British, and the conquest of so-called free lands (the famous frontier of the West) – that is, through the genocide of the indigenous people who inhabited them and the unpaid labour of African slaves. In the first half of the twentieth century, republican institutions were supported by a particular kind of democracy that only capitalism could produce: parallel to the New Deal and the creation of welfare, a social democracy (for whites only) began to emerge.

This new democracy would fully develop only after the Second World War, leaning on economic forces rather than institutional realities. In mature and stagnant capitalism, consensus was based on commodities, and social and individual consumption, controlled by business, while public consumption was managed by the state (welfare), and only secondarily by voting, unions, and political participation. Beginning in the 1970s, the counterrevolution would prefer this political system to the democracy of the New Deal – that is, the democracy built under the capital/labour compromise.

The state of political parties and the European welfare state of the Trente Glorieuses were caught in a double stranglehold of the American matrix: in conjunction with the development of an 'absolute, meticulous, systematic, prescient and mild' power (as described by Alexis de Tocqueville) – in other words, *consumption* – the privatization of welfare is capable of transforming even social services (health, education, housing) into forms of individual consumption.[30] Meanwhile, imperialism drove monetary and financial centralization that regulated and *controlled private and public consumption through individual and sovereign debt (of states), and no longer through wages.*

The Keynesian principle of full employment shifted towards access to consumption, to (small) property, to the possessive individualism of the financier, the income earner, and the entrepreneur. On the contrary, precarious, underpaid, servile labour spread from the South to the North and now constitutes the political norm for consumption in the society of opulence.

The devices for the control and production of subjectivity are manifold, but the specificity of mature capitalism is to achieve *freedom and equality* through the circulation of goods. Tocqueville saw the emergence of an 'immense and tutelary power' precisely from American democracy. This power, however, escapes the categories of 'tyranny and

---

30  Alexis de Tocqueville, *Democracy in America*, trans. Henry Reeve, London: Saunders and Otley, 1835, available at gutenberg.org.

despotism' because it assures an 'innumerable crowd of like and equal men who revolve on themselves without repose, procuring the small and vulgar pleasures' that condemn them 'irrevocably to infancy'.[31]

What can make 'citizens amuse themselves, provided they think only of amusement' if not consumption, which Tocqueville, in his time, could hardly have foreseen? The power inherent in the circulation of commodities perfectly corresponds to that described by the French liberal – it 'willingly works for their happiness', of which it 'wants to be the sole agent and arbiter ... what remains but to spare them all the care of thinking and all the trouble of living?' Invasive and pervasive, accompanying every gesture, every form of behaviour, every desire – this power is exercised not on abstract citizens, but on real proletarians: on their biological needs, but also on their most personal desires.[32]

Consumption, consumers, marketing techniques, and ubiquitous advertising perfectly correspond to a democracy capable of producing a 'well-ordered, easy and quiet servitude' that can be combined with 'some external form of freedom'.[33]

The process of individualization led by consumption and debt can be usefully understood with the help of Carl Schmitt, who analysed the tendency of the state, starting with the establishment of the absolute state, to create a situation in which individual and state directly face each other, without any mediation. This ideal situation is realized in the French Revolution, which the German jurist described using the work of Condorcet: within the state, there are no longer 'powerful groups and classes. The *associations puissantes* [powerful associations] have vanished. While they existed, *un despotisme armé* [an armed despotism] was required to contain them. Now individuals confront a unified totality. Thus, *il faut bien peu de force pour forcer les individus à l'obéissance* [a little force is needed to keep individuals obedient].'[34]

---

31 Ibid.
32 Ibid.
33 Ibid.
34 Carl Schmitt, *Dictatorship: From the Origin of the Modern Concept of Sovereignty to Proletarian Class Struggle*, trans. Michael Hoelzl and Graham Ward, Cambridge: Polity Press, 2014.

It is clear that, with the advent of capitalism, this individualization (and the equality that makes it possible) can be continued and fully accomplished by a force that is no longer institutional – by consumption itself. Without any mediation, consumption faces the individual directly, not only before the state, but also before capital. Consumption is the most effective device for individualization, and it has almost never been investigated in this light.

Social democrats and reformists mourn the disappearance of intermediate bodies (workers' unions, employers' unions, tradesmen's associations, and so on), which they would like to resurrect, when in fact this eradication is an indispensable strategic objective of capitalism: as soon as the balance of power allows it, capital resets *civil society* to zero. Instead, Foucault thinks that the latter is inseparable from *Homo economicus*. For him, civil society guarantees a non-economic social bond, a kind of spontaneous social pact within which the economy finds its place. Schmitt's position seems to me more credible: he holds that the ideal of capital and the state is to dispense with any civil society at all – that is, any 'powerful groups, classes and associations' that an individual can join and rely upon for mediation with the state. Rather, Schmitt's state prefers to confront the individual directly. From this point of view, the counterrevolution embodied in consumption/debt has been a great success, because it has succeeded in undermining all kinds of mediation, until (civil) society ceases to exist, leaving only individuals.

Consumption can also tell us a lot about the nature of power, as analysed by Pasolini, Baudrillard, and Lacan. It is the expression of a power that does not repress, that never says *no*, but rather panders, urges, incites, always saying *yes* (Foucault). The *positive* power of consumption seems to compensate and sublimate the *negative* power of sovereign centralizations and the burgeoning polarizations of class, sex, and race. The figure that fully realizes the subjectification of the consumer is the tourist, who is definitively established as the model of contemporary capitalist subjectivity in the counterrevolution, with tourism becoming one of the most important industries.

The complete realization of the positive, however, unleashes an unprecedented machine of annihilation: the tourist, an absolutely deterritorialized consumer, while sacrificing their own subjectivity to the cult of consumption, destroys the social, economic, cultural, and linguistic relations of the cities and in the places where they circulate, making a tabula rasa of every kind of environment they pass through (ecological, cultural, social). Its positive action turns everything it touches into nihilism: tourism is the pinnacle of contemporary capitalism's identity of production and destruction.

But to understand the power of consumption it is also necessary to analyse the nature of debt, its condition and presupposition. Debt is a *positive* power that drives individuals, businesses, and states to spend. Yet it is also – and above all – a terrible *negative* power that, since the 1970s, has been sowing death and violence around the globe through austerity and structural-adjustment policies imposed by international financial institutions. These policies have annihilated economies, protection systems, and social and political rights, first in African countries, then in Latin America, then Southeast Asia, and finally in Europe (Greece). The negative force is such that the subprime debt crisis exported around the world by the US, which became a sovereign debt crisis, opened the phase of the current Ukraine war. Debt wields life-and-death power over the peoples of the world.

In the new democracy of the circulation of goods, images, and information, workers and production are disappearing less than thirty years after they functioned as the regulative idea of politics. Party democracy and the capital-labour compromise are easily routed by the pairing of the dollar's debt imperialism and the democracy of circulation and consumption.

Our current democracy, a depoliticization of class and party democracy that existed in Europe for a very brief period (1945–68), no longer makes much political sense and is rightly ignored by voters (abstention), who are aware that *decisions* are centralized elsewhere (in the quadrilateral Fed, Wall Street, Pentagon, and oligopoly monopolies) and that *participation* is reduced to the consumption of goods, images, and information.

Social democracy is based not on a political pact (as described by Hobbes, Rousseau, and others, and of which the capital-labour compromise is still part) but rather, to put it succinctly, on the shopping cart. This is the main reason for the failure of exporting democracy to the countries of the South. Americans cannot guarantee this specific model of social democracy (it costs too much), and, for that matter, the despoliation of the global South remains the condition of affluent society.

Institutional democracy can perish (limited to sporadic elections that rendered the motto *one person, one vote* vain from the very beginning), democratic rituals can lose their meaning (why and for whom should one vote when the parties present no substantial difference?), neofascists can be integrated into the institutions and undermine the very foundation on which postwar democracies were built, the oxymoron of *democratic ruler* (presidentialism) can now impose itself in every country, but *consumer democracy – precisely because it is non-institutional – is not in the least affected*. Raging inflation matters much more to the citizen-consumer than any of these problems. Consent has not been completely withdrawn from the state-capital machine, only because commodity democracy has not yet entered a crisis of no return. Despite the fact that *progressive democracy* has been transformed into an oligarchy through the hegemony of finance capital, the overall legitimacy of the political system endures through the fantasy of freedom and equality, secured, in the North, by the circulation of commodities.

Corresponding to this power of consumption, non-political power (in the classical sense) is a process of verticalization of institutionally defined democratic power. The centralization of political power is older than the centralization of capital (Marx), but with imperialism and the First World War it was greatly accelerated.

Here I would like to reiterate an analysis I undertook, along with Éric Alliez, in our book *Wars and Capital*, based on the work of Nicolas Roussellier. As world conflict breaks out, governments, not armies, prove best suited to mobilize the nation and population for total war. It is a war of governments before it is a war of armies, because the knowledge and management of the resources that will be activated belongs to civil power and, especially, to executive power. War will henceforth be *deep war*, capable of involving the whole of the population – labour, industry, and public opinion – rather than just being the task of an armed detachment of a nation. Industrial war requires a reconfiguration of executive power that does not end with the conclusion of hostilities but continues to the present. By learning to direct a nation at war, the executive has opened the way to the return of the military into the very definition of the nature and function of political power. Conducting war through the conceiving and organizing of executive power lays the path for a political-military (or political-military-industrial) executive.

While the First World War revealed the crisis of a military model based on the separation of decision-making (army general staff) and its execution on the battlefield, 'in the constitutional political sphere the separation of legislation and execution is equally questioned'. Immediately after the First World War, the new executive power continued its work of depriving legislative power of its authority. The need for faster and more effective political action is felt everywhere. Carl Schmitt defines this new governmental practice imposed by a centralizing executive as the 'motorized legislature', or 'the increasing motorization of the machine to legislate'.

The centralizing dynamic of executive power was never denied, even by the democracies that emerged from the war against Nazi fascism. It continued undaunted even during postwar reconstruction and decisively intensified with the counterrevolution of the 1970s. But its climax is being reached during neoliberalism's alleged struggle against all forms of concentration of power.

The *economic, political, and subjective transformative power* of consumption is a terrain on which class struggle is played out and, as such, it is surely *one* of the causes of the impending civil war. Using Marxian categories, we will now analyse the clash that threatens to destroy what remains of the social democracy of consumption, the last bastion in defence of institutional democracy and its process of centralization.

The power of consumption runs through individuals, splitting them, according to the division in the condition of the worker already discussed by Marx. On the one hand, it makes each individual both abstract and universal, equal to every other individual to whom advertising promises the satisfaction of every desire, and manifesting a power that is bound to limitless consumption, always saying yes. On the other hand, real (not just imaginary) access to goods is neither universal nor egalitarian, because it depends on the proletarian condition of the individual, in this case trapped in concreteness, in singularity. The consumption of the young insurgent of the French *banlieues*, of the precarious worker in underpaid jobs, of the woman providing free domestic work, of the racialized servile labourer, or the minimum wage earner must first pass through exploitation, submission to welfare, or the power of a bank (credit or microcredit).

The real consumption of proletarians runs up against all kinds of limits. The universality, abstraction, and equality of the individual consumer (and their infinite capacity to spend) shatters against the negative power of consumption, which, depending on the needs of capital accumulation, imposes austerity, sacrifice, debt repayment, welfare cuts, wage freezes, privatization, and, today, inflation.

The strategic role of *individualization* driven by consumption can be analysed in radically different ways depending on whether one adopts Marxian or Foucaldian tools. The French philosopher understands consumption as the *normalizing process of differentiation* of individuals, and limits its power to the production of their differential subjugation. Marx, on the other hand, puts the emphasis not on *difference* but on the *division* that runs through the individual. Division in Marx *always entails an expropriation*: the capitalist's expropriation of the product in production is also, simultaneously, an expropriation of consumption, and of the communal capacity to consume – that is first destroyed, then captured, and later completely configured by the capital-state, which subsequently imposes it on individuals, now isolated. This is a normalizing differentiation of consumption and consumers, but which, unlike in Foucault's model, is inseparable from abstraction and expropriation.

The expropriation of consumption is also the expropriation of the management of *reproduction* that passes to capital from the proletariat, from its autonomous forms of life, at the centre of which is the condemnation of women to domestic labour in mononuclear families. Without this free labour, consumption and reproduction would cost capital prohibitive amounts of money.

Again, using Marxian tools, division and dispossession can be considered the foundation not only of power, but also of class struggle and revolution, understood as collective subjectification. Foucaldian differentiation, on the other hand, focuses on the shift from the normalization of differences to their ethical-aesthetic subjectification of forms of life, precisely because it involves neither division nor expropriation. Marx, on the contrary, thinks of the rupture of division and the expropriation of the expropriators as the precondition of the relation to self! Clearly, these are two radically different conceptions of power and subjectification.

Consumption's abstract and singular aspects that divide the individual have clashed in an increasingly clear and violent way since the financial crisis started. The class struggle in the French *banlieues* still confirms that every revolt always contains the looting and appropriation of commodities. Revolt is the logical and rational consequence of the miraculous form of their appearance in the real and in images: if their production is miraculous, appropriation must be free.

## Towards world civil war?

The process of institutional verticalization has never been interrupted by neoliberal governmentality. On the contrary, governmental practices in executive branches undermine juridical systems; their laws and procedures organize the centralization of various state bureaucracies, so there is a mutual reinforcement of executive power and the administrative state.

Sovereignty becomes one with government, in the sense that *the government becomes sovereign*; the executive constantly overrules the legislative by issuing regulations, decrees, and administrative measures that no longer go through parliament. The need to have some kind of an absolute power within democracy is proper to every democratic constitution because all, without exception, evolve towards presidentialism. Political practice is no longer framed and governed by general laws, but ad hoc acts that issue specific administrative (and especially police) measures each time for every particular case. This rests on *decision* and not law; and the thing that decides is policy. These policies are determined by the action of the state-capital machine that mutes the rule of law and drains liberal and neoliberal forms of government. This is d*ecision*, because under the thin layer of democracy and the rule of law, even more menacingly after the 2008 financial crisis, civil war flows.

During the pandemic, centralization crossed another threshold, and, with the war in Ukraine, is taking another step forward. The Biden presidency intensified the process of centralizing the executive power of American imperialism. The necessary subordination of the value chain to the political-military strategy (global NATO) required the centralization of the executive which, in less than two years, issued 106 so-called executive orders (which don't need be converted into law) and 177 memoranda (procedures necessary to enforce laws, but which often contradict the laws themselves, ensuring increased power in the hands of the president).

The centralization of the political system no longer integrates conflict (as it did for a brief period between 1945 and 1968) under the impetus of class struggle in the global North (in the global South, there have always been wars of conquest and civil war). Quite the opposite: after becoming the engine of accumulation and institutions of the Trente Glorieuses, conflict was opposed, devalued, repressed, and criminalized as early as Thatcher and Reagan. The dialectical relationship between institutions and struggles, the foundation of the postwar capital/labour compromise, was publicly denounced in the early 1970s because it resulted in increased demands for wages, income, and social and political rights by the oppressed, according to the Trilateral Commission.

The collapse of the financial system marked a further step in this strategy of confrontation, of rejection of democratic mediation through parties and unions (even reformist ones), so conflict became radicalized – especially after 2008. The Arab Spring, the Chilean and Iranian uprisings, and the different experiences of reformism developed in Latin America all seemed short-lived because there were no conditions for a compromise.

Worldwide inflation unleashed by the monopolies and the Fed, coupled with the reduction of state social expenditures directed to the financing of armaments, have brought down another possible mediation: that of the private and public consumption that guaranteed consensus and pacification more than the democratic institutions themselves.

France is an exemplary case of how, in the global North, there has been a gradual shift from the conflict of the Trente Glorieuses to a situation of civil war that is gradually becoming less hidden and more like open warfare. Its specificity is precisely that it knows no mediation, no compromise, and no negotiation (as is always possible in wars between states) – there can be only winners and losers.

The clash in France over pension reforms (spring 2023), like the *gilets jaunes* movement before it, revealed a government determined not to make the slightest concession to the social movements that opposed the extension of the retirement age (even though they were led by reformist unions). When the echoes of the French '*mars*' had not yet died down, the uprising in the *banlieues* after the police killing of a young man, Nahel Merzouk, from a working-class neighbourhood took place within a political framework determined, as always, by the exclusion of any mediation with the colonized of the interior.[35] Those who are treated as natives of the republic (representatives of the South, living in the North) must be economically integrated, as poor, precarious, servile labour, and must be politically excluded (racism towards Muslims is a strategic axis of all governments). The same attitude of rejection was adopted towards ecological struggles, dissolving the organization Les Soulèvements de la Terre (Earth Uprising).

This formidable sequence of struggles was governed by the action of the police and justice system, which continually adopted laws to legitimize and legalize their actions. The police union's statement in defence of the policeman who killed the young Nahel Merzouk must be read as a sign of the intensification of the confrontation: 'Today the policemen are fighting a battle because we are at war' against the 'savage hordes' of the youth of the working-class neighbourhoods, defined as 'harmful';

---

35  Translator's note: Again, the French *mars* as in the month of March.

'tomorrow we will resist and the government must take note'.³⁶ The police accompany and facilitate the centralization of executive power because they are *the only institution capable of handling the state's rejection of the conflict*. In return, the government grants them maximum freedom in all respects, and the judicial branch covers for them.

France's confrontation for more than two centuries with revolutions, uprisings, and civil wars, domestically and in the colonies, has often involved repressive techniques accompanied by legal provisions that must legitimize them (and recommend them) to states around the world (the last resounding case: the Argentinian coup plotters of the 1970s had borrowed techniques tested in the Algerian war). In 2017, the French government ended the state of emergency that had been in effect since the November 2015 attacks. This special legislation had been instituted during the Algerian war, and was reinstated in 2005 during the *banlieues* uprisings as a testament to the continuity of French colonial policy, outside and inside the nation's borders. But the suspension of the state of emergency is only formal, because the exceptional provisions were integrated into the common law, first on an experimental basis in 2017, then definitively with the law of 30 July 2021. During the long struggle against pension reforms, these exceptional laws, now integrated into common law, were widely used, and hardly anyone noticed how the measures taken by prefects in various cities were normalized state-of-emergency devices. Walter Benjamin's statement – 'The tradition of the oppressed teaches us that the "state of emergency" in which we live is not the exception but the rule' – had found its institutionalization.³⁷

When economic, social, and patrimonial divisions become politicized through a sequence of struggles, as in France – ranging from the *gilets jaunes* to struggles against pension reforms, from ecological demonstrations to revolts in the *banlieues* – the police and the judicial system are the institutions on the front lines. Since the beginning of his

---

36  Damien Renoulet, 'Mort de Nahel: Un communiqué de syndicats de police enflamme la gauche qui parle de "sédition"', RTL, 30 June 2023, rtl.fr.
37  Walter Benjamin, 'On the Concept of History', in *Selected Writings*, vol. 4, *1938–1940*, ed. Howard Eiland and Michael W. Jennings, Cambridge, MA: Harvard University Press, 2003, p. 392.

presidential term, Macron has been governing *with* and *thanks to* the police. The power exercised over various social strata is the *government of civil war* – the exact opposite of the governmentality proposed by Foucault: 'Basically power is less a confrontation between two adversaries ... than a question of government.' It is a mode of action 'neither warlike nor juridical'. Power should not be 'sought on the side of violence or of struggle', but on the side of government.[38]

The real action of power against this long and formidable sequence of struggles is all that Foucault denies, removes, exorcises: it is the material, daily exercise of power normalized by a state of emergency; it is violence and struggle, it is warlike (police) and juridical. The regime's brutality has only grown from struggle to struggle, culminating in the repression of the *banlieues* revolt where it mobilized its entire repressive apparatus and the entire legal arsenal of the judiciary branch.

While the *negative* action of power is clearly seen, the *positive* action is latent.

Ordinary law not only supplanted the laws of the state of emergency, but the courts carried out state and ruling-class vengeance against those who dared to rebel. The violence of the disproportionate punishments meted out to young insurgents were tributes to the sanctity of property and order.

One might have the impression that social movements do not recognize this change of political phases, the closing spaces of agency put in place by the end of neoliberalism and accentuated – this time definitively – by war. The idea that social movements can develop by themselves – grow and expand without passing through moments of confrontation with the enemy; that they can plot escape routes, organizing exodus and defecting without determining ruptures, and without building power relations and forms of organization capable of supporting them – is now an illusion belied every day by the exacerbation of class, gender, and race differences.

---

38  Michel Foucault, 'The Subject and Power', in H. Dreyfus and P. Rabinow, eds, *Michel Foucault: Beyond Structuralism and Hermeneutics*, Chicago: University of Chicago Press, 1983, pp. 208–26.

The chimera of democracy as a political system capable of giving expression to differences, of organizing their reconciliation, of fostering synthesis for the development of the system, which had lasted since 1945 but was sunk by the events of '68, is now definitively shattered. This utopia, having failed at the institutional level, seems to have been adopted by the new social movements that bet on the linear development of differences, the only problem of which would consist in their own empowerment, as if this could unfold independently of the hostile relationship that civil war establishes. Instead, what irrevocably emerged from the 2008 crisis was that class differences are irreducible and contradictory. Rather than the proliferation of class differences, like the philosophy of becoming and political Spinozism hold, these differences lead to the radicalization of confrontation. In this way, revolution becomes a necessity. The political defeat suffered during the cycle of struggles that emerged after the 2011 financial crisis in Egypt, Chile, and Iran is being repeated without any discussion on the strategies to be adopted in the new political phase inaugurated by the war.

All attempts to depoliticize conflict through neoliberal governmentality have failed. The task of controlling and containing it today is equally shared by authoritarian, neofascist, racist, and sexist regimes, as well as democratic parties. Institutional democracy competes with these regimes in enacting veritable fascist and racist laws, laws of declared civil war on immigrants (Muslims are yesterday's Jews) as a place to experiment with the management of frontal confrontation. The government of democratic Denmark – first liberal, then socially democratic – introduced the concept of *non-Western* into law: a non-Westerner is someone who has only one Western parent, even if they were born in Denmark. Each year, neighbourhoods are reviewed and subjected to racial segregation, with the inhabitants of those areas that are considered ghettos suffering doubled penalties for any crimes committed. One year after birth, those children deemed non-Western have to spend thirty mandatory hours a week in kindergarten to assimilate Danish values. Social housing can make up only 40 per cent of the neighbourhoods, so 60 per cent of public housing will be sold to private individuals (resulting in gentrification). This is a victory for the far right, which does not even need access to power to see its ideas implemented. The democrats are doing it for them.

There are those, such as Roberto Esposito, who still think that they can govern the conflict by building a dialectical relationship with institutions. They are simply in the wrong epoch, because the scenario before us is that of world civil war.

Only a real threat of socialism opened a short period of democratization (in the North). The condition for making the conflict work in and for Western institutions was the Russian revolution, revolutions in the global South, and class struggle in the North. Having defeated the revolution, we are at the end of the cycle of accumulation that started in the 1970s, and the system now reveals its nature: war and civil war have returned.

## Democracy or oligarchy?

The hegemony of finance/monetary capital and its centralizations produce oligarchic political systems (the other face of consumer democracy). This is particularly evident in the United States, which the Wall Street boys also imposed in Russia after the collapse of the Soviet Union.

Throughout the period of market triumph and free competition, instead of a multiplication of the centres of power and decision-making, as neoliberalism would have it, three main monopolies managed by oligarchic groups emerged, taking control of the US Congress, Senate, and Department of Defense, controlling the functioning of the US economy with methods, tools, and procedures that should give pause to every good ordoliberal and neoliberal. First, the oligarchic group that runs the military-industrial complex (also referred to as Pentagon capitalism) has for years been pushing for war against the US's new enemies (Russia and China). Second, the oligarchy of oil, gas, and mining rents has lobbied enthusiastically, with apparent success, to block Nord Stream 2. Finally, perhaps the most important oligarchic group consists of the combined finance, insurance, and real estate industries (real estate has enormous economic power, as 80 per cent of bank loans are issued for the purchase of houses); through impressive coordination, this group caused the greatest financial crisis since 1929, the subprime crisis, which kicked off the current phase of inter-state warfare and low-intensity civil war.

The work of oligarchical lobbies to impose their interests on the political system is not complicated: 50 per cent of the democratic representatives of the American people are millionaires or billionaires.

The acceleration of centralization processes that occurred during neoliberalism could only progressively limit democracy to the point of bringing new fascisms into government, all over the world. This new fascism does not need thugs, nor does it need to assume the form of reactionary revolution (as it did between the two world wars), because there is no Bolshevik danger, no revolution threatening the landowning classes. Political movements are now powerless since the revolutionary strategy has been lost – they do not threaten the existing order. Societies are divided and social polarizations are reaching nineteenth-century levels, but there is no revolutionary theory or practice capable of transforming these divisions into political alternatives.

The epilogue of the Trump and Bolsonaro presidencies are clear signs of how, for the moment, a part of big capital, the administration, and the military have no interest in pushing the fascist hypothesis to its extreme because – again for the moment – it is running no real risks, except possibly of the will to power and profit of the state and capitalism itself. The growth of new fascism is a sign, however, that war is coming, or is already among us. *Fascism = war*, the revolutionaries used to say, and it is still true.

The policies of the state-capital machine can have different modes of governance: fascist, liberal, populist, oligarchical, democratic, or dictatorial, depending on the situation and specific conjunctures. It is the concept of governmentality that is wrong, because it is identified with capitalism, while that is but one of the possible modes of control and management.

Neoliberalism has multiplied the devices of power, pluralized them beyond the action of the state, implicating corporations and different territorial, regional institutions, but also international authorities (such as the IMF and the World Bank) in an attempt to disperse power downward and upward. Instead of being a liberating and creative action capable of realizing the individual through the market, this process has led to centralizations and polarizations (domestically, through class; externally, between states) that governmentality, the market, and free competition are no longer able to control.

In the same way that classical liberalism paved the way for fascism, neoliberalism, with its desire to multiply the devices and centres of power, instead paved the way for populism and new fascisms – and thus for war and civil war. The neoliberal illusion, like the classical liberal illusion, lasted a blink of an eye before slamming against the centralizations of capital, politics, and the state, forcing it to give way to reactionary, *warlike*, and *legal* ways of managing conflict.

# Chapter 3

*Since the time when the infinite geographical surface of our globe shrunk into a finite and interdependent space of action, all wars have been transformed into civil wars.*

*The starting point of a historical-ontological analysis must be the contemporary civil war.*

Reinhart Koselleck

## War and neoliberalism

No neoliberal policy will be able to impose onto US imperialism a return to competition and the market – policies which vassal states must instead adopt, in turn cascading down onto their subjects, demanding respect for competition and the market – *because monopoly is a political necessity that comes before the economic necessity of capital*. Michal Kalecki taught us a principle that imperialism still rigorously applies today and is misunderstood by critics of neoliberalism: profit is first and foremost about power and class relations, before being an economic issue.

In the early part of the twentieth century, monopoly was already a response to class struggle: the concentration of production and labour to beat the threat of revolution through rationalization, through productive restructuring based on pitting the unskilled worker against the vanguards of the professional worker. The absolute monopoly of money and further integration of war into the state-capital machine still act against the threat of revolution, but now on a global scale. This strategy, appropriate to the threat of worldwide revolution that developed through the twentieth century, was put in place after 1971 and the onslaught of the Vietnamese revolution.

Throughout the phase defined as *neoliberalism*, economic centralization and political centralization each intensified and exacerbated the other, instead of resolving their own contradictions, both in terms of relationships between states and between classes.

Once again, the different state-capital machines clashing in the world market entrusted war and civil war with the task that could be achieved by neither politics nor economics: that of redistributing power and the international division of labour. War and civil war rise to the forefront: before the economic cycle (production, market, and competition) comes the political cycle, in the precise sense that class struggle and class civil war precede and dictate accumulation. Like classical liberalism, neoliberalism is also forced to surrender to the regime of truth – class struggle, civil wars, and wars between states.

Neoliberalism and ordoliberalism problematize the war/economy relationship according to the classical canon, remaining faithful to the conception of the economy as an alternative to war. But, especially since the twentieth century, every turning point, every restructuring of economic production, and every change of power in the world market has been determined not by new rationalities, not by technological or productive *revolutions*, not by productive competition – but by war. These wars have not been provoked by crises reminiscent of Marx's time, but rather by wars of the kind we have seen since Lenin!

*The globalization of markets, currencies, consumption, production, and technology was anticipated by the globalization of war.*

It was the first and second world wars (and the revolutionary civil wars) that completely reconfigured the world market and the powers acting in it: the collapse of European and colonial empires; the passage of hegemony from England (sterling) to the US (dollar), and the emergence of the socialist pole. The Korean and Vietnam wars forced the US into inconvertibility and superimperialism. Later, in the 1970s, civil war in Latin America paved the way for neoliberalism as a continuation of civil war by other means.

The organization of imperialism around the dollar and a debt economy passed through civil war waged in situations where the new US hegemonic project was likely to arouse strong resistance. The first very clear signal of a change in political phase (the prelude to a historical reorganization of the world market) was the CIA's imperialist Operation Condor in Latin America. The US neoliberal programme was able to operate in Chile and most of Latin America only after Augusto Pinochet's coup d'état (in Argentina the transition was equally or even more ferocious and bloody). The physical elimination of revolutionaries paved the way for general submission to the principles of the market, debt, and competition. As early as the beginning of the 1970s, the hierarchical relationship between the two forms of power was affirmed: imperialism commands, decides, *exercises the power of life and death* – and, only once the situation is *normalized* (controlled), does it bring in Milton Friedman, Friedrich Hayek and the neoliberal economists who, along with the military, *rule life*. Foucault's claim that the power 'to give death' was reconfigured into a power to 'manage life' is an insult to the thousands of militants murdered on the altar of imperialism throughout Latin America. The *management of life* presupposes the *giving of death* as its political condition, because this phase is only reached once the revolution has been defeated. This diminished and mutilated life, integrated into production and consumption, which continue its subjugation by other means, can be imposed only *after* class struggles have been obliterated by the use of force. The operation of positive mechanisms of power follows the action of the negative, which Foucault tried hard not to see.

Even ordoliberalism is a policy whose effectiveness could only manifest itself after the defeat of the German working class at the hands of Nazism. The debate over which of the ordoliberals were Nazis is of little interest (although there were some). Instead, reiterating that their policies required victory over the German labour movement is absolutely fundamental. Neoliberalism was born practically at the same time as Nazism, as a fierce critique of the Weimar Republic, but it would become an effective policy only after Nazism had annihilated the subjectivity of Europe's most important labour movement. This is the condition that made its integration into capitalist development possible. In the 1970s, another blow was dealt and the world revolution was defeated, albeit in less bloody a fashion in Europe as compared to in South America and other parts of the world. This would make a broad extension of ordoliberal politics outside Germany, into Europe, possible.

## War: Prerequisite for the international division of labour and power

Even today, the reorganization of the international division of labour will be decided not by the market, nor competition, nor the actions of entrepreneurs, nor technological innovation, but by the ongoing armed struggle. It is the armies and the geopolitical armed clashes that define economic space and determine the configuration of the local, the territorial, and the micropolitical within it. Once a new architecture of world power has established who commands and who obeys, it will provide markets, competition, technological innovation, entrepreneurial initiative. It is never the other way around.

For these obvious reasons, war should be incorporated into the concept of capital, since it is the main source of the division of goods and labour and because only its outcomes determine any kind of world order in which production can be defined. Instead, Marxists and economists of every school stubbornly separate war and economics, seeing the latter as an alternative to the former.

But even in times of what is called 'peace', relations between the dominant imperialist power and its vassals are structured by the threat of war or its actual exercise. After all, sanctions, trade blockades, and control of technological exchanges are already acts of war. The reproduction of superimperialism requires continuous wars to defend the dollar and to eliminate anyone who threatens its supremacy when finance is not enough.

In the short upward cycle of accumulation (during the 1980s and 1990s), ordoliberal and neoliberal theories served the function of pacifying the power relations that, in the 1970s, had been upset by the civil wars and counterrevolution of US imperialism, trying to impose a positive, productive vision of power that incites and urges, instead of merely repressing. Foucault abusively extended and universalized this phase-specific concept of neoliberal power, denying its presupposition of civil war. This presented it as a force that develops, expands, and fosters life, as opposed to its portrayal in classical liberalism, which placed limits (negative function) on state power through economics.

Neoliberalism is indeed a technique of governance, but one that must intervene to bring order, to control, manage, neutralize the polarizations, imbalances, and class asymmetries that the dollar and the Pentagon provoke, trying to anticipate civil wars, revolutionary ruptures, and the class divisions that monetary superimperialism necessarily arouse.

*It is certainly governance, but it operates under the new imperialism.* It intervenes after war has determined the victors and the vanquished, and functions as *governance of the vanquished.*

Neoliberal politics is the continuation of class war, the war of conquest, the war of subjugation, the war between states waged by imperialism, which, by other means, must stabilize, consolidate, and award the victors. It must spread the logic of profit/revenue/debt production throughout society once the situation is normalized by force. It must transform all social relations by preparing the defeated subjectivities to be docile and submissive to finance's usurpation and capture.

Neoliberalism asserts that its policies are completely autonomous, that these policies do not depend on any power other than itself. Only this power and this power alone holds up and directs all politics, the economy, and society. But there is a strict power hierarchy between dollar imperialism and neoliberal policies. The former controls the latter and holds the modalities of governmentality, progressively transforming them into authoritarian, populist, neofascist, and warmongering management – modalities more consonant with trying to contain and suppress resistance to the further centralizations and polarizations that the end of optimistic globalization imposes.

## The constituent power of revolutionary civil war

An important clarification: when speaking of war, I always mean first civil war, and better yet, global civil war. What has disrupted European societies since the French Revolution is not war between states, but civil war: no longer the civil wars of religion, nor war between factions of the aristocracy or the bourgeoisie, but a continuous class civil war – sometimes underground, sometimes out in the open – hence the need for the economic, political, and military centralizations to control labour and society.

Class civil war sparks the demise of the state, as it was configured by the Treaty of Westphalia: a state capable of maintaining internal 'peace, security, and order', and of displacing the external enemy. Police rule over society, sovereignty decides war between states. The irruption of the masses will radically challenge the state's monopoly over politics and decision-making, as power is claimed and exercised by non-state subjects (workers, women, slaves, the colonized). As its main goal, the revolution aims to repoliticize what the police and governmentality have depoliticized, transforming internal conflict into the rupture of the established order. With proletarian revolutions taking place on capitalism's peripheries and in the South, where war and civil wars rage without interruption, the state is dispossessed of another of its prerogatives, the *jus belli* that it alone was able to exercise: Haitian slaves, for example, declared war on the colonial empires, defeating the two most important ones (England and France), and the Bolsheviks inaugurated the first world civil war with their revolution against capital and the Russian state.

Political Spinozism made constituent power fashionable, so even the smallest struggle would be an expression of it. But in modernity, constituent power is a direct consequence of civil wars, insurrections, and revolutions (every revolution is necessarily a civil war, although not all civil wars are revolutions!). Every constituent opening is not the child of a generic ontological power of the masses, of class, of the multitude. Rather, it needs a strategy to rupture constituted power, to inflict defeat upon the class enemy: the latest example is provided to us by Chile where only the great insurrectional days of 2019 could create the possibility of declaring a constituent phase. The overthrow of the constituent phase against the social movements that had produced it was probably due to the fact that this constituent phase was *not interpreted as a continuation of the civil war by other means* (a class perspective on the post-insurrectional situation was not held, in contrast to the enemy).

In modernity, all great constitutions – all great political, institutional, legal, social, and economic upheavals – have been produced, paradoxically, by 'the scourge of the *people*', civil war: the American revolution, the French, Soviet, Mexican, Chinese, Vietnamese, Cuban, and Iranian revolutions were examples of the hardest of all wars, and led to a radical shift in economic, social, and political systems, and the values at their foundation.

European democracies were born out of partisan wars against fascism. Even China's great development emerged from a more or less low-intensity, more or less violent civil war (the Cultural Revolution). It is only after the political victory of one side over the other, of the assertion of those who wanted Western production even in a socialist country, that capitalism asserts itself.

So we might formulate a general law: *first revolution, then production; first class warfare, then economy, law, and political system.*

War and civil war are economic, social, and political forces, or, to put it more precisely, war constitutes the political conditions for these forces to emerge and develop. The mode of production, the political system, and the form, for better or worse, that a society will take depend on war. The tragic case of the Spanish Civil War provides us with many negative lessons in this regard. Franco's victory imposed a sort of asphyxiated capitalism, a radically reactionary political and social system, different from other European countries.

Civil war is a formidable machine of production and subjective transformation. The constitution of new political subjects, unprecedented forms of collective action, and the qualitative leaps and ruptures produced in subjectivities are formed within these conflicts, a fact neglected by modern theories that, paradoxically, put the 'subject' (Foucault), the 'production of subjectivity' (Deleuze and Guattari) and the 'subjectification' of the multitude (Hardt and Negri) at the heart of their ideas. The transformation of how we feel and suffer, our affects and sensibility, is inseparable from the great political ruptures of the masses.

Despite its tremendous force, civil war is the great absentee of the theoretical renewal of the 1960s and 1970s, except in Foucault. But his willingness to make it a matrix of social relations (however briefly) is useless in analysing contemporary wars and civil wars for two fundamental reasons.

The clash under discussion is not Hobbes's civil war, nor is it the Greek *stasis*. It takes shape during the primitive accumulation of capital and manifests itself through a multiplicity of wars against populations: wars of land appropriation and the expropriation of peasants, the necessary conditions for the existence of the proletariat and factory labour; wars for the conquest of women, the necessary condition for reproductive labour; and the war of conquest of slaves and natives of the Americas, which are necessary conditions for servile labour. The multiplicity and transversality of these civil wars are the necessary conditions for the development of capitalism and its production. Primitive accumulation (and the wars that define it), far from being limited to the two centuries preceding the industrial revolution, is contemporary to every stage of capitalist development and is still the indispensable condition of any change in accumulation models and the form of the state.

While Foucault describes the civil war of the formation of the French working class, he does not analyse the changes of wars and civil wars produced by the transformations of capital accumulation and state action. He describes a capitalism and civil war that have not existed since the late-nineteenth century. His competitive capitalism was overcome and erased by economic (monopolies), political (executive), and military (the world war) centralization in the late-nineteenth and early-twentieth centuries. The Foucauldian civil war is still nineteenth century and peaked during the Paris Commune. Not only was it defeated by the armed intervention of the French and German armies, but the imperialism/centralization coupling erased its very possibility. Lenin (and Mao in even greater depth) would start from this double awareness to rethink civil war as a partisan war against imperialist war.

The shift from competitive capitalism to monopoly capitalism corresponded to a radical change in war and civil war, because both became global. The Russian revolution inaugurated the era of world civil wars in and against the first imperialist war, an era from which we have not yet emerged. Hannah Arendt and Carl Schmitt (and later Koselleck) would also define the Cold War and the post–Second World War anti-colonial revolutions in this way.

*The Eurocentric viewpoint of the French philosopher struggles to grasp the paradoxical world dimension of internal conflict.* World civil war does not mean, in the first instance, fratricidal struggle, but, rather, the breakdown of the balance of relations between states that had long guaranteed internal peace. Already fractured by the French Revolution and the world wars of the early-twentieth century, that balance was permanently broken by American imperial asymmetry, and especially by twentieth-century socialist and anti-colonial wars and struggles for national liberation (Leninist and Maoist partisan war). The fixed bipolarity of the Cold War was a temporary and short-lived phenomenon. As soon as the Soviet Union collapsed, world civil war, which had not actually subsided by any means, resumed its hegemony over local conflicts.

Foucault never confronted this global qualitative leap made by wars and civil war in the twentieth century. *The reality is that civil war has always been world civil war*, because capitalism is immediately born as a world market and the formation of its classes and states are produced within this dimension. Capitalism has never existed without polarization between centre and periphery, between North and South, since it started developing in the sixteenth century. That is not to say, however, that war and civil war have not evolved differently in these spaces. In the North, after primitive accumulation, civil war went underground, while the working class was integrated into production and reproduction of capital and the state; in the South, civil war, the state of exception, and wars of conquest would know no process of integration, but would rage seamlessly, expressing absolute violence (Frantz Fanon), without mediation. In the twentieth century, these two processes became intertwined in a single and differentiated world civil war, with a vanguard of oppressed peoples of the global South.

The other side of the world civil war is total war; that is to say, it becomes impossible to circumscribe the war spatially and temporally because it continues through the economy, information, currency management, technical-scientific competition, and so on. With the fall of the Berlin Wall, world civil war and total war fed off each other and returned to the centre of today's political agenda.

The concept of biopolitics has been so successful precisely because it ignores wars and world civil wars, just like the concept of governmentality. The COVID-19 pandemic, held up by Esposito and Agamben as proof of the relevance of the concept of biopolitics, shows us a power that seems like harmless population management when compared to inter-imperialist warfare (where *bio* has little relevance).

Globalization, which is actually the world accumulation of capital, must be read in two different and complementary ways: as the construction of a world market; and as world civil war, even if the second aspect is silenced, removed, and denied, including by critical theories. But what has been removed resurfaces, sooner or later, as a reality (the war in Ukraine). The perspective that leads with civil war is not a warmongering or militarist point of view, but nor is it a pacifist one. Civil war is not the content of politics but, in capitalism, it is the 'ever-present presupposition of war, always present as real possibility'.[1]

The ever-spreading revolt in France and throughout the world more generally (uprisings are increasing year by year) seems to portend a world civil war, rather than a revolution, because the radicality and continuity of the struggles, while objectively all directed against power, do not produce subjectifications capable of thinking and practising rupture – that is, revolutionary action.

---

1 Carl Schmitt, *The Concept of the Political*, trans. C. J. Miller, Quakertown, PA: Antelope Hill Publishing, 2020.

The future looms as simultaneous world civil war and total war, which, if not transformed into revolution, will bring death and destruction.

## Neoliberalism: Prototype for contradictory critical thinking

The double standard of power by which imperialism works, which we have already seen at work in the previous chapters, requires a different kind of analysis that neoliberalism and biopolitics cannot propose because they recognize only governmentality, without being able to tell us (or not wanting us to see) what controls them, keeps them alive, and will make them disappear: war and new fascism.

This double standard is a differentiated exercise of power through which we must examine economic and political phenomena. Imperialism asserts two different concepts of state sovereignty: full sovereignty, which is at the same time economic and political, and which is exercised today by large states (the US, China, Russia, India); and limited sovereignty, exercised, for example, by small European states.

With the economy comes, according to Foucault, a 'new mechanics of power', that is 'absolutely incompatible with relations of sovereignty'.[2] Actually, the economy is crucial to the stabilization and consolidation of an imperial *sovereign* power that combines state and capital, a governing power over a territory (the United States), and an economic power that aims to control the entire planet, inaugurating a new and unprecedented concept of sovereignty.

Sovereignty has to be doubly redefined because, on the one hand, one can judge its exercise only by measuring it on a world scale, and, on the other, it should not be referred solely to the state (as it is in the European political tradition), but also to the state-capital war machine in which the political, economic, and military cannot be separated. All this was

---

2 Michel Foucault, *Society Must Be Defended: Lectures at the Collège de France, 1975–76*, trans. David Macey, ed. Mauro Bertani and Alessandro Fontana, London: Picador, 2003.

already clearly established by the previous hegemonic phase of financial capitalism.

Dollar imperialism *reconfigures the state-capital sovereignty of the US*, reinforcing it. We are not witnessing a crisis of the nation-state but rather a differentiation of it. In large states, the conjunction of the force of capital and the force of the state gives rise to a further centralization and concentration of a power that acts on a global scale, building a new concept of sovereignty and state that displaces traditional legal-political sovereignty and cannot but escape Foucault's categories. The economy is not an impersonal device consisting of the myriad of self-interests; it is not a subjectless process. It certainly has a strategic head: the *collective subject* embodied by the state-capital machine of imperialism that manifests an unprecedented will for economic totalization and political sovereignty.

Of course, this strengthening of sovereignty concerns only the US and the other big states (China, India, Russia). Other statelets are imperatively invited to surrender whole chunks of their sovereignty to Uncle Sam. European states, Japan, Australia, and the UK are limited-sovereignty states, totally at ease in this colonial function they have to fulfil with a devoted sense of oligarchic duty. Others (China, Russia, the global South in general) are less at ease, and this drives the ever-impending possibility of confrontation and war.

In turn, vassal states – whether they choose their subordination voluntarily as in Europe and Japan or suffer it, like most states of the South – exercise their sovereignty, however limited, over their subjects.

Foucault confuses the liberal tradition and its 'disqualification of the political sovereign' with the actions of the state-capital machine that cannot function without sovereignty.[3] Assuming that mercantilism is the attempt to establish a sovereign that is legal-political but also economic, Adam Smith's political economy would show that it is 'a theoretical and political error', according to the French philosopher. In

---

3   Michel Foucault, *The Birth of Biopolitics: Lectures at the Collège de France 1978–79*, London: Palgrave Macmillan, 2008, p. 283.

reality, a different argument can be made because the state plays an essential role in *The Wealth of Nations*.

Would *planning* then be an attempt to overcome this 'curse formulated by political economy' of the impossibility of an economic sovereign, the French philosopher wonders?[4] If Foucault seems to hesitate, the imperialist state-capital machine has long since solved this problem by reinforcing the function of the political sovereign and the economic sovereign, by melding their power and centralization.

Foucault builds his critique of sovereignty and affirms governmentality as its alternative starting from an assumption that imperialism proves wrong. The 'legal and economic worlds' are, and have been since the seventeenth century, 'heterogeneous and incompatible'. On the other hand, starting at the end of the nineteenth century, these two worlds have become even more firmly intertwined, making their heterogeneities compatible without, however, blurring or losing themselves completely.

The first and most important sovereign function (the power to decide who is an enemy and thus who are friends and allies) is expressed annually, in official documents by the US government. But this would have no effectiveness if it were not accompanied by economic and techno-scientific *sovereignty*. The limited sovereignty of small European states, on the other hand, shares neither of these powers.

Competition, and not only sovereignty, also functions under the dual-regime rule. The *economy* (capitalism) must be thought of as a hierarchical organization between classes, between businesses, and between institutions, and not as the result of spontaneous action by individuals who, from below, through competition and the market, constitute hierarchies. Hierarchical division is the starting line.

The closer you get to the top of the hierarchy, the more monopoly – concentration of economic, political, and military power – asserts itself, and competition disappears or is minimized; the further down the hierarchy you go, the more you find yourself in subordinate spheres, functions, and subjectivities, and the more competition dominates. Small and medium-sized businesses certainly compete, but those who profit

---

4   Ibid.

and benefit are the monopolies, large commercial groups, and multinationals on which they depend. Competition at the bottom of the hierarchy reaches its peak in the labour market and management of the oppressed, but those who decide the fate of the labour market and the oppressed are still the monopolies and the state.

While competition among capitalists results in monopoly by eliminating competition, among the oppressed no form of monopoly (union, party, organization) should arise, because here competition, rather than eliminating itself, reproduces itself by spreading and intensifying.

Even the state monopoly of the legitimate use of force is subject to a dual regime. Large continental states increase their military power, while small nation-states, unable to use force in the world market, are, in the European case, mere subsidiary armies of the continental American state. At the same time, they fully exercise their monopoly of the ever-increasing use of force over their respective populations, an operation that is entrusted mainly to the police.

The dual regime of power shows all its violence and arbitrariness on another neoliberal principle: capital cannot be conceived without the intervention of legal systems and the rule of law, which, together, set the rules of the game (market competition) for all players. Actually, setting rules is clearly a sovereign privilege, reserved only for the dominant power.

The US is not bound by any rule, nor any law. Instead, it imposes the dollar standard, and the standards of production, consumption, and communication, as well as the legal system, to which international industrial or financial disputes (especially concerning debt) are now subject.

The double standard of imperialism clearly states the reality of its operation: the victors, the Americans, define the economic, political, and legal norms, and, after enacting them, have the power to follow them or not, according to convenience, or can create more, always in their own exclusive and unquestionable interest.

The United States acts within the system (immanent power) and, at the same time, outside and above it (transcendent power). This dual action constitutes the very definition of sovereignty (Schmitt). The difference lies in its worldwide operation in the dual political and economic form.

The absurdity and hypocrisy of ordoliberal and neoliberal policies are manifested in the claim to apply the *three golden rules* to all states, rules that everyone is expected to inscribe in their constitution: *monetary stability; balanced budget; and free and undistorted competition*. The dual regime of analysis and judgement also applies to these. If applied to the US, these rules would result in the country's immediate economic and political collapse because the Fed, in order to capture planetary wealth as a whole, continuously plays on imbalances, raising and lowering interest rates: the dominance of the dollar is built on a trade balance deficit that must be permanent because no *free and undistorted* competition to the US financial and monetary system can be accepted.

Achieving balance, enshrining the obligation to balance the budget in the constitution (the famous *economic constitution*) is a rule for vassals. US power is based on imbalance, indeed on imbalances in the plural. Only the Germans, who continue to lose battle after battle (the latest being the war in Ukraine, which verifies the old NATO strategy, still in effect even after the collapse of the USSR, expressed by its first secretary Lord Hastings: 'To keep the Soviet Union out, the Americans in, and the Germans down'), can impose it on their subordinates (Italy, for example) after first having it included in their constitution.[5]

German ordoliberalism – with its economic ideology, golden rules, and economic constitution – has heavily contributed to making Germany the first loser of the war in Ukraine. For years, the Germans wove economic relations with East European countries, building a truly integrated system of production. But their economic leadership has melted away like snow in the sun, with Germany unable to use its economic satellites to prevent the sabotage of its economy by the US, which has instead worked to impose its political-military might on the East European countries. Ordoliberalism manifests a weakness that US neoliberalism does not have, because it is not supported and controlled by any power comparable to dollar imperialism. It only believes in the economy, competition, the market, and the state that guarantees them through economic constitution. This is the real difference between

---

5 'NATO Leaders', NATO, nato.int.

neoliberalism and ordoliberalism, not the one established by Foucault. The former has imperialism behind it; the latter, a strong economy.

### Rent and human capital

Ordoliberalism and neoliberalism still have an industrial conception of capitalism: businesses are the structuring principle of the economy; each individual must transform themselves and function as a business. What is central to contemporary capitalism is rent, not business. In other words, financialized businesses have themselves become a source of rent. Already when the great American automobile industry – the heart of industrial capitalism (Fordism) – was restructured, those who controlled it and made the decisions were banks. The business was described as a 'bank that sold automobiles'. The financial services of the automobile industry produced 40 per cent of the profit, employing 35,000 people. The remaining 60 per cent was produced by more than 200,000 production workers.

The choice in favour of finance was quickly made (and so was the consequent deindustrialization), and supported, moreover, by neoclassical theory, which had already attacked head-on the distinction established by classical economics between value and price in the previous phase of the hegemony of finance capital, precisely in order to legitimize rent – precisely to break down the difference between profit and rent, making them equivalents. Any price, whatever its origin, is economically productive and contributes to the increase of GDP, something explicitly denied by classical economists up to Marx. A subprime stock certainly has a price. Its value, on the other hand, like that of derivatives, is not easily determined, because it is absolutely arbitrary, having no basis in any cost of production. The free market of the classics wanted to get rid of rentiers, but today the oligarchies of rent hold the keys to the economy and power everywhere, and not only in Russia.

All critical theories have followed Foucault on this entrepreneurial blunder, and go along with him on an *industrial* definition of human capital. But human capital, rather than constituting a portfolio of assets, must diversify the disbursement of its wages to pay for the different industries of rent. The 'financial exploitation' mentioned by Lenin as early as 1917 has been embodied at the micropolitical level in the lives of American workers who have to spend three-quarters of their wages on repaying debts of all kinds to banks and insurance companies: home debt, car debt, credit card debt, health insurance debt, education debt, and so on.

The investments that the human capitalist would have to make (training, health, housing, and more) to increase their value are all credit, so, rather than resembling an entrepreneur, human capital appears more as an indebted worker who has already mortgaged part of their wages before even starting to work. Financial pillage lays its foundation very early in the lives of individuals.

Foucault tells us that the 'wage is an income produced by capital and not the price of labor power', and neoliberals go looking for it in the early-twentieth-century texts of Irving Fisher ('income is simply the product or return of a capital'). Marx, more cautious, warns us, because turning the worker into capital is not a neoliberal novelty, it is part of what political economy has always tried to do. This 'insanity ... in the second half of the 17th century ... used to be a favourite conception (for example, of Petty), but it is used even nowadays in all seriousness by some vulgar economists and more particularly by some German statisticians'.[6]

---

6  The concept of human capital that Marx criticizes in the third book of *Capital* is more interesting than the one we find in Gary Becker or Foucault, because it is understood through finance and not through production. Certain economists of his era, in line with the definition later given by Fisher, equated labour power with monetary or financial capital and wages with the interest that such capital would produce. Marx points out that if labour power were capital, one could sell it and thus collect the value-capital corresponding to its price (one could say the same thing about his industrial version of the neoliberals: if labour power were a business, one could sell it). But the value of human capital is inseparable from the body. Only in the system of slavery, Marx continues, does the worker have 'capital-value' corresponding to purchase price (perhaps it is precisely the unspoken desire for a new and modern form of slavery that lies behind the ideology of 'human capital'). Marx speaks of an absurdity that critical theories have accepted as the reality of the contemporary worker: 'instead of deriving the valorization of capital from the

Even the so-called *anthropological* change to the individual is produced more effectively by debt, pension funds, and rent; in short, by money that opens the door to consumption, rather than the model of the entrepreneur. The conversion of subjectivity that contemporary capitalism implements is based on the pillars of *debt and consumption*. What seems more effective than the entrepreneur model is the *religion* that Walter Benjamin describes, at the same time 'indebting and guilting', founded on the most abstract form of money: credit. But credit is credit for consumption (of the individual, of businesses, of states); religion is a religion of consumption, its rituals taking place by buying and consuming goods of all kinds. Twentieth-century capitalism, first in the United States where the process had already begun in the 1920s, shifted its main axis – at least in the West – from labour (toil, sacrifice, pain) to consumption (pleasure, desire, and gratification, with neither toil, nor sacrifice, nor pain). Through Benjamin, we can grasp the *subjective* face of consumption that complements the *objective* function Sweezy had identified in the pull of accumulation for financialized societies and the political face that I have tried to reconstruct through Tocqueville and Schmitt.

Consumption's power of subjugation lies in being cult, praxis, behaviour, a religion without dogma and without theology, says Benjamin. In reality, it is an idolatry rather than a religion. We are immersed, twenty-four hours a day, in words, images, symbols, and practices of consumption. In the Middle Ages, every aspect of life was religion; today, every aspect of our daily life (eating, dressing, sleeping, washing, dwelling, loving) corresponds to a commodity and an advertisement that is solicited, that assaults us, that, battering us, accompanies us even when we sleep, because commodities and advertisements have invaded even

---

exploitation of labour-power, they explain the productivity of labour-power by declaring that labour-power itself is this mystical thing, interest-bearing capital' – capital that produces income, writes Foucault without hinting at his agreement or disagreement with such absurdities. However, Marx concludes, whether in the industrial or financial version, human capital must work, must be directly or indirectly subordinate and dependent, in order to obtain a wage. Karl Marx, *Capital*, vol. 3, trans. David Fernbach, London: Penguin, 1991, p. 596.

our unconscious. Consumption knows no rest, it is limitless; it has eliminated holidays because it is itself a continuous feast. Consumer capitalism has waged a long, fundamentally successful battle against Sunday, the day when one might interrupt the ordinary course of life by opening up to *what exceeds* (traditionally, the sacred). By making Sunday lose all sacredness, what was previously profane has become sacred. Everything works 24/7: television and its advertising, but also stores, online sales, supermarkets – veritable temples where consumers exercise their idolatry, precisely because it is a religion of worship alone, without theology, without dogma.

Work, no matter how much certain people say it corresponds to life, can never have the invasive presence of consumption. Only through consumption can we speak of a global, totalizing experience, because it invades the most everyday, mundane – but also most intimate – behaviours. There is no gesture that is not accompanied and thus shaped by a commodity. Labour, even if exploited, is still cooperation, collective action – *community*; while consumption is individualism, narcissism brought to the point of paroxysm.

Ideally and symbolically, consumption is the realization of interclassism, but one that continues to be fractured and hierarchized by class polarizations (income, wealth, labour). Consumption is the ethical-aesthetic turn of capitalism, because it promises self-realization. Commodities are the instruments of the production of the self (lifestyle, forms of life, life as a work of art). If there is a pastoral power that guides souls and transforms bodies, it must be sought here. At its centre is the woman's body as an absolute commodity.

Consumption makes production disappear in two different ways: we know nothing about how or where things are produced (the counterrevolution is based on the production of cheap commodities, the result of the servile, underpaid, dispossessed labour of workers in the global South). The supermarket is the continuous repetition of the miraculous disappearance of labour and the equally miraculous appearance of commodities.

The great victory reported by capitalism against wages was achieved through pairing consumption and credit. The money that opens access to the cult of consumption is provided by credit, because wages have been frozen for years.

In the pantheon of the gods of capital, the consumer occupies a prominent place. As a model of *subjectification*, they are surely more effective than the entrepreneur who still suffers, in spite of everything, from the Calvinist (protestant) ethic of performance, toil, and self-sacrifice. Money acts with an invasive and pervasive force that the entrepreneurial model does not have. What is real for everyone – no one excluded – is not so much the figure of the entrepreneur, but rather the situation of the consumer/debtor. It is their dependence on debt, as an alternative to wages (frozen), welfare (cut), or pensions (continually reduced, now coinciding with statistical life expectancy), that acts on subjectivity.

'Debt is the American way of life', and this is what needs to be reproduced on a global scale.[7]

It is time to end the use of the enemy's vocabulary (*self-employed entrepreneur, human capital*), which is the obvious sign of a political and theoretical defeat internalized and reproduced even by critical theory. The imperialist counterrevolution has destroyed only one monopoly: the trade union monopoly. It has enlarged the economic monopoly and, at the same time, created an enormous, precarious, competitive, individualist economy, where an increasing number of individuals work without having employment, without a job, but also often even without having a direct employer. In the South, this phenomenon is even more prominent than in the North and has been called the *popular economy*. In Argentina,

---

7   bell hooks: 'My partner had no sense of shame. Time and time again, he told me "Debt is the American way of life."' This 'anthropological' conversion is not produced by the entrepreneur (ideology of neoliberal academics), but by 'obsessive fantasies about having money'. 'The issue for most poor and working class people is not that they do not make money but that their fantasies about what money can do far exceed reality . . . I find that many working-class and poor people I know spend an inordinate amount of time fantasizing about the power of money, about what money can do.' They certainly don't fantasize about a career as an entrepreneur. It is through access to credit that capitalist ideology creeps into subjectivity. 'This lack of awareness stems in part from the fact that widespread credit and debt allow so many people to consume above their means and have lifestyles they cannot afford.' bell hooks, *Where We Stand: Class Matters*, New York: Routledge, 2000.

40 per cent of the workforce, particularly women and migrants, is in this kind of situation.

Such people create their own jobs, invent their own wages and income. These poor and indebted workers who oscillate between welfare, work, and debt should not be described as self-employed. The popular economy, rather than deferring to the tradition of employers (entrepreneur, capital) understands this in terms of the three political traditions of the exploited: 'Unions to fight capital, a cooperative movement for autonomy from capital, and feminism to value themselves against capital. Three movements for people not to be in need, to create their own economy, to resist the lack that unemployment imposes.'[8] Alexandre Roig perfectly expresses the difference between being *human capital* and being, in a new way, against capital, because this labour force is always in a class war that cannot and should not be understood

---

8   The inheritance that is needed must be found not in the history of the bosses but in that of the class struggle, in the history of movements. In the labour movement: 'Progressively, the negative category of "unemployment" will be replaced by a positive proposal: the "popular economy" [*economía popular*]. And it thus proposes a change of direction for politics. It does not aspire to return to "work", but to promote the work that already organizes daily life. Build and strengthen what has already been done for a living. Thinking of a union from this perspective is proposing that the subject continues to be the organized worker who challenges wages and rights, but from another point of view.' In the cooperative movement: 'The traditions of self-organized labour coexist in the popular unconscious of our country and in the practice of many other territories, Argentina being one of the countries with the largest number of cooperatives and mutuals in the world. In Latin America, this way of organizing labour is even stronger because of its affinities with the organization of the community economies of many indigenous peoples.' In the feminist movement: 'The problem of the economy as a whole, and in particular of the popular economy, ends up being how this labour is made visible and valorized. And the problem of valorization leads to an encounter with another movement: the feminist movement. One of the big questions that feminism has asked through struggle is: how is historically invisible and unvalued work visible and valued? As in the case of caring tasks, reproductive work or social-community work. This question is what allows, precisely, to resist the logic of financial capitalism: to see the relationship, even if it is hidden. The popular economy seeks to interrupt the flight of financial capital from the scene of conflict with labour.' Alexandre Roig, 'Economía popular: Tres momentos de un movimiento', Medium, 11 October 2022, medium.com.

using the definitions of the class enemy.⁹ For example, it is hard to imagine the American worker internalizing this absurd and contradictory terminology of power. Once they ascertain that since 1973, pay cheque after pay cheque, their wages have not increased, but rather decreased; once they learn that the politics of human capital have transferred 10 percentage points of GDP from wages to profits (that is, real capital); once they realize that the only thing that increases is their debt, they calculate that, according to the entrepreneurial norm of costs and benefits, the power that human capital supposedly has to transform his subjectivity from subordinate worker to entrepreneur is simply hot air. But self-styled human capital has the opportunity to make plenty of discoveries of this kind. In fact, year after year, as they verify that their ability to *act* and their *freedom*, instead of expanding, retracts like wages, it is more likely that, instead of becoming their own entrepreneur, their subjectivity will be caught up in the vortex of fear, frustration, and resentment. Rather, their subjectivity seems to be developing towards the new forms of fascism (Trump) that superficially reflect and give vent to their frustrations.

Only psychoanalysis could explain the unfolding of an impossible process of accumulation carried out by the self-employed: the doubling of the subject, their entrepreneurial part exploiting the part that works. More seriously, if human capital were, as Foucault would have it, a 'machine that produces streams of income', its production over the past fifty years, calculated using the principles of entrepreneurship (costs/benefits), would prove it a failed enterprise.

Foucault makes Becker's work on criminal law the paradigm of the functioning of the theory of human capital from which new modes of

---

9  'Today it is fashionable to talk about race or gender, the unpopular topic is class: it makes us tense, nervous, in doubt when we ask where we stand. In less than two decades our nation has become a place where the rich really rule ... Now I choose class because I believe that class warfare will be the fate of our country if we do not confront classism together, if we do not deal with the widening gap between rich and poor, between the haves and have-nots. This class conflict is already connoted in terms of race and gender. It is already creating divisions and separations.' hooks, *Where We Stand*.

neoliberalism would emerge: no longer would it be a system in which a will acts upon a will (domination), but rather, the individual would be placed in a certain situation (mostly competitive), with certain rules. By leveraging freedom and ability to calculate costs and benefits, the subject's action, constrained by the game and *the rules of the game*, should correspond to what governmentality requires of them. These results are achieved not by acting directly upon the players, but rather on the game and its rules – the environment and norms – that is to say, through soft power. Criminal policy in the United States has never functioned according to these principles. It has merely thrown 2.5 million Blacks and Hispanics in jail, the largest imprisonment in the history of all mankind, following classic American racist policies: it targets players based on skin colour. Becker also tries to justify racism with this game theory.

In any case, the much-vaunted behavioural conduct that governmentality is supposed to ensure does not lead to entrepreneurship. We must not look for great anthropological change in the figure of the entrepreneur, but in the subjugation that combines fascism, racism, sexism, and the further leap forward it takes with war. The economy of the market and competition is transformed into a war economy, and the production of the subject now has mobilization and ideological readiness for civil war as its goal, as we are now seeing in the US, Brazil, Peru, and elsewhere – or readiness for war *tout court*, as with the confrontation in Ukraine.

As long as neoliberalism (and biopolitics) fails to grasp the processes of subjugation of the oppressed consequent to the change of political phase (the self-employed entrepreneur is the ideology of the ascendant face of imperialism, rapidly articulated), it cannot grasp the modes of subjectification of power, the becoming subject of the process of political and economic centralization that is not the big businessman, but the oligarch. Oligarchies and corruption are the modes of subjectification of rent economies.

## 100 Orders

The US's 2003 occupation of Iraq, which aimed to *export democracy* to the peoples who still guiltily ignored it, is almost a caricature of the *hierarchical relationship between imperialism and neoliberalism*. It describes a capital/state cycle, purified and simplified but containing the essence of its functioning, as well as the unscrupulous use of liberalism and its equally unscrupulous abandonment. It thus constitutes a summary of my arguments here.

The *economic* cycle began in 2001 with an invasion that established the winners and losers: who commanded and who had to obey. In 2004, the US government commissioned Paul Bremer to apply neoliberal governmentality to the defeated state and the subjugated population so as to stabilize and reproduce the power acquired by force – that is to say, impose democracy.

Margaret Thatcher's famous phrase, 'economics are the method: the object is to change the soul' of the individual is only true if the method is applied to defeated individuals.[10] The transformation of subjectivity according to the principles of human capital has defeated subjectivity as a condition.

Bremer announced the 100 liberal decrees (the '100 Orders') that Iraqis and their state had to transpose and execute in order to become true democrats.[11]

Prominent among these commandments was the rule that has always guided American policy (especially in the case of poor, agricultural countries) and had already been put in place in Latin America after the Second World War: make subsistence farming impossible, for food must depend on American agribusiness.

Iraqi farmers could no longer use the seeds and processes that had been handed down for millennia (agriculture was born in these parts, 10,000 years ago, in the so-called Fertile Crescent) because

---

10   Margaret Thatcher, interview by Ronald Butt, *Sunday Times*, 3 May 1981.
11   Coalition Provisional Authority, 100 'Orders', govinfo.library.unt.edu/cpa-iraq/regulations.

they had to be bought from the American agro-food corporations (Monsanto).

Order 81, paragraph 66 commanded: 'Farmers shall be prohibited from re-using seeds of protected varieties or any variety mentioned in items 1 and 2 of paragraph (C) of Article 14 of this Chapter.' In plain English, farmers had to destroy all seeds every year, and to buy them back from 'authorized suppliers' (US multinational corporations).

The other major guiding lines of the 100 Orders are a summary of neoliberal policies, which are actually policies of imperialism to facilitate the dollar's plunder: everything public was to be privatized (dismantling of social and public services); profits produced by US investors could be repatriated in full instead of serving the country's development (pillage and robbery); it applied regressive taxation favourable to foreign or local capital; it established new property rights for foreign companies over Iraqi businesses so they could buy out the most profitable ones; it opened up the ownership and control of banks to allow quick absorption by American and British banking and financial groups; and it restricted the right of association and strike of workers, and especially public employees.

This form of expropriation of an occupied country is prohibited by international law. But the US is not bound by law like an ordinary vassal state, because it makes the rules. The new state, also built on neoliberal principles, turns these commands into impersonal laws, in perfect harmony with the ordoliberal rules that strive for the nature of capital to be not only economic but also legal. The production of freedom is reduced to the freedom of appropriation, of financial and industrial plunder.

But, under governmentality, under *peace*, under economics, war and civil war continue to build and will soon resurface openly. The Americans lose another war in the global South and are forced to leave the country. The cycle closes: from war to war, through neoliberalism.

## Return to cyclical theory: The political controls the economic

These two cycles are inseparable but civil wars, revolutions, and class struggle precede and direct the economic cycle. The political economic cycle of the imperial machine does not coincide with the history of neoliberalism. In order to be able to separate the two realities that are normally automatically conjoined, one must reconstruct the cycle of imperialism and the function that neoliberalism plays in it.

What Foucault criticizes in Marx – the fact that he circumscribes the general 'laws' of capital accumulation and thus describes a *single capital*, instead of grasping the development of different types of capitalism – is Foucault's strong point. It allows us to identify the contradictory foundation of capital that its development will only deepen. There are indeed various types of capitalism, *because there are different types of state with which capital is coupled*, but all converge around key moments that precisely define the beginning, development, and end of the business cycle, and all affect different combinations of the state and capital machine. The US private debt crisis, transformed into a sovereign debt crisis, is the ultimate convergence: the great synchronization of all capitalisms – that is, of the different state-capital machines.

The cycle of imperialism arises from wars (of conquest, civil war, between states), and there follows its relative pacification (governmentality) in which the radical conflict is not annulled by the action of liberalism but continues, expressed through other means. War, momentarily governed, resurfaces with a violence that exhausts neoliberalism itself. Neoliberalism intervenes in one part of the cycle, its ascendence, when imperialism seems to develop without tension or contradictions – a momentary illusion we must not believe.

It is the history of capitalism, not liberalism (ordo- or neo-), that is confirmed and reaffirmed by the current war in Ukraine and the imposition of imperialist conflict. Neoliberalism claimed to avoid the economic catastrophes and wars that classical liberalism had failed to avert, and has thus died of this impossibility. Neoliberalism cannot possibly maintain this claim, since what it consciously or unconsciously tries to erase (class struggle, war, monopoly, economic and political power) is what has always been present and which leaps to the forefront in deciding the destiny of the world – and, as it resurfaces, it also decides the fate of neoliberal governmentality.

The cycle of imperialism *does not result in a new rationality, in a new reason for the world*, but in a new war and a new fascism: in a new and growing economic, political, and ecological destruction.

Theories that have disavowed war lack the tools to grasp the failure to which neoliberal policies are destined. They fail to see how class and inter-state wars flow like a karst river under the peaceful, modernizing, and rationalizing neoliberal categories. So, they criticize only what power highlights, what it puts before their eyes: the glittering false truth of the market and competition.

The US, a country that introduced the new norms of imperialism and its governmentality by imposing them on the whole world, is emblematic of neoliberalism's failure. The sovereignty of the state-capital machine is undermined internally, in its own territory. *The low-intensity civil war across the US is the first of the consequences of the dollar imperialism that neoliberalism was supposed to govern.* The dollarization of the world, the control of the world market exercised from a position of universal debtor, creates a radical deindustrialization. The destruction of industry and the working class, while grinding down union monopoly through the export of factories, the debt economy, and the development of the rent, exacerbates class struggle, continually risking a fall into civil war that the techniques of governance cannot control.

Governmentality is a subsidiary technique that seeks to stabilize what has been violently destabilized. It has the impossible task of balancing what the sovereign state/capital continually unbalances. Imbalance is its manner of operation, which clashes violently with *balance*, the keyword of ordoliberal and neoliberal ideology. It matters little whether this equilibrium is presented as attainable through the spontaneous action of social forces or the assiduous intervention of the state: synthesis, conciliation, or 'homeostasis' (Foucault) *is always impossible*.

Ironically, the affirmation of the theories of the free market and its power of self-organization and self-regulation (albeit with different methods – through spontaneity for classical liberalism or through state intervention for ordoliberalism and neoliberalism) always occurs at the moment when the state-capital coupling unleashes enormous imbalances – polarizations of income and wealth between classes, but also between states – which can only be *balanced* by war. This is the second time that power has played this trick on us, but repetition has not served to awaken critical theory to what is happening.

## What is neoliberalism? An ideology?

Among all the theories from the school of '68, I have chosen to consider Foucault, because it is precisely his work on ordoliberalism and neoliberalism that synthesizes all the contradictions, misunderstandings, and errors of analysis regarding capitalism. His ideas have been debunked by capitalism's forceful return in the 1970s, and in particular since the turning point of the counterrevolution in 1973 (combined civil wars in Latin America; the energy crisis and the invention of petrodollars). I will continue to follow Foucault's paths in recognition of his merits as well as to demonstrate the limitations and the many failures of critical thought.

Power functions by producing its own truth: for power to be effective it must create its own regime of truthfulness. Foucault takes his conception of the relation of power to truth, like many other concepts, from Nietzsche: 'truth is . . . not something that exists and is to be found, to be discovered'; it 'is an active determining'.[12]

If the market and competition constitute neoliberalism's regime of truth, what are we to infer when we know that prices are set not by the regime of competition (nor by the market) but by relations between economic-political forces, between industrial monopolies, between rent oligarchies; and that only the price of labour power is left to savage competition among the oppressed? When it becomes evident that the 2008 crisis has debunked, one by one, all the so-called neoliberal principles and laws? How are we to define neoliberalism when it constructs the

---

12  Friedrich Nietzsche, *The Will to Power*, trans. Walter Kaufmann and R. J. Hollingdale, New York: Vintage Books, 1968.

veracity of the market and competition, and keeps silent, concealing and ignoring the real sources of power that instal and dismantle it?

From this point of view, neoliberalism functions as an ideology. How could we call it anything else when ordoliberalism and neoliberalism, the offspring of two different hegemonies of finance capital, construct narratives in which war, currency, credit, debt, and the power relations they establish are simply not there (as indeed they are not in *The Birth of Biopolitics*)?

Certainly, this ideology cannot be called false consciousness, because it is consciously produced by networks of intellectuals, financed by capitalists of all kinds, disseminated by the media, legitimized by politicians, and supported by the military and the state. Nor is it a superstructure because its concepts are an 'active determining', constituting discursive devices that concatenate and enter into conjunction with material ones that, in turn, function as another kind of active determining. Together they produce the *real* of neoliberalism. But in what sense can this *real* be recognized as *true*?

Foucault (and also Deleuze) argues that there is no ideology in our societies because everything is visible, nothing is hidden. This does not always seem to be the case – at least not with financialization, not in the case of the dollar, and not in terms of the relationship of American currency to the political and the military.

In Foucault's sophisticated theory, when it comes to truthfulness (the regime of truth), it is not truth and falsity that is at stake, but the devices, techniques, and discourses that allow us 'to say as true and to affirm as true a certain number of things that we now know are not true'. This means that neoliberalism, like ordoliberalism, produces concepts that are *true* and *false* at the same time.

Here, too, the double regime must be applied to decipher the workings of power: they are *true* concepts because they correspond to discursive and material devices that impose competition on proletarians in the organization of labour and the labour market, because they manage the social consequences of the action of the debt economy and financial crises, and because they create favourable conditions for dollar imperialism's capture mechanisms, predisposing society to be milked by finance.

They are *true* concepts because the market and competition are applied to education, the healthcare system, and social services in general – not because they create gains in productivity, but only because they function politically as devices for the centralization of power and as disciplinary and control techniques facilitating imperialist capture.

Instead, they are false concepts because they dumb down the real articulation of power on which the life and death of neoliberalism also depends; they avoid problematizing a power that is not subservient to competition and the market but imposes them on all vassal states and all proletarians on the planet.

The functioning of a true/false concept can be demonstrated effectively in the arguments of economist Robert Lucas, a representative of the Chicago school who received a Nobel prize for his work on money that would function as a mere 'veil' of transactions, with no influence on the distribution of income. He argues that debt has no importance because, contrary to what even a Greek or Argentine or Thai or African child understands, it does not enrich creditors and impoverish debtors. Debt is deemed *neutral*. By insisting that debt does not matter, he claims that neither currency nor debt can lead to financial crisis, a claim made again just before 2008.[13]

These statements are clearly *false*, but the academic community, the media, and policymakers recognize and legitimize them as *true*. And policies constructed on the basis of these false utterances have *real* effects. The production of false/true categories is not limited to the market and competition but covers the whole spectrum of economics and politics (cutting taxes for the rich promotes growth; the richer the rich get, the more their wealth trickles down on the poor and the more society benefits). An intellectual battle for the triumph of truth against the falsehood of neoliberal categories will not change the real situation. Truth is a political issue before having anything to do with knowledge.

Marx, before Nietzsche, had grasped the reality of contemporary truth no longer being transcendent, but rather immanent to the activity

---

13  Robert E. Lucas Jr, 'Supply-Side Economics: An Analytical Review', Oxford Economic Papers, New Series, vol. 42, no. 2 (April 1990), pp. 293–316.

of human beings: 'The question whether objective truth can be attributed to human thinking is not a question of theory but is a practical question. Man must prove the truth, i.e., the reality and power, the this-sidedness of his thinking in practice.'[14]

Just as in politics, truth in economics is nothing but the power of praxis, the ability to prevail over the opponent. If revolution does not prevail, it has no truth. If capitalism prevails, we shall have, as we do, *its* truth.

The concepts of imperialism that neoliberalism manages for a time are neither true nor false; they are *powerful*, in the sense that they are the categories of the victors imposed on the vanquished.

But then, what is neoliberalism? Again: it is the continuation of the financial/monetary war waged by dollar imperialism by other means. Its *real* truth regime is monetary imperialism that neoliberalism must naturalize through the abatement of conflict. It is a set of both material and discursive techniques ancillary to new imperialism, used to stabilize, reproduce, and consolidate its worldwide supremacy (the so-called *peace* of governmentality). Neoliberal *rationality* comes after the establishment of relations between forces; the market comes after the action of a power that is not the market; norms and rules come after a power that is not a norm, that is not a rule. The market functions once it has determined who commands and who obeys, the legal comes into play once force has created difference. When neoliberalism fails to produce appeasement, it will be cast aside.

## Rationality and its critique

In *The Birth of Biopolitics*, Foucault not only confirms the abandonment of war as a method of analysing the real, but also of class struggle. Once the latter is dropped as well, history becomes a succession of rationalization techniques and governing techniques, and the state would be not an

---

14  Karl Marx, 'Theses on Feuerbach', in Karl Marx and Frederick Engels, *Selected Works*, vol. 1, Moscow: Progress Publishers, 1969.

'autonomous source of power', but nothing more than the *effect* of a multiplicity of practices of governmentality.[15]

The shift, clearly enunciated, is from Marx to Weber. The former uses what Foucault calls 'the contradictory logic of capital', while, for the latter, the problem is no longer contradiction, but the 'irrational rationality of capitalist society'.[16]

The philosopher fully adopts this change of viewpoint, so that the whole analysis of neoliberalism deals exclusively with its rationality; the differences between liberalisms (classical, ordo-, neo-) are differences in rationality. With the introduction of governmentality, the problem is no longer the contradictions of social class and capitalist wars; rather, social class and war become its optimization techniques, its functionalities, its systemic decisions.

Rationality is a concept that, translated, means the depoliticization of the economy, welfare, and the state – all of which had become highly politicized by class struggle. The shift from contradiction to rationality is the shift from conflict to its neutralization.

The presupposition of this new method is the pure and simple elimination of imperialism, that is, of class relations that respond not to the logic of governmental reason but to the logic of the irreconcilable conflict between classes and between states.

It is perturbing to see how an author who believes in a reconfigured concept of power (and has been highly influential in this field) completely misses how power – whose strategies depend on the activation and deactivation of neoliberalism – suppresses the hierarchy that establishes the supremacy of dollar imperialism and the subordination of governmentality.

The elimination of Marx and his logic of contradiction, which Foucault interprets as succumbing to dialectic, is a relevant political operation. The theoretical displacement (from contradiction to rationality) removes the negative, which is the element that grounds contradiction in Marx. The negative – which poses the problem of exploitation, domination, war as well as rupture, revolt, revolution – is overcome

---

15   Foucault, *The Birth of Biopolitics*, p. 77.
16   Ibid., p. 105.

(removed) in two different ways: through a *governmental reason* capable of providing an answer to the problem of the irrationality of capitalism, and through the replacement of the negative (contradiction, class conflict, and war) with the positive actions of power.

This shift from Marx to Weber thus explains why power changes in nature by becoming *productive* (power that incites, makes things possible, urges) and why *repression* is as inadequate as contradiction (both are negative forms of power) in explaining the real. Power is transformed into a force that produces, fosters growth, and increases the power of life. *The negative disappears from both sides of the relationship, both from the action of the oppressed and from the action of power.*

The *positivization* of the negative was a constant through the thinking of the 1960s and 1970s. Today, this attempt to disavow the negative, in class struggle, war, and fascism, all which stubbornly resist becoming positive, is revealed all its weakness. What has been removed returns even more violently with the absolute negativity of war, precisely because it has only been minimally foreshadowed.

After Foucault, books on the rationality of neoliberalism are redundant; believing they exercise a severe critique of neoliberalism, they in fact make its apology. Dardot and Laval, in *The New Way of the World: On Neoliberal Society*, were already cultivating all the misunderstandings about neoliberalism that continue to be expressed in the books of Wendy Brown and Barbara Stiegler, as in every leftist criticism based on the courses at Foucault's Collège de France).

## Foucault 'the Revolutionary'

The curious thing about Foucault is that one can criticize him in his own words, demonstrating his great political instability. In fact, before he embraced rationality and functionality as principles on which to base the analysis of the economy (which is therefore already no longer capitalism), before the analytical tools of the real were competition, the law of supply and demand, and cost/benefit calculus, war and civil war were, for a few years, the method he used to understand and interpret the real.

These early views will be discussed below; they are not far removed from the views of some twentieth-century revolutionaries, and they lay the foundation for a more effective point of view that can account for the actuality of war, which neither biopolitics nor neoliberalism can do.

'Right, peace, laws were born in the blood and mud of battles', in the same way as the market, competition, neoliberal peace, and the law that accompanies them.[17] Twentieth-century wars, civil wars, and colonial wars forged the hegemony of imperialist power and the subordinate regime of the dispositions of governmentality and biopolitics.

Peace and war do not merely substitute each other (where one begins, the other ends) – they also coexist. Governmentality 'does not begin where the sound of arms ceases'; the market 'does not begin when war ends'.[18] In the sense that war continues its work during peacetime, economics, rights, and law comprise the continuation of war by other means.

In dollar imperialism, under the market, governmentality, and competition, 'war continues to rage'. It develops 'within all mechanisms of power, even the most regular ones. War is the engine of institutions and order: peace, in the smallest of gears, makes war warily. In other words, war must be deciphered under peace: war is the very figure of peace.'[19]

If one fails to decipher the dual regime of power, there is no way to understand the current war. But the power to glimpse the war under the apparent peace of the victors presupposes a partisan point of view, a class perspective that, in the Foucault of the early 1970s, is very similar to the theories of early-1960s Italian *operaismo*. Society is divided by class struggle, and it is from the specific position one occupies in this division that one can and must look at the world. We cannot

> occupy a position of *totalizing* or *neutral subject*. In this general struggle he is talking about, the person who is speaking, telling the truth, recounting the story, discovering memories and trying not to forget anything, well, *that person is inevitably on one side or the other*: he is involved in the

---

17  Foucault, *Society Must Be Defended*.
18  Ibid.
19  Ibid.

battle, has adversaries, and is looking toward a particular victory... This discourse about the general war, this discourse that tries to interpret the war beneath peace, is indeed an attempt to describe the battle as a whole and to reconstruct the general course of the war. But that *does not make it a totalizing or neutral discourse*; it is always a *perspectival discourse*. It is interested in the totality *only to the extent that it can see it in one-sided terms, distort it and see it from its own point of view* ... The truth is, in other words, a truth that can be deployed only from its combat position, from the perspective of the sought-for victory ... *It is the fact of being on one side* – the decentered position – that makes it possible to interpret the truth, to denounce the illusions and errors that are being used – by your adversaries – to make you believe we are living in a world in which order and peace have been restored.[20]

After writing these lines, Foucault returned, with the concept of governmentality, to occupy the position of a totalizing and neutral subject, abandoning the reality of division and the subjective implication it contains.

In reality, there is no alternative. If one does not take the partisan point of view, if one does not pierce the totality from the point of view of the oppressed, one is continually deferred to the side of power. It is the failure to rigorously maintain a class perspective, the failure to firmly define one's own field of belonging, that leads Foucault to the bitter realization (symptom of a crisis that the subsequent ethical-aesthetic phase is far from overturning): here we are, 'always with the same with *inability to cross the line*, to pass over to the other side ... always the same choice, on the side of power, of what it says or causes to be said'.[21]

Choosing sides and a point of view is either an extra-theoretical presupposition (Marx) to which one remains faithful, or one will constantly oscillate between one side and the other.

---

20  Stephen Morton and Stephen Bygrave, eds, *Foucault in an Age of Terror: Essays on Biopolitics and the Defence of Society*, London: Palgrave MacMillan, 2008. My emphasis.
21  Michel Foucault, *Essential Works of Foucault: 1954–1984*, vol. 3, *Power*, New York: New Press, 2000.

From the neutral and totalizing categories of governmentality, amputated by imperial power, it is impossible to decipher class warfare. If we allow ourselves to be enclosed in the Foucauldian trap of neoliberalism and governmental rationality, of neoliberal reason seen from a neutral and totalizing point of view, we will not understand anything about war, which will then present itself as exogenous to the economy and the class struggle: an *irrationality* completely unrelated to the rationality of globalization (this is how the Russian enemy and its war are defined).

Instead, we must follow the direction of deciphering war under the peace of the victors, which was also the method of the revolutionaries of the first half of the twentieth century. In order to do so, we must abandon neoliberalism and biopolitics in all their versions and return to social class and their conflicts.

# Chapter 4

## Theories of money and dollar imperialism

Dollar imperialism holds great implications for a theory of money (but also of power). The inconvertibility of the dollar with gold has made it clear that currency, rather than having an ontological relationship with exchange, with labour, or with production, has one with the political system: with the state, with war, and with public debt. Or rather, it has this relationship with the political nature of the state/capital machine.

Now, currency came into being in precisely this way five thousand years ago in Mesopotamia, during the Neolithic period, and had the same functions that we find in our new monetary imperialism. Studies on Mesopotamia were developed by Karl Polanyi, and taken up at Harvard by the Institute for the Study of Long Term Economic Trends, which organized regular meetings and seminars on the subject and published five volumes 'rewriting the beginnings of the economic history of Western civilization'.[1]

---

1 Karl Polanyi, *The Great Transformation: The Political and Economic Origins of Our Time*, New York: Beacon Press, 2001; Michael Hudson, *Killing the Host: How Financial Parasites and Debt Destroy the Global Economy*, Petrolia, CA: CounterPunch, 2015.

The genealogy of currency shows us what dollar imperialism has revealed: namely that its true nature is *debt* and *power*, *debt* and *war* (debt without war makes no sense). When we say that the origin of currency is political, we mean that its existence always depends on a centre of power rather than on production; we also mean that we must replace the automatisms of economic laws (that would find their most abstract expression in currency) with the political-economic-military strategy of the state/capital machine, as indeed dollar imperialism teaches us.

The production of money has an extra-economic origin and is the main reason why *economic science* does not understand it, immediately recognizing it as something foreign to its logic. This is also evident in the history of the dollar: before the market, the price, and economic laws, there are power relations, impositions and compromises, threats and agreements between forces. But we can also argue that the history of currency shows us that politics precedes being, that strategy precedes ontology, that conflict defines both.

Five thousand years after its appearance, virtual money, scriptural money, symbolic money is again operational and imposing its nature. Perhaps money has always worked this way and it is so-called economic science that has given us a distorted view of it. History, archaeology, and the study of Neolithic languages in Mesopotamia completely undermine the natural progression supposedly established by classical economics (and also by Marx, a faithful disciple), from which money should spring: barter, exchange, production, credit, and debt. Credit money is placed not at the end but at the beginning of this economic evolution. Currency emerged not from trade, but from debt and credit established by political/religious power; it has an intimate relationship with war, army, and conquest.

Before being an economic phenomenon, money was a political strategy. It has now been established by economic history and anthropology that credit and debt preceded exchange. Nietzsche criticized a political economy in which everything begins with exchange – in which human behaviour must be sought in our attitude to exchange. By placing the creditor/debtor relationship at the origin of civilization, the German philosopher brings out not only measure, value, valuation, and price, but also the very subjectivity of humans (our memory, our ability to promise, and to predict).

To confirm Nietzsche's hypotheses, we possess a rich documentation regarding the emergence of currency in the Neolithic period. The essential cuneiform writing that remains from that era concerns finance: the famous tablets are nothing more than IOUs – recognitions of debt and calculations of interest or taxes to be paid to the ruler or temple. Three thousand years before the birth of Christ, political and religious power invented a refined system of credit/debt that also included interest and compound interest, from which were derived money and its functions of measurement, calculation, payment, and reserve.

Money was born as virtual currency, scriptural currency, coin – as a *sign* to levy tax on behalf of religious and political power. *Extractivism* is not a new technique of wealth appropriation that appeared with rent and predatory capitalism; it originated with debt and credit, which are extractive techniques, not instruments designed to facilitate exchange or measure labour.

The monetization of society and the economy is the work of imperial administration. The general equivalent does not arise from exchange and barter, as Marx believed; it is instead established by officials who arbitrarily set a price for grain and establish an equivalence with silver (a silver shekel weighing 8 grammes has the same value as a gur, or 250 grammes of grain). Currency served mainly to pay debts contracted with the ruler (taxes payable) and to establish a price grid essential to power's calculations and accounts, necessary for the measurement of labour time and land yield. This currency served to finance the operation of great institutions, temples, and palaces, allowing it to circulate and spread throughout society.

To make up for the time that separated sowing from harvesting, the Sumerians invented a technique that allowed them to *buy time* (consume before paying, and before producing one's wages). Peasants borrowed seed from political or religious powers, or bought goods on credit, or consumed refreshments at the bar, establishing a tab to be paid at harvest time. The peasants and other actors in the economy could thus repay the palace (administration) that had advanced the monetary resources. Exchange is made possible, facilitated, and extended by the existence of virtual currency established by political power. The monetized economy and the market arise from the tribute that subjects owe to the constituted power.

The creation of currency is a powerful device for controlling time, governing the activities of subjects, and imposing on them the rhythms of work and tax payment schedules. These financial systems built on debt, even at the time, quickly created strong social inequalities, polarizations of income and wealth that resulted in the impoverishment of debtors and the enrichment of creditors. These deep differences and the resulting formation of oligarchies have been around since the Neolithic period. Power was regularly forced to cancel debts (*jubilee*). The palace and temple cancelled debts, freed debtors who had fallen into slavery, and redistributed land – not for humanitarian reasons, but to preserve a population of peasants and small landowners who provided soldiers for war and labour, and resources for the temples and palaces. The impoverishment of the population caused by debt threatened to produce an implosion of the whole society. The oligarchy of the time was much wiser than contemporary oligarchies whose diktat is that all debts must be repaid without exception – save for those of the United States, obviously.

This truth of currency – its being immediately political, a device of a power strategy – is lost with the emergence of economics as a *science*. Economics carefully avoids establishing a relationship of money to political power, but in two different ways: classical economics makes it emerge from exchange and thus reduces it to an entirely economic affair, while neoclassical theory makes it a mere *numéraire* that has no influence on prices, incomes, and the economy. Léon Walras's neoclassical general equilibrium theory also dispenses with currency. Economic exchange is reduced to barter that is not mediated by currency. Each individual brings goods and services to the market, where an auction commissioner sets prices through supply and demand without the intervention of currency.

For neoclassical theory (the model for orthodox economics), money is neutral, changing neither prices nor income distribution. If money changes market equilibrium, it means that the monetary system is mismanaged by the authorities (monetarist position).

## Marx and money

The Marxian theory of money contained in the third book of *Capital* takes a big step forward because it monetizes the economy. There can be no economy without money. Marx has a very original position on money, but one that remains ambiguous. On one hand, money cannot be neutral because it is the sine qua non for access to goods by both the consumer (worker) and the capitalist. Money heavily influences transactions, income distribution, and class differences, not least because credit amplifies and accelerates production and the concentration of economic power, creating imbalances and thus crisis. On the other hand, in classical economics, money arises from exchange, and has a purely economic, mercantile origin. The relationship with political power and the state is a relationship of instrumental use; it is not a strategic relationship, because the genealogy of money is explicable through economics.

The Marxian ambiguity implies that the money of the world market excludes both 'symbolic money, mere tokens of value, which are designed for specific use in certain states, and . . . credit-money'.[2] Currency can never disengage from this objective measure constituted by the totality of international exchange, as the dollar does today: 'But it should always be borne in mind that, in the first place, money – in the form of precious metal – remains the foundation from which the credit system, by its very nature, can *never* detach itself.'[3]

With this conception of money, the Fed could never intervene in prices because they would be determined by the autonomous functioning of exchanges. I do not want to reconstruct the whole of Marxian

---

2  Karl Marx, *Capital*, vol. 2, ed. Frederick Engels, trans. I. Lasker, Moscow: Progress Publishers, 1956, ch. 4, available at marxists.org.
3  Karl Marx, *Capital*, vol. 3, ed. Frederick Engels, New York: International Publishers, 1959, ch. 36, available at marxists.org.

money theory; I merely highlight the problems inherent in its conception of the functioning of money as an automaton, which is fully expressed in what Marx calls the 'autonomous movement of value', capable of overthrowing human activity into an impersonal movement of things (or even a *subjectless process*, as it will later be called). Again, I would instead like to show that what is crucial here is *political and military strategy, so that class struggle precedes not only production, but also money*. Monetary and financial management can, and in fact does, emancipate itself from the objectivity produced by the autonomous operation of exchange. What it cannot get rid of is class struggle.

Marx's problem, long before economics, is ontological-philosophical in nature; it is the *fetishism of the commodity*, as it is called in the first book of *Capital*: relations between humans are transformed into relations between things, and it is the latter that command the action and fate of the former. This fetishistic description of the movement of money is the negative version of the impersonal functioning of the economy, while the positive version is provided by market theorists: human actions coordinate and self-organize thanks to the market, which overthrows the individual subjectivity of each economic actor through the objectivity of prices, thanks to competition.

What disappears here, in the automatic functioning of money, is *strategy*, the action of a will against other wills, something that a working theory of dollar imperialism (and an awareness of currency's Neolithic roots) restores to us in its entirety. Of course, strategy is not a simple relationship between *subjects*; it always passes through *things* – but this does not mean that the latter dominate the former.

If economic action is not simple intersubjectivity, neither is it interobjectivity (based on relationships between objects). Action always has an intentional element, but this does not mean that the subject is individual. Action is always confronted with the action of other wills, with which it must struggle in order to be able to unfold: there is always a relation between forces. Economics comes next – first is class struggle. Only the victory of capitalists over proletarians gives rise to *objective* economic processes, laws, and automatisms.

The fetishism of capital manifests itself in all its fullness with finance capital, with interest-producing capital, which embodies the culmination of subject–object reversal according to Marx.

The formula M—M' – money producing money, or money 'unassisted by the processes of production and circulation' – is, according to Marx, a 'meaningless condensation' in which it '*appears as a mysterious and self-creating source of interest* . . . Thus we get the fetish form of capital and the conception of fetish capital.'[4]

Simple objects, pieces of paper, 'accumulated claims, or legal titles, to future production' take on a life of their own: they have their own movement, their own laws that give the illusion of constituting *real capital*. For Marx, they constitute 'fictitious capital', and an 'illusory' production.[5]

> The independent movement of the value of these titles of ownership, not only of government bonds but also of stocks, adds weight to the illusion that they constitute real capital alongside of the capital or claim to which they may have title. For they become commodities, whose price has *its own characteristic movements and is established in its own way*.[6]

What we must retain from Marx's pages is not his assertion that the power of money asserts itself through its automatism, through automatic movement (money as automaton), but the fact that money, interest, finance, and credit have their own laws and movements that can make them independent from real (industrial) capital. The *fictitious capital* exploiting this relative autonomy subordinates itself to *real capital*. Finance (in complicity with the state) ends up controlling production. This is an internal and necessary tendency of capitalist development that has been openly manifested since the end of the nineteenth century with imperialism.

It is thanks to this supposed independence that dollar imperialism has been able to establish itself, and it is always thanks to this relative independence that the strategy between economic and state powers is

---

4   Ibid., ch. 24.
5   Ibid., ch. 29.
6   Ibid. My emphasis.

effective. The transition from the hegemony of industrial capitalism to the hegemony of financial capitalism is an internal necessity for capitalist development. The finance temporarily brought under control by political power during Keynesianism (the euthanasia of the rentier) and reduced to a mere financial service structure of industry will quickly overthrow its subordination. With the declaration of the dollar's inconvertibility, it resumes its function of guiding and organizing exploitation and domination, not only in the factory but also in society as a whole, across the globe.

If we must take the Marxian assertion about capital seriously, it is then not possible to counterpose productive capital to parasitic capital, profit to finance (rent), because these are two sides of the same process. We must draw all the consequences of this idea, rather than hesitating as Marx sometimes does. We have to acknowledge that, starting at the end of the nineteenth century, a hierarchy has been established between finance capital and industrial capital where the former dominates the latter – rent controls profit – to the point of blurring them.

My thesis is not to argue that the automatism of monetary and financial value does not exist, but, on the contrary, that it can only be constructed and function after strategies are established – after choices regarding political, economic, and military power have decided the winners who command and the losers who obey. It comes after power relations have established who benefits from automatism and who is dispossessed by it. This is what dollar imperialism shows to those who want to see.

The limitation of Marxian theory emerges clearly when it analyses the role of public debt solely from an economic/industrial point of view: the fact that the accumulation of public debt can function as capital accumulation shows the reversal that takes place in the credit system between real and fictitious capital.

In dollar imperialism, the political function of public debt shows its full force. It is the fundamental weapon for the accumulation of profit and rent (there is nothing fictitious about it), which can now hardly be distinguished. It is on the basis of the public deficit that the power of the US has been intentionally politically constructed, and is continually reproduced.

The dark side of financial capitalism that neoliberalism must not mention – getting drunk instead on the market, competition, supply, and demand – takes us back to strategy: to the power relations in which it is increasingly difficult to establish any clear separation between political-economic and military. Currency may have the most rigid laws and the most cogent systems, but the history of dollar imperialism tells us that it is not an automatism at all. This history allows us to understand that all markets are preceded by strategies that use the workings of money for purposes of domination. They can only achieve these strategies of domination through the development of finance, however: by controlling and guiding its laws.

The history of the dollar clearly shows impositions, prohibitions, norms, agreements, threats, and rules, imposed with the carrot (if the subordinate states agree or if a compromise is reached between the contenders), or with the stick (the dominant power will not hesitate to use force if the dominated do not cooperate). *The market exists, but only between winners and losers* that economic science disguises as harmless, peaceful actors exchanging goods as equals rather than as enemies facing one another in a bloody confrontation.

In dollar imperialism, interest-producing capital, like credit, functions as a tool for world wealth capture (I reconstructed four such tools in Chapter 1). These tools thus have an absolutely central political function, because they allow dominant powers to use the debtor/creditor relationship to enrich themselves, to impose their wills, and to keep nations and entire continents subservient.

The category of *fictitious or illusory capital* is misleading, and risks creating misunderstandings of all kinds, because this financial capital corresponds to something absolutely real, an effect that is suffered by millions. Wealth is extracted, and the subordination is real.

Finance capital has become autonomous from production – as Marx says, it has its own laws. It is this autonomy, not its automatism, that has been politically exploited. Not only have the subordination of industrial capital and the subordination of commercial capital been built on this autonomy, but so has the subordination of sovereign states that do not have the financial capital and military force at their disposal to push into the world market.

It is from this point of view, and not from the purely economic point of view, that one must interpret financial capital. Its activity, coupled with the force of the state (the state-capital machine) means that, on a global level, war and military power relations are inseparable from economics; this combined power is capable of affecting not only production or society, but markets, on a planetary level.

This combined power is money in the world market, nothing else.

Marx's claim that the M—M' formula considers 'capital, without regard to the conditions of reproduction and labor' is only superficially true. The conditions necessary for the formula to work are quite different and go far beyond Marx's categories of reproduction and labour. Between M—M', there are not only financial dispositions (treasury bills, derivatives, stocks, the stock market, central banks) – there is the *world market* with its unequal exchange; the *heterogeneity* of economies, more or less developed, more or less industrial, more or less commercial; the multiplicity of types of labour (wage, precarious, domestic, servile, slave); the great mass of unpaid labour ... Above all, however, we find the state, war, and the army. There are power relations between classes on a global level (including those of centre and periphery, the competition between delocalized workers in the global South and those in the North), and power asymmetries between states, and between capitalisms. We still find colonialism, pillage, dispossession. Financial capital has the ability to capture not only *wage labour* but the whole of social relations, and this is why irresistible development is not in industrial capital, but in financial capital (the former being an indispensable part of the latter, but still only a part). What is equally important is that, without imperialism, without war, the M—M' formula is impossible.

This Marxian ambiguity around currency must be resolved by resorting to Marx himself – to the Marx of class struggle. Capital is a *social relation* that cannot simply spill over into a relation between things, because it is *class struggle* before it is production, because it is a relation of *war* before it is an economic relation, and because it is a strategic relation before it can become an *automatism* – all the more so if we do not merely speak of capital's economic laws on the one hand, and the state's sovereignty, citizenship, and laws on the other, but of the state-capital machine, where sovereignty and capital cannot be separated. Having said that, their joint action retains specific differences in how they function and their specific objectives, as we shall see.

## Money flows and power

As I have said elsewhere, Deleuze and Guattari offer an important theory of money that reaches the same conclusions as the Harvard study group cited above. In *Anti-Oedipus*, they view credit money as what gives *infinite debt* its capitalist form. This point of view is still very much tied to Volume 3 of *Capital* and the Marxian description of credit money, but money is already debt.

In *A Thousand Plateaus*, their theory is further refined and shows currency arising from taxation (as it did in the Neolithic period), and not according to the principles of classical economics (that is, from mercantile exchange).

> As a general rule, it is taxation that monetarizes the economy; it is taxation that creates money, and it necessarily creates it in motion, in circulation, with turnover, and also in a correspondence with services and goods in the current of that circulation. The State finds in taxation the means for foreign trade, insofar as it appropriates that trade. Yet it is not from trade but from taxation that the money-form derives . . . It is through taxation that goods and services come to be like commodities, and the commodity comes to be measured and equalized by money.[7]

But the contribution that perhaps matters most is the relationship established between monetary flows and force, between money and power, between money and war. This relationship is easily deciphered in dollar imperialism. Deleuze introduces a qualitative difference between

---

[7] Gilles Deleuze and Félix Guattari, *A Thousand Plateaus: Capitalism and Schizophrenia*, trans. Brian Massumi, London: Continuum, 1987, p. 489.

economic flows that seems specifically relevant here: investment flows are of a different nature than money flows embodied in the purchasing power of wages or income. The heterogeneous nature of flows is expressed through differences in power that express different possibilities for action. Money is a sign, a currency such as the dollar or the currency of the Sumerians, but it can be a *powerful* or *powerless* sign.

Investment money is *powerful* because it determines and establishes *future* production and labour power, while wage money is *powerless* because it is a mere medium of exchange with already produced objects (*until it becomes the object of class conflict, of the rejection of political domination*).

Wage (or income) flows are flows of purchasing power that express only a certain power of exchange with commodities. They are a set of means of payment that are exchanged for goods for reproduction. Of lesser power, they are subordinate to financial flows that instead hold a power of prescription, of choice, of decision – a force that has the capacity to anticipate production, power relations, and modes of subjection to come. The power of the financial currency does not derive from a higher or lower purchasing power; the strength of a capitalist does not depend on the fact that they are richer than a worker, but on the extra-economic force that accompanies, sustains, and singularizes the economy. 'However rich you may be, however great your purchasing power, money as purchasing power determines a series of powerless signs which receive their power from another flow – financing. And just as money as purchasing power is regulated by the laws of exchange, the other flow is regulated by all the other laws, that is, those of the creation and destruction of money.'[8]

Here, we already find a first relation, not between money and the economy, but between money and the state, political power, and sovereignty – that is, between money and force. The creation and destruction of money is a prerogative, first of the sovereign, then of the state (through its Central Bank). Private banks can also create money (and they create a lot more of it than the state – 90 per cent of money is created by banks)

---

8   Gilles Deleuze, 'Les conceptions de l'énoncé. Flux de financement', lecture, 4 June 1973, Vincennes, available at le-terrier.net/deleuze.

but, unlike the latter, they cannot issue it to save themselves from bankruptcy, while the state can and must prevent the implosion of both finance and the capitalist system through sovereign monetary creation. This is what has always happened throughout history and what central banks did during and after the 2007–8 crisis. It is a 'sovereign privilege', not an economic function.

This relationship is, once again, quite evident in dollar imperialism.

Dollar imperialism derives all its strength from its ability (an extra-economic ability, because it is secured by a power that is both political and military) to create and destroy the currency over which it has a monopoly. Through the play of interest rates, it can increase or decrease investment flows, it can decide on the allocation of these investments, and, again through money, it can make capital go out or come back in. In other words, it can encourage investment abroad or create the conditions for capital to return to invest in the three American markets of treasury bills, derivatives, and the stock market itself. The whole process is guaranteed not only by the economic and innovative strength of American capitalism, but also by military strength.

This power is the monetary flow that controls the world market, sustained and determined by the flow of war – by the political/military/economic force of imperialism.

## The state/capital machine

We must, however, enlarge the framework defined by Deleuze to grasp the wholeness of the process and the (different) function played by the state and capital. The financing flows of dollar imperialism run through the world market. The state-capital relationship, which was already closely established in the First World War, constitutes a war machine in which these two powers combine their strength while retaining relative autonomy. This autonomy is a source of increased strength, but it is also a contradiction that can lead not only to crises but also to war.

Marx's industrial capital becomes financial capital, but keeps, indeed enhances, its will for limitless expansion. But the hegemony of finance capital cannot come to fruition without a double state intervention, *first into the world market, and second, directly into finance.*

The tendency of capital to universalize itself, become cosmopolitan, and continually push the boundaries it encounters and which it creates, can be accomplished only through the intervention of the state. In no case is capital able to immanently remove limits to its development, through the economy, through Schumpeterian crises of destruction/creativity. In the world market, the displacement of these limits requires the intervention of imperialism.

In classical imperialism, colonial empires all had a centre of accusation, the state. Without its armed forces, it was impossible to conquer free spaces, that is, to bring war to bear on the colonies' unlimited resources and declare ownership of them against European competitors, both on the continent and in the world market. In dollar imperialism, the spaces of the global South are no longer free, and globalization clashes with the limits of former colonies that have become sovereign states. Despite this, as Ciao Liang argues, the US is fighting an 'endless war' (constantly since 1945) not against terrorism, but to preserve the monopoly of the dollar that colonizes without occupying, that dominates through finance and debt.

On the other hand, the second intervention of the state is internal to the dynamics of financial accumulation. In dollar imperialism, capital is both cosmopolitan and American at the same time, because the creation/destruction of money (on which the start of each economic cycle depends) always flows from a national power centre: the deterritorializing force of money, knowing no borders, needs the territorialized force of the state whose full sovereignty is exercised only within certain borders.

This is a contradiction without possible synthesis, a tension that cannot be overcome but must be managed as such (strategy). The state-capital machine shows all its strength, but also its burgeoning internal contradictions, when the hegemony of finance capital asserts itself. It is clear that this contradiction cannot give rise to any resolution. Imperialism is precisely the device of strategic management in which these contradictions are reproduced instead of resolved, and by reproducing themselves exponentially, they end in war.

The will of financial capital to expand relentlessly – its vocation to universalization, to lose its Americanness – pushes it to the limits of financial collapse and, even further, leads the entire capitalist system to war. At this point, it is only the state and its monetary creation that can stop this process of self-destruction (which, like production, knows no limits) and save the system. *Currency (state) saves finance (capital).* And it saves not only finance, but also businesses. Actually, the state has been building a real welfare for enterprises for years.

Each component of the state-capital war machine needs the other, but their functioning is not harmonious because they (capital and the state) respond to different, though complementary, logics. Their contradictory evolution is one of the main sources of crises and wars. Using another terminology, we are saying what Luxemburg already knew when confronted with a different hegemony of finance: capital tends towards a globalization it can never achieve, because it cannot disengage from the state through money as it believes it can (precisely because money has *a sovereign and not an economic origin*). All at the same time, capital is cosmopolitan, universal, but incapable of getting rid of its nationality, of its state, which sooner or later seizes it (to save it). Without state intervention (that is, political intervention), capital would have collapsed long ago.

Finance, which tries to assert its autonomy by dominating and subordinating the state, actually has an absolute need for state intervention, because it needs currency. It needs sovereign power to exist and reproduce itself, but above all to get out of the crises it inevitably slips into. Its power is relative. It develops vast financial flows that far exceed those the state can manage. But these massive flows of money – which make anything seem possible, with which one imagines that anything can be done – *cannot save themselves when necessary.* Left to their own endless expansion, they implode. Ultimately, the world market clearly demonstrates the relationship between money, finance, and state/war: the contradictory combination of the immanent, cosmopolitan, deterritorializing power of capital; and the transcendent, national, territorial power of the state.

Money, the most abstract form of capital (in the sense that it is the abstraction of ever particular form), is always founded on specificity and anchored in a particular and specific state (American, Chinese, Russian, and so on).

But the opposite is also true: while the state, especially the American state, retains its sovereignty, this is not a classical, Hobbesian sovereignty. The dependence of capital on the state therefore also goes the other way: the state without capital – without wages, income, welfare, or consumption – constitutes an empty sovereignty. State interventions cannot be deduced from an autonomous logic; they are determined by the cycle of capital, with its crises and stagnation. Its force is exerted on what gives consistency to contemporary sovereignty – that is, on the activities of capital and the disasters it produces (financial crisis, impoverishment, health and ecological crises). It is not the state but the cycle of capital that dictates what, when, and how sovereignty should intervene.

In this sense, we need to think about articulating state and capital together, emerging from the separation of economy and politics, both in terms of development and crisis. It is clear that no autonomy of the political, no autonomy of the state is possible, just as no economism of Marxist or capitalist origin is possible.

## Industrial capital and financial capital

To delve deeper into the relationship between *money* and *force* in imperialism, we must take a step further than Deleuze and Guattari and distinguish between the *investment flows* of *industrial capital* and *finance capital*. Both have a relationship to the use of force and thus the state, though they are different from each other.

Investment flows in industrial capital require the *purchase* of a particular commodity: labour-power. These are flows that involve the use of force because they must create *workers*, which do not exist in nature, then subordinate them, bind them to the factory, and fix them to the organization of labour. These flows cannot be economic without also being political; they cannot be political without forcing subordination and obedience. This domination is inconceivable without three modes of the use of force: the war of conquest that dispossesses the peasant of the land and the means of production; the violence of laws against the vagrancy forced upon them by dispossession; and the probable closures of workhouses (in parallel, force is used in other wars of subjugation against the colonized, women, and the enslaved). But even after they have been bent to the slavery of wage labour and forced through the factory gates, the worker is not simply subjugated by the impersonality of machine operation and labour organization. The machine system, like any automaton, cannot command alone; it needs the supervisory work of the boss (an expression of despotic power, according to Marx). Without the boss's despotic violence, there would be no production.

The investment flows of industrial capital cannot impose themselves without help; the economy cannot be conceived as a process of self-organization and immanent self-regulation. The rationality of industrial capitalism and its governmentality exudes violence, the use of force, and more or less armed coercion from every pore. Upon the basis of these types of violence, the habits, routines – the automatisms – of wage labour (and domestic, servile, or slave labour) and consumption can be constituted. These automatisms seem to have a natural consistency: capable of reproducing themselves through the mists of time, they take possession of the individual for a certain time, during a specific period. The subjugation of the vanquished is then reproduced by governmentality, to which different modes of violence (sexist, racist, class-based) are joined.[9]

In the world market, money flows also require the use of force, but of a different nature. Capitalism was born as a world market but it is only with imperialism in the late nineteenth century that the globe was entirely subjugated to the various state/capital machines fighting for their slice of the pie. The hegemony exercised there was held by those who controlled the circuits of money and finance sustained by economic production and the legitimate monopoly of force managed by the state.

Flows of finance capital also require flows of power, but of a different nature than industrial capital, because the world market is always

---

9  On the distinction between war and violence, see Maurizio Lazzarato, *Guerra o rivoluzione: Perché la pace non è un'alternativa*, Rome: DeriveApprodi, 2022.

shattered, divided, and balkanized by the action of different state-capital machines. The construction of a smooth space of globalization is always an illusion that lasts for the blink of an eye (the ascendant phase of the cycle of accumulation), because its construction is possible only due to the irregular spaces where states act.

Financial and monetary flows must not only command different types of labour (wage, domestic, servile, slave), but also intervene in foreign states, nations, and populations, and in heterogeneous economies (industrial, mercantile, underdeveloped, subsistence).

Dollar imperialism faces bitter and violent opposition from other state-capital war machines, but also from revolutions, struggles for national liberation, wars, and so on. Capital, even when embodied in mighty multinational corporations and immense financial flows, does not have the capacity to withstand a confrontation that always risks escalating into war.

Here, neither national state intervention nor despotic power exercised in the factory is enough; it takes a type of imperialist force capable of exerting its power over the world market, controlling the seas and skies. That is, it takes more than 700 military bases located in 100 countries; it takes an army; it takes the threat and practice of imperial warfare. Production, financial, and monetary flows are, at the same time, flows of war, determined by power relations between states and state alliances.

The contradictory convergence and divergence between state and capital is fully manifested as finance capital becomes hegemonic, because the space of action is the world market.

It is here, on the world market, that financial accumulation must refine and mobilize the state-capital machine and its contradictions even more intensely. In US imperialism, the tensions of this alliance assume even greater significance. The universality to which American financial capital seems to contradict the territorial sovereignty of the state, but, without the latter, without its army and its deadly capacity to use force, to wage war, capital would never be able to participate in the world market.

Use of force is indispensable because imperialism is, by definition, a multiplicity of imperialisms: there cannot be a single global state; a universal state is a contradiction in terms. This is what the Americans did not understand, convinced that one imperialism – their own – was not only possible but necessary for the good of humanity. The existence of one imperialism was due to a contingent situation, a singular political situation (the fall of the Soviet Union), from which other imperialisms would soon emerge, as is logical. The illusion that blinded the United States after the collapse of the Soviet Union quickly faded, and the war in Ukraine is the latest and most dramatic manifestation of this reality.

## A return to imperialism: The functions of state and capital

In order to describe the workings of the state-capital war machine and their necessary conjunction/disjunction, we must analyse its economic and political cycles and not limit ourselves to the static analysis we find in both ordoliberalism and neoliberalism. Depending on the phases of the cycle, one of the two components of the machine seems to prevail. In reality, they act together, even though the two logics may momentarily collide.

The cycle begins with the state, because class formation is an extra-economic phenomenon that requires the deployment of a war of conquest (the civil wars in Latin America, for example, or strikes in the North). The state is still at the beginning of the economic cycle, because it is the one that initiates capital liberalization, tax policies, and labour market laws.

In the ascending phase of the cycle, capital seems to disengage itself from its relationship with the state and assumes its own cosmopolitan dynamic. However, it quickly faces a wall of crises that it has built from limitless valorization, ever accelerated by credit and financial tools. The ascendant phase of globalization should not be interpreted as the sole work of the power of capital, but of the conjunction/disjunction of the latter's strength and that of the state – that is, from *political capitalism*.

In the downward phase of the globalization cycle, we should not talk of the *return of the state*, because state action was there all along.

The magnitude of the 2008 financial crisis was a sign that the ascending cycle of capital was over, and the cycle was entering another phase.

The state had to intervene, first to save banks, financial institutions, and insurance companies in order to prevent the collapse of the system and make the people of the various countries pay for the bailouts. Globalization then began to creak, the cycle reversed, and winds of war began to blow. When the crisis turned into war, the state intervened a second time, this time even more forcefully.

US imperialism's will to globalize has been shown as impossible, once again. Even at the end of the cycle that began in 1971, war between states reappeared. Dollarization failed, the international order constituted on its shoulders crumbled, and pacifying governmentality was powerless because fascism and civil war began to divide societies (in the US, Brazil, Peru, Chile, Egypt, Iran, and elsewhere).

War is the logical outcome of this crisis, and now the state not only intervenes but dominates the economy, which is no more than a (still very important) part of the new strategy of the cycle of imperialism and armed confrontation.

The imperialist cycle that began with war (of conquest, of subjugation) ends with war (between states, now large states).

Understanding capital as a general process of accumulation based on class divisions – on the domination of one class over another, and whose violence leads to war – is undoubtably more useful than the ordoliberal and neoliberal refrains of *market, competition, and human capital* that sound increasingly out of tune (because they result in an impossible equilibrium).

## Imperialism as analysis of power

Dollar imperialism also allows us to renew the analysis and critique of power, of relations of domination, resistance, and rupture. Critical thought, and particularly Foucault – whom we have chosen as a symptom of its virtues and vices – has sought a way out of the impasses of Marxism and revolution (dialectics, the philosophy of history, labour as the essence of man, progressive historicism, the concept totality) in Nietzsche's thought. If we take on the new concept of power that emerges, we must do so by integrating the kernel of the Marxian analysis of capitalism and its power relations; this is difficult, if not impossible, to find in Nietzsche and his readers (Foucault and Deleuze, first and foremost).

The multiplicity of power relations found in the German philosopher (a plurality of forces that are dynamically and conflictingly composed in a game that is never stable but always becoming) *is bent in a specific way by capitalism in the dualisms of class, race, and gender.*

Power cannot be analysed without capital, as Foucault tended to do with the concept of governmentality, because capitalism, with imperialism, constitutes a specific subjugation of forces: *it organically integrates the state* (legal, political, military) and *capital* (non-legal and non-state force), reaching new levels of centralization and spreading its devices of control and capture over the local, over the micropolitical (over the multiplicity of forces). Centralization and micropolitics are not opposed to each other, they are two sides of the same power. Foucault never reached this level of analysis because he never integrated modern forms of capitalism – that is, imperialism – nor its *global* wars, nor its *global* civil war.

After Nietzsche, finally in the 1960s and 1970s free of associations with Nazism, we still have capitalism with its class oppositions, we still have imperialism with its contradictions between states and between capitals, its negative and destructive charge. Indeed, since the 1970s, capital has asserted itself as a brutal and savage counterrevolution. *So, after Nietzsche there is still, necessarily, Marx – and especially Lenin.* Foucault, convinced that our contemporary problem is not capitalism but *too much power*, thinks the opposite; hence all the limitations we have noted in his analysis of neoliberalism and governmentality.

There is a basic difference between Foucault's and Deleuze's readings of Nietzsche, on the one hand, and, on the other, the revolutionary tradition. It is a difference in *method*, or rather, of perspective. The book that Deleuze dedicated to his friend Foucault contains all the misunderstandings and ambiguity of his microphysical or micropolitical method and brings out the differences in approach and analysis with Marxism, but also with feminism and decolonial thought.

For the revolutionary tradition, *the foremost power relation is oppression, which means appropriation, division, and domination* (of class, gender, race). Materialist feminism affirms its close relationship with Marx through Christine Delphy's programmatic statement: 'It is the only theory of history for which oppression is the fundamental reality, the starting point.'[10]

The great strength in Marxism, and later in feminism and decolonial thought, consists in a historical-political point of view: classes do not exist in nature; they must be created through wars of conquest and subjugation. The defeated – workers, women, slaves, and the colonized – will then be subjugated to capitalism's exploitation and domination through governmentality. Marxism starts *from appropriation and division* (of workers, women, slaves), Foucault and Deleuze *from difference and multiplicity*.

What we do not find in Nietzsche is domination qualified by the state-capital machine, in which a power of division and appropriation, conquering first and dominating later, is affirmed, and at the same time also the power that resists, escapes, or turns against it. In Nietzsche, we find exploitation, oppression, and domination, but not their capitalist qualification. Instead, exploitation is *positively* conceived as the 'essence of the living', claimed as 'the original fact of all history' and, consequently, not only ineradicable, but to be reproduced as a condition of civilization.[11] He says one can only imagine a society without exploitation, as socialists do.

Starting from oppression and from the appropriation of capital means asserting a partisan point of view, because oppression is proof that society is divided, and, as such, one cannot assume a general interest perspective, that is to say, the ideology of governmentality.

A point of view means subjectivity. The wills *to* power in capitalism are subjectivities, processes of collective subjectification, just as the wills *of* power, of workers, women, and the racialized who counter capitalist power are also subjectivities and collective processes of subjectification. These are neither subjectless processes nor techniques of governmentality, but policies and strategies on either side of the relationship. In

---

10 Christine Delphy, *The Main Enemy: A Materialist Analysis of Women's Oppression*, London: Women's Research and Resources Centre Publications, 1977.
11 Friedrich Nietzsche, *Nietzsche: 'On the Genealogy of Morality' and Other Writings*, ed. Keith Ansell-Pearson, trans. Carol Diethe, Cambridge: Cambridge University Press, 2017.

capitalism, there is not the impersonal *one* but the subjective *who*, manifesting through division, conflict, violence, and wars.

Starting with oppression is affirming a political *difference* that must first be denied because, starting with the reality of appropriation, exploitation, sexism, and racism, it is impossible to affirm anything without first defying subjugations (affirmation without denial is the donkey in *Zarathustra* who brays his eternal 'yes' without ever being able to say 'no', a perfect image of much contemporary thought and politics).

The partisan viewpoint where we might begin all criticism and all politics also applies to the *multiplicity* that Foucault introduces, again citing Nietzsche. There is no single power relation capable of determining social reality as a whole: 'A society is not a unitary body, in which one and only one power is exercised. Society is in reality the juxtaposition, the link, the coordination and also the hierarchy of different powers that nevertheless remain in their specificity . . . Society is an archipelago of different powers.'[12]

This is certainly true, but the problem lies not in the alternative between interpreting power from multiplicity or from a unique relation (as a certain Marxism would tend to do, according to Foucault), but the *point of view from which this multiplicity is analysed*. Foucault, through the concept of governmentality, paradoxically looks at the immanence of these relations from above, from the *outside*, and thus has a global, bird's-eye view, moving completely away from Nietzschean perspectivism. His position is neutral, without perspective, so there are *no divisions that compel sides to be taken*. Instead, starting from oppression means grasping power relations from *within* and *from a singular, partisan point of view* (the power of man over woman, boss over worker, white over Black). This is not reality *as it is*, but reality as it is *for us*, the oppressed, exploited, subjugated; it is a condition for knowing and transforming reality. True immanence is only this partisan perspective that reorganizes power's supposedly complete vision from its own oppression in order to attack it better. The truth of the whole does not reside in

---

12   Michel Foucault, 'The Mesh of Power', trans. Christopher Chitty, *Viewpoint Magazine*, 12 September 2012, viewpointmag.com.

analytical objectivity; it comes only from the unfolding of struggle, from the will to prevail over the enemy.

Immediately after '68, the multiplicity of power relations began to be understood, starting with lesbian feminists, as a pluralism of forms of oppression that nonetheless constitute dominant and dominated dualisms (man/woman, white/Black, capitalist/worker).

Power is not external to the oppressed, but runs through them, Foucault continues, because the oppressed also exert force and can construct a strategy of resistance and/or attack (again, Nietzsche). The oppressed are perfectly aware of this: they know that power is found neither on one side of the relationship nor on the other, but in clash, in struggle, and that they need a strategically oriented knowledge for this conflict, a knowledge that cannot build itself without attacking and prevailing over the enemy.

It is not the same thing to begin analysis from *power*, or even *desire*, rather than beginning with the condition of the oppressed and the point of view of the vanquished. *Starting from oppression, fundamentally, also means starting from conflict in capitalism* – conflict before production, *class struggle before relations of production*, and *civil war before productive forces*. Starting from oppression also and especially means starting from the appropriation of bodies. The war of subjugation through which classes are constituted is expressly ruled out by both Foucault and Deleuze as the origin of power, but curiously not by Nietzsche. The latter makes it the foundation of all political order: 'rulers and masters' must first have been 'predators and conquerors', which is precisely the sequence of the process of capital's constitution – first the war of conquest that later continues through other means in the exploitation of wage, domestic, and colonized labour.

In 1983, at the end of his life, Foucault again repeated the phrase 'replace domination with . . . governmentality', which, translated, means replacing capitalism with neoliberalism, exploitation with the market, force with competition.[13]

---

13   Michel Foucault, *Power/Knowledge: Selected Interviews and Other Writings 1972–77*, Brighton: Harvester Press, 1980.

For Deleuze, too, the effects of domination are not attributable to conquest, appropriation, or violence – that is, to an act of force – but to 'strategy, to devices, to maneuvers, to techniques, to operations' (governmentality). Deleuze does not even remotely assume that the latter is one of the faces of imperialist strategy, irreducible to governance, to diffuse, dispersed, local micro-power.[14]

The microphysics of power, as indeed micropolitics, implies that we give up both the 'theory of the contract' and the 'model of conquest', Deleuze continues. Instead, we must remain faithful to Marx who, before Foucault, had seen a *non-juridical, non-state, and non-contractual power* at work in the operation of the factory and capitalism, while nevertheless holding firmly to the concept of appropriation and expropriation (of bodies and knowledge) as its foundation.

There is no possibility of manufacturing docile bodies (workers, women, the colonized) without first a political victory over subjectivities expressed through the expropriation and appropriation of bodies themselves. There is no way to produce *individuals*, or *subjects*, without the normalization created by wars of subjugation and conquest.

Power relations, Foucault suggests, 'by virtue of their inequality, constantly engender states of power, but the latter are always local and unstable'. But where do the 'unbalanced, unstable, heterogeneous, tense force relations' – between men and women, between whites and racialized peoples, between capitalists and workers – come from, if not from the war of conquest, the war of appropriation, the war of subjugation of workers, women, slaves, and the colonized?[15]

The political significance of dualisms is not functional, as in the categories of government microphysics, but political, because it expresses the fact that society is divided, radically divided (*ab origine*) by the capitalist and state power of appropriation. Society is divided into classes and, according to the revolutionary tradition, these divisions cannot be

---

14  Gilles Deleuze and Félix Guattari, *Anti-Oedipus: Capitalism and Schizophrenia I*, trans. R. Hurley, M. Seem, and H. R. Lane, London: Athlone, 1984.
15  Michel Foucault, *The History of Sexuality*, vol. 1, *An Introduction*, trans. Robert Hurley, New York: Vintage, 1990.

overcome or even reconciled. Deleuze asserts that 'this new functionalism, this functional analysis' (the micro integrated by a multiplicity of macro institutions such as the 'state, family or religious hierarchies . . . production, the market') is compatible with a class point of view.[16] We can legitimately doubt this.

Again, following Nietzsche, Foucault correctly defines power: 'power is not an institution, it is not a structure . . . it is the name given to a complex strategic situation' – which, evidently, I would add, also uses institutions and structures to exercise itself (and is therefore always, without exception, asymmetrical, heavily unbalanced in favour of capital and the state).[17]

It is not enough, however, to start from strategy (the relation between forces equally capable of exerting force); what is required is the historical-political qualification of the dominant and dominated forces. Despite the asymmetry determined by the wars of appropriation, these forces oppose each other; they struggle against each other. Just as Foucault indicates, we must start from the power relation of a non-dialectical strategic situation in which the oppressed also have the power to change the situation, to overthrow these power relations. However, these relations must be specifically qualified by the oppression implemented by imperialism.

In order to understand the nature and origin of inequality, not in general, but in and of capitalism, we must go through a concept of strategy that is not generic (as Foucault does), but specific and differentiated.

It is necessary to overturn the historical order of the process of constituting capitalist power established by Foucault. Foucault believed the dominator–dominated relationship is a result of the strategy that manages to reduce the multiplicity of power relations to this dualism. Instead, it is necessary to first start from the negative action of power that produces the dualisms of the dominant and the dominated, that is, from wars of conquest (wars in the plural because capturing and subjugating is of multiple bodies – workers, women, slaves). Second, it is

---

16  Deleuze and Guattari, *Anti-Oedipus*.
17  Foucault, *The History of Sexuality*.

necessary to move to governmentality, the 'positive' action of power that continues the war of conquest by other means, that is to say, using 'devices, techniques, strategies' of pacification and control of the multiplicity of the behaviour of the vanquished, and fix them to the objective and subjective functions of worker, woman, slave. In this phase, power makes us act, makes us do things; it multiplies the devices of power, and even grants us certain pleasures (consumption), but power quickly encounters a limit in the very functioning of the state-capital machine. Third, finally, this plurality of economic and political activation and appeasement processes ends up – under the pressure of capitalist centralizations, totalizations, and polarizations – exasperating the asymmetries and hierarchies that lead us to war between states (the Clausewitzian strategy), or to revolution (the Leninist, Luxemburgist, Maoist, Ho Chi Minhian strategy – so far, there haven't been others).

Power is productive, as Deleuze and Foucault say, because it creates the *real* of the worker, the woman, and the slave, but the productive phase goes through *three modes of war and three different strategies*. We can define the *negative* and *positive* action of capital as, always and in any case, an act of war ('sometimes open, sometimes hidden', say Marx and Engels in the *Manifesto*).

For Foucault, in 1976, forces are codified by war and the political, but not by capitalism, it seems. 'The relationships which for a long time had found expression in war, in every form of warfare, gradually became invested in the order of political power.'[18]

Power, on the other hand, was radically changed by the appearance of capital, and especially by the development of imperialism after the 1870s, which integrated the power of the state, war, and the power of capital. Both reconfigured sovereignty and the economy, further pushing centralization.

Despite this fact, Deleuze and Foucault both insist on the local diffusion and multiplicity of centres of power, a cartography that refers back to neoliberalism and governmentality. Deleuze defends an exercise of power that *makes the economy the result of imperialism and its three*

---

18   Foucault, *The History of Sexuality*.

*processes of economic, political, and military centralization.* First, power is never global but always local; its exercise 'has two very different meanings: power is local because it is never global, but it is not local or localized because it is diffuse'. Second, power does not drive centralizations: 'Power is characterised by immanence of field without transcendent unification, continuity of line without global centralisation.' It makes local and diffuse management the general form of power. According to Deleuze, the 'continuity of its segments' (school, factory, prison, army) does not produce a 'distinct totalization'.[19]

The critique of sovereignty, totalization, and globalization in the age of imperialism is one of the major contradictions in Foucault's *Birth of Biopolitics*, here reproduced by Deleuze, because capital and the state continually tend to centralize, globalize, and unify, concentrating power in the hands of the few at the same time that it exercises its diffuse power in the local, in the micropolitical, and throughout the social fabric.

On the other hand, it is true that all these dynamics of the globalization, totalization, and centralization of power *are never completely fulfilled; on the contrary, they are doomed to fail*. But when these processes falter, are challenged, or show faults, capitalism always has the possibility of producing a *distinct totalization*, which is called war, fascism, and/or Nazism (centralization and diffusion are inseparable even in Nazism). This is what has been happening for years.

We could distinguish between a *relative* distinct totalization and an *absolute* distinct totalization. The former is seen in monopolies and executive political power, whose processes of unification and totalization are always unfinished, never fully realized. *Distinct and absolute totalization*, on the other hand, occurs when these processes converge in war, simultaneously manifesting a sign of strength and of weakness: strength because there is a will to close, to bring to completion the centralization and globalization that otherwise regularly fail; weakness because the force that is required brings capitalism and the state-capital machine into a new phase where uncertainty, risk, and chaos dominate, which can lead to catastrophe (historically, Nazism).

---

19   Gilles Deleuze, *Foucault*, trans. Seán Hand, London: Continuum, 1988.

The two French philosophers, taking absolutely no account of the phenomenon of imperialism, seem to have succumbed to the postmodern image of power that is belied by its habitual and repetitive result – monopolies and war.

Deleuze not only defends Foucault and adopts his definition of power and governmentality, but indeed flips the hierarchy that we have reconstructed, because *government precedes the state-capital machine*: 'government comes before the state,' he says. First there is the multiplicity of power devices, and then the state, which is nothing but a sum, an overlapping of devices for governmentality. We have tried to show that governmentality cannot, under any circumstances, precede the state-capital machine because it is radically subordinated to dollar imperialism. Commanded by and dependent on monetary and financial imperialism, it lasts for a time – until contradictions, asymmetries, and polarizations between classes and between states are no longer manageable by the widespread form of apparently peaceful control. At this point, other devices more suited to defend the interests of ownership classes – including populism, neofascism, and war – enter the field.

'Power-relations ... simultaneously local, unstable and diffuse, do not emanate from a central point or unique locus of sovereignty' from which derivative and descendant forms radiate, Deleuze insists.[20] There is no centre more central than others, no perspective more true than another, but the *praxis* of civil war means that there exist a dominated and a dominator: a centre and a truth that one political force asserts against other forces, other truths, other centres. There is a perspective that asserts itself not because it is *true*, but by leveraging direct and indirect violence.

Power is powerful and powerless at the same time; it has its zone of power but also of powerlessness, say Deleuze and Guattari. Power is a relation between forces, where one commands and the other obeys: the one who has to carry out the order can carry it out, refuse, revolt, or flee. Power is always simultaneously power/impotence. In the contemporary condition of capitalism, characterized by the dominance of finance and

---

20   Ibid.

currency, Deleuze and Guattari propose that political power manifests its impotence because it has little room for manoeuvre: 'Politics operates by macro decisions and binary choices, binarized interests; but the realm of the decidable remains very slim.'[21] The ground on which to exercise decision is certainly limited – sovereignty is in crisis, repeat the theorists of empire; but it has sufficient and necessary strength to decide who are enemies and who friends. Imperialism has its zone of power and of powerlessness; but it also has sufficient and necessary force to declare war (economic, technological, and military). Imperialism – when the political-economic machine of capture does not work according to its expectations, when the diffuse and dispersed totalization of governmentality fails – does not hesitate to unleash, today, as yesterday, wars of all kinds, and to bring new-old fascisms back into play. In both Foucault and Deleuze, Nietzschean perspectivism becomes a harmless philosophical category, relieved of all its political force. Their last, conciliatory conceptions of micropower bear witness to this.

## Imperialism: Permanent phase of capitalism

At least until 1970, both Deleuze and Guattari used the category *state monopoly capitalism*, which contained the two fundamental concepts of imperialism – monopolies and the state – tied to war. In later writings, these concepts disappear. They are not found in Foucault, nor in Negri, who replaced them with a postmodern conception of power (explicitly described, together with Hardt, in *Empire*) that is exercised through governmentality, disciplinary societies, control societies, and biopolitics.[22] According to Agamben, power takes on the guise of administration

---

21 Deleuze and Guattari, *A Thousand Plateaus*.
22 Empire is one of the last expressions of postmodern thought which, like all fashions, quickly died out: a supranational organization, an optical illusion that has never seen the light of day, would replace imperialism. Supposedly, we have entered 'the era of secondary internal conflicts' in which 'police operations' replace 'imperialist and inter-imperialist wars'; the 'United States would be called upon to assume the central role' in the construction of the Empire and only 'an American coup d'état'

in biopolitics: 'Governance, the exercise of government, exceeding and contaminating the traditional powers (legislative, executive, judicial), now exercises – in the name of administration, and in a discretionary manner – the functions and powers that once belonged to them.'[23]

The statement does not seem to correspond to the actual exercise of state power, because it is the executive centralization that always commands administrative governance. And it is the capitalist centralization of currency that directs international organizations such as the International Monetary Fund and the World Bank. Reagan's and Thatcher's liberal and neoconservative shift was what dictated the administration's change in fiscal, monetary, and social policies.

This version of biopolitics is symptomatic of an era, because it only takes into consideration the duplicity of the political machine (government/state) and excludes capital, which in fact radically alters both the state and its administrative, military, and political functions through its processes of centralization and imperialist expansion over society and the world. One cannot speak of the 'political machine' without considering capital's invasive development because, from the very beginning, its economic action is inseparable from its political action.

A 1966 quote explains what happens to critical thought (and to Deleuze himself) once the concept of imperialism is excluded: 'Whatever

---

would prevent its coming. In the Empire, governmentality, networked power and diffuse control succeed centralizations; racism works 'not in terms of binary divisions and exclusion but as a strategy of differential inclusion'; businesses also produce by integrating differences. Financial capital is confused with currency, so that state monetary action, which has continued for a century, as has imperialism in order to save capitalism, is eclipsed. The North/South relationship must be read as unification of the world market, and not as division, a centre–periphery polarization. The resulting globalization is, after all, a happy one: Empire is a good thing 'in itself not for itself' – in any case better than the capitalisms that preceded it 'because the potential for liberation has increased', so progress is always among us, while a new philosophy of history, barely veiled, let out of the door re-enters through the window and ferries us towards an increase in the power of the proletariat (the multitude)! One could go on much longer, but let us conclude: Empire is a reassuring vision of a fundamentally pacified capitalism that, like all lies, has short legs!

23   Giorgio Agamben, 'On Anarchy Today', trans. Ill Will, 26 February 2023, illwill.com.

the complexity of a phenomenon, we can distinguish primary forces, of conquest and subjugation, from reactive, secondary forces, of adaptation and regulation.[24]

Capitalism, without monopolies – without the processes of *sovereign* centralization (economic, political, military), wars, imperialism, or 'continuous primitive accumulation' – is reduced to a force of adaptation and regulation, of which governmentality is the paradigm. On the other hand, capitalism stubbornly debunks any sort of governmental pacification, practising conquest, exploitation, domination, and subjugation through *sovereign* verticalizations that result in wars between imperial powers as well as civil wars.

Against the eurocentrism of Western Marxism and various critical theories (including those of Foucault and Agamben), Samir Amin held that the nature of capitalism has always been imperialist. The point of view from which one looks at capitalism – the North or the South – is not the same at all. His perspective also differs from the revolutionary Marxism of the first part of the twentieth century because imperialism did not impose itself during the great depression (1873–95), but prior to that, with primitive accumulation. 'Lenin described the imperialism of the monopolies as the "highest stage of capitalism". I have described imperialism as a "permanent phase of capitalism" in the sense that globalized historical capitalism has built up . . . the center/periphery polarization.'[25] Lenin's imperialism is a permanent phase of capitalism. Polarization produces the imperialist rent with which the capital-state machine pays for social peace and the integration and control of conflicts that develop in the North, in the institution.

Amin repeated this in another way: 'Accumulation through expropriation is permanent in the history of historical capitalism', which is therefore 'imperialist in all stages of its development, in the precise sense that it is polarizing'. The Egyptian-born economist was one of the first (as

---

24 Gilles Deleuze, *Pure Immanence: Essays on a Life*, trans. Anne Boyman, Princeton, NJ: Princeton University Press, 2005.
25 Samir Amin, 'The Trajectory of Historical Capitalism and Marxism's Tricontinental Vocation', *Monthly Review* 62, no. 9 (February 2011), monthlyreview.org.

early as 1960) not to confine primitive accumulation to the fifteenth and eighteenth centuries. Deleuze and Guattari in turn affirmed, as do most contemporary Marxists, the continuity of primitive accumulation. But only Amin (and certainly not David Harvey, whose concept of 'accumulation by dispossession' he adopted because it was more elegant) deduced two consequences of the utmost importance.

'With imperialism, the main contradiction of the capitalist system tends to become that which pits monopoly capital against the super-exploited masses of the periphery; the center of gravity of struggles against capital tends to shift from the center to the periphery of the system. This is what Lenin admirably expresses when he proposes the new formulation, "Proletarians of all countries, oppressed peoples, unite."'[26] This simple addition – *oppressed peoples* – manifested a break and a qualitative leap from Marx's time. While Western Marxism and particularly Italian *operaismo* might brand these positions as Third Worldism, the twentieth century has only confirmed this perspective. Revolutions were only produced in the South, against Marx's *Capital*, as Gramsci pointed out.

The second consequence is even more important, because Amin distinguished the political force of civil wars and revolutions in the global South from the political force of workers' struggles. The effects of the former are incomparable to the changes generated by workers' conflicts in the North. The rupture of the centre–periphery polarization at the foundation of capitalism since its inception was carried out in the South, where primitive accumulation was never integrated and mediated by production, and where class opposition did not take the form of the conflict between productive forces and relations of production.

> The 'South' is the 'storm zone', one of permanent uprisings and revolts. Beginning in 1917, history has consisted mainly of these revolts and independent initiatives (in the sense of independence of the tendencies that dominate the existing imperialist capitalist system) of the

---

26  Samin Amin, *Unequal Development: An Essay on the Social Formations of Peripheral Capitalism*, Hassocks: Harvester Press, 1976.

peoples, nations, and states of the peripheries. It is these initiatives, despite their limits and contradictions, that have shaped the most decisive transformations of the contemporary world, far more than the progress of the productive forces and the relatively easy social adjustments that accompanied them in the heartlands of the system.[27]

One need only think of the consequences of the Chinese revolution, which is one of the main reasons for the shift of capitalism's centres to the East and South and the main cause of the current war.

Amin criticized Western Marxism for its inability to grasp what was also happening at home, saying it 'has ignored the decisive transformation represented by the emergence of generalized monopoly capitalism. The intellectuals of the new Western radical left refuse to measure the decisive effects of the concentration of the oligopolies that now dominate the production system as a whole, in the same way that they dominate all political, social, cultural, and ideological life.'[28]

---

27  Amin, 'The Trajectory of Historical Capitalism'.
28  Ibid.

# Chapter 5

*Every revolution dissolves the old society and in so far it is social. Every revolution overthrows the old power and in so far it is political.*

Karl Marx

*Without war, no revolution.*

Reinhart Koselleck

*Gradualness explains nothing without leaps. Leaps! Leaps! Leaps!*

V. I. Lenin

## Times are a-changin'

The war in Ukraine is a symptom that the hegemony of US imperialism is coming to an end, and its slow decline is triggering not only wars between states, but also more or less low-intensity civil wars (Brazil, US, Peru), veritable insurgencies (North Africa, Egypt, Chile, Iran (Iraq?)), and a generalized world civil war of growing intensity. But it is also a symptom of the end of a civilization, Western civilization, and its absolute supremacy over the rest of the world that has lasted for centuries.

This civilization is at the same time universally asserting itself and drawing to a close. Capitalism and globalization, whose development had secured its hegemony, have entered a phase of destruction, without creation, of destruction *tout court*.

We no longer experience the continuous and empty time of globalization, but the discontinuous, broken, tumultuous, contradictory time of its unravelling: a time marked no longer by the economy or by governmentality, but by the conflict that neoliberalism was meant to avert and has instead brought out with greater violence, in wars and civil wars.

We face the return of the state, the return of history (but neither history nor the state had ever abandoned us) – which is another way of saying the return of the time of politics, no longer as administration and governance, but as long-denied, removed, and repressed class struggle.

The times are a-changin'. No longer Kronos, the continuous and linear time of normalized domination and exploitation, but an unhinged time, which makes the *world economy* falter, and from which Kairos emerges: Kairos, the time of rupture, discontinuities, disjunctions leading to catastrophes (in the sense of change, a mutation of state), implosions, destructions – but also the creation of new possibilities and opportunities that were unimaginable before 2008.

These are tragic times, because such possibilities are inevitably intertwined with conflict, confrontation, and civil war. It is a tragic situation, because *let live and make die*, which Foucault relegated to sovereignty's distant past, now unfolds in full force with war and is articulated even where war has not yet shown itself; tragic because civil wars return to the fore, although in a low-intensity form, for the moment; tragic because, within this clash, the very inhabitability of the planet is a problem pushed aside by conflicting imperialisms.

Tragic times are times of choices and decisions.

## How to understand war

Let us now try to analyse how major states (imperialisms) position themselves in the new phase opened by the 2008 crisis, and how social movements try to move within the same political phase opened up for them by the 2011 cycle of struggles. The two processes (war between states and social struggle, civil wars, insurgencies) intertwine and feed off each other.

States seem to be fully aware of what is at stake and are acting accordingly: a new imperialistic world order that the West (the US and its allies) wants to control as usual, while China, Russia, and the global South are struggling for a multilateral order – a multilaterality, however, endowed with unilateral power at the regional level, perpetuating in both unilaterality and multilaterality oppression, domination, and exploitation.

In order to orientate ourselves in the new political phase, we have to know of what political process war is a continuation, as we said at the beginning of this book. We can now answer this question because we know from what political process war comes: it is the continuation of dollar imperialism and the class and inter-state struggles it has provoked. But it is also a continuation that takes us into another dimension, another time. The continuation of politics in war actually constitutes a discontinuity.

It opens up another political phase marked by instability, uncertainty, and unpredictability; these qualities have always played a role in capitalism but are now exacerbated by war, because 'all that is solid melts into air' when time reopens.[1]

'War is the realm of chance,' Clausewitz sharply states.[2] Chance (the *fortune* that Renaissance Italians understood as totally unpredictable power) opens the situation to unknown and radical alternatives because catastrophe can also result in implosion, chaos, barbarism, or

---

1  Karl Marx and Engels, 'Manifesto of the Communist Party', in *Karl Marx and Frederick Engels Selected Works*, vol. 1, Moscow: Progress Publishers, 1969, available at marxists.org.

2  Carl von Clausewitz, *On War*, ed. and trans. Michael Howard and Peter Paret, Princeton, NJ: Princeton University Press, 1989, p. 101.

revolutionary rupture. It is in this sense that we should interpret the catastrophism proclaimed by early-twentieth-century revolutionaries. The state-capital machine periodically produces a historically determined catastrophe, but therefore its own historically possible *end*. We are now past the time when the clueless or irresponsible would say: 'It is easier to imagine the end of the world than the end of capitalism.'[3]

The accumulation of profit and power has reached a point of real catastrophe, because it leads to war. The future is as dark as ever, but the other side of this tragic time is an era of radical change.

We can draw a parallel with what Lenin wrote in 1917 just before the October Revolution, because we know that the salient features of capitalism as analysed a century ago are still present, although expanded. The conditions leading to war are similar and different at the same time; its deflagration seems diluted in time compared to the concentrated events of the First World War. Lenin's work cited in the second chapter contains an analytical method for the causes of war that, compared to contemporary methods, is still incomparably more illuminating. The uninformed regard Lenin as a dead dog. Instead, the last serious, thorough, and politically sound debate on war and its relation to capitalism and capital's relation to the state took place in the early twentieth century, with Lenin front and centre.

The very first lines of Lenin's 'War and Revolution' immediately highlight the gulf separating the consciousness of his time from that of today: 'The question of war and revolution has been dealt with so often lately in the press and at every public meeting that probably many of you are not only familiar with many aspects of the question but have come to find them tedious.'[4]

For some time, the two categories *war* and *revolution* (each the subject of analysis and heated debate among revolutionaries at the beginning of the twentieth century) have been completely excised from critical

---

3 Mark Fisher, *Capitalist Realism: Is There No Alternative?*, Ropley: O Books, 2009, p. 1.

4 V. I. Lenin, 'War and Revolution', in *Collected Works*, vol. 24, Moscow: Progress Publishers, 1964, available at marxists.org.

thought; they have become taboo. War and revolution have undergone a theoretical eradication that we are paying a heavy price for. They have also dropped off the radar of social movements, which are now completely focused on their own specific power relations. But these concepts also cause cognitive panic (especially in the media), the West having convinced itself, with the end of the Soviet Union, that democracy and liberalism have definitively won, and that it no longer has any enemies besides a few terrorists. The reappearance of what should not have existed – war in Europe, as the theatre of world conflict – ignited hysterical calls for a just war against an irrational enemy.

The outbreak of the armed conflict in Ukraine took everyone by surprise, as if war was a twentieth-century contraption and that our new cognitive, biopolitical, informational, platform capitalism, the site of all possible innovations and modernizations, could never contemplate it. How is war possible if peace had been reigning for seventy years, and if war had been nothing but a distant past for entire generations?

Peace is a relative concept in capitalism because it is inseparable from war. Sometimes, for democrats and liberals, war is difficult to discern because it flows under the economic and political institutions of a superficial peace; at other times, because war takes place in distant territories that, despite being part of the world market, seem to have no relation to *our* peace. The task of deciphering war under peace is not even considered. So when war manifests in all its destructive force, it seems to drop out of the clear blue sky.

We find ourselves today in a situation similar to that which preceded 1914. War had not been raging in Europe for years, and capitalism was weaving economic relations between nations that no one, it seemed, had any interest in questioning, because war is (it was said then as it is now) bad for business. These statements ignored a double truth: capitalism exists only as a world market, and economics is not different from war, but merely its continuation by other means.

When peace reigned in Europe, Lenin was already saying, 'but this was because domination over hundreds of millions of people in the colonies by the European nations was sustained only through constant, incessant, interminable wars'. Now, as then, 'we Europeans do not regard [these] as wars at all, since all too often they resembled, not wars, but brutal massacres, the wholesale slaughter of unarmed peoples . . . [they are] "little" because few Europeans died in those wars, whereas hundreds of thousands of people belonging to the nations they were subjugating died in them."[5]

Lenin's phrase could be redeployed against the astonishment at the war that has irrationally interrupted the peace of the global North. It invites us to reconsider both the concept of peace and the concept of war by measuring it against the world market. The analysis of the ordoliberals and neoliberals is obsessively focused on the global North, the US, and Europe, while US imperialism has a global vision the whole time, partly because it has grappled throughout the twentieth century with the wars of liberation that took place in the global South against secular colonial rule. Any conception of power that does not take into account this global dimension (Foucault) is weak, and risks missing the deeper reasons for the current conflict.

Since the end of the Second World War, the United States has waged an impressive number of wars in the global South (all of them lost, by the way) with the direct help of the Europeans, the Japanese, and other allied countries. And it is precisely the countries of the global South that are challenging the hegemony of the dollar and its devices of capture that have stripped them of their wealth and sovereignty, using the classic principles of colonization. Actually, wars waged by the colonized to free themselves from the yoke of European colonial empires have never stopped since the late 1800s, but have been in constant metamorphosis. Anti-colonial struggles first took democratic-bourgeois forms, then, from 1917 on, Bolshevik and revolutionary forms, to become capitalisms today, but capitalisms heterogeneous to the American model.

There is an important difference between the First World War and the present war: the Great War was a clash between imperialist countries of the global North for the partition of the global South, for exploiting its people and their resources, without which the cycle of capital simply

---

5  Ibid.

could not start. Two groups of capitalist powers faced each other. One group included France and England, which had already consolidated their colonial empires and commanded the world market unchallenged. Against this 'mainly Anglo-French group, we have another group of capitalists, an even more rapacious, even more predatory one, a group who came to the capitalist banqueting table when all the seats were occupied' and demanded a new division of the colonies and the world market.[6] On the basis of the innovations introduced in capitalism ('state-controlled capitalist production, combining the colossal power of capitalism with the colossal power of the state into a single mechanism'), Germany claimed its share of the colonial spoils.

Two power groups also face each other today, but with very different characteristics. The main contention of the Great War, the global South, has now become an economic and political entity of its own that, after its revolutions, has accepted the rules and workings of capitalism, even if it has not fully conformed to the American model. Unlike a century ago, it is a force demanding its share of the capitalist banquet. The countries gathered in Samarkand in September 2022 embody this desire for 'a new redistribution of power' that the Americans cannot accept, and that Europeans delude themselves into thinking they can reject.

But there is, simultaneously, something deeper in this confrontation. China, India, and the countries of the South in general do not understand with what legitimacy the West pretends to continue to control and decide the fate of the world, as it has done for centuries. What is at stake are the fundamental Western *values* – once the Soviet Union was routed, the West thought it could export these, just as it exported goods to every corner of the planet – that are radically challenged. It is the West's supremacy that is no longer accepted as a natural fact.

To think that the origin of the current war is the Russian invasion is ridiculously naïve on the part of the defenders of democracy and enemies of the (strictly Russian) oligarchy. It is, rather, as Lenin described the imperialism of his time: 'If they have clashed, it is because they could not help clashing . . . [They] were bound to clash, because a

---

6  Ibid.

redivision of this supremacy, from the point of view of capitalism, had become inevitable."[7]

## Attacker/attacked, or the categories of imperialist ideology

On approaching and evaluating the ongoing war, Lenin gives us valuable insights. Public opinion in the global North has been focused on the attacker/attacked dualism as a way to decide which side to take. Lenin considers these two concepts a distraction because they prevent us from asking the right questions.

> Forgetting the history of finance capital, the history of how this war had been brewing over the issue of redivision, they present the matter like this: two nations were living at peace, then one attacked the other, and the other fought back. All science, all banks are forgotten, and the peoples are told to take up arms, and so are the peasants, who know nothing about politics. All they have to do is to fight back! . . . The question of which of these two robbers was the first to draw the knife is of small account to us.[8]

Lenin proposes shifting the debate, focusing not on the contingent fact (*who attacked*, the incident that lit the fuse), but on the level of capitalism's global functioning: the world market and the financial control that organizes the capture of rent/profit, then as now.

> Who's to blame for banks being set up which handle hundreds of millions of rubles, for these banks casting their nets of plunder over the whole world, and for their being locked in mortal combat? Find the culprit if you can! The blame lies with half a century of capitalist development, and the only way out of this is by the overthrow of the rule of the capitalists . . . Such questions are not settled voluntarily in

---

7   Ibid.
8   Ibid.

this world of capitalists. This issue could only be settled by war. That is why it is absurd to blame one or another crowned brigand. They are all the same, these crowned brigands. That is why it is equally absurd to blame the capitalists of one or another country. All they are to blame for is for having introduced such a system.[9]

Lenin, unlike Western Marxists, also understood perfectly the evolution of the revolution, brought about by the entry of the oppressed peoples into the struggle, and this led him to reconfigure his strategy once he saw the failure of revolution in Europe. Lenin marks a fundamental shift, not only because war is integrated into and inseparable from capitalism, but especially because, for Marx, revolution would necessarily be European and would later spread around the world. Lenin, on the other hand, described being 'on the eve of a world revolution' that had its vanguards outside Europe, in the global South. What was more difficult for him to grasp was that the twentieth-century world revolution would usher in the political decline of the West.

## The new political phase

To try to define our current political conjuncture, one that we will likely be in for quite some time, can we take the current war as a confirmation of Arrighi's prediction in *Adam Smith in Beijing*?[10] Are we in fact witnessing a substitution of imperialist hegemony? Is China replacing the US at the head of the world market? Are we heading towards a Chinese century after suffering an American one?

One can doubt it. The reasons that make Arrighi's prediction unlikely, at least in the short to medium term, are numerous, and they conjure up a much less linear, much more problematic situation.

---

9 Ibid.
10 Giovanni Arrighi, *Adam Smith in Beijing: Lineages of the Twenty-First Century*, London: Verso, 2009.

The current war does not resemble a new version of Thucydides's Trap, in which an emerging power attempts to oust the hegemonic power and the confrontation results in military conflict. The Harvard International Relations researchers who coined the term found that, throughout history, in the sixteen such cases analysed, as many as twelve resulted in a military confrontation between the hegemonic and the emerging power.

China does not have this strength, because it does not have the economic, technological, and military power to replace the US. The Chinese Communist Party seems to be fully aware of this.

US imperialism has made the dollar the world economy's nexus, the point at which the world circuit of capital opens and closes, begins and ends. US currency was the engine of globalization because it ensured investment and the liquidity needed for production and trade. The budget deficit dictated the dollarization of the world, and Wall Street guaranteed the capital outflows and inflows that fostered either economic development across the globe, or recession. China is still a long way from being able to play the role of big debtor in the world market, capable of flooding the world with renminbi with its structural debt (on the contrary, it has a large trade surplus); it does not yet have the ability to have a simultaneously domestic and international currency.

This is not to say that, once the war in Ukraine is over, we can return to the state of globalization that existed prior to the confrontation. On the contrary, the war has accentuated the divisions that already fractured the world market. Globalization is even more balkanized than before. The Germany-Russia-China axis has perhaps been permanently broken by the American military initiative. Europe is in a position to see its economy further weakened, its trade with the East increasingly difficult. The West is trying hard to isolate Russia, which is successfully recycling its trade with non-Western countries. China, the main target of the war, is the object of decoupling, disengaging the North and the rest of the world from trade with the emerging power and preventing it from acquiring indispensable new technologies. The US is always grappling with the civil war while funding the America First initiative to the tune of billion-dollar subsidies – yet another deadly blow brought against the so-called free market.

Latin America's desire to have a currency that breaks its dependence on the dollar supports Chinese and Russian plans that move in the same direction (de-dollarization). Several southern countries are beginning to trade using their own currencies, disengaging from the dollar. The monetary/financial system risks shattering into regionalization and multilaterality, each corresponding to political projects for autonomy from US currency. One economist predicts a future currency war that has actually been going on since 2008, and is hidden (for those who prefer not to see) at heart of the current clash between imperialisms.

We have never emerged from the 2008 crisis: the monetary policies of the central banks – quantitive easing – have, yes, flooded the economy with money, but without succeeding in making it trickle from the financial sphere to the real economy, demonstrating that the economic model of the last fifty years is at a dead end.

This enormous availability of liquidity has accentuated the predatory character of contemporary capitalism, combined with the inability to restart production, a tendency (more rent and less production) that was already at the heart of the subprime crisis and has been exacerbated by the central banks' attempts to rescue financial capital. Money has functioned as a mechanism of capture, of expropriation of wages and incomes that were already under heavy downward pressure.

The asymmetry that characterized dollar imperialism has become even more pronounced, and the countries that have suffered most from financial bloodletting (the global South) and the cost of globalization are no longer willing to bear this de facto taxation that feeds the investments necessary for their exploitation and subordination.

Great unknowns are thus looming: not only because we are not witnessing a classic substitution of one hegemony for another, as was the case with the dollar and sterling, but also because the ecological crisis and the political-economic strength of the global South pose problems for which capitalist logic has no solution.

The virtuous circuit of the dollar has reversed into a vicious cycle, and the phase that the war has now opened up does not seem to be leading to a classic restructuring of the mode of production on a global scale. Rather, what has begun is a process of *chaotic destruction* that has little to do with Joseph Schumpeter's creative destruction. The classical replacement of one mode of production with another that is more productive, higher performing, and more profitable for capital collides with two realities. On the international chessboard, there are not only political economic powers fighting each other (none of which holds the keys to a new development of the world market), but also something unprecedented. The possibility that planet Earth will become inhabitable for the human species is now a tangible and measurable reality. The war in Ukraine was immediately associated with an energy crisis that shot profits through the roof – $185 billion, an all-time record – for the five largest oil monopolies (Total, ExxonMobil, Chevron, Shell, and BP). While nothing was being done before to solve the problem of fossil fuels, the engine of production, today this same energy has not only become irreplaceable but is prohibitively priced for the losers of the war (Europe is being forced to bear the energy costs of both individuals and businesses, which hinders its competitiveness). Inside the war is another war of fossil-energy hoarding, and the ecological transition (if it was ever on any state agenda) is now postponed to an unlikely aftermath of the war. The world economy has never been more dependent on fossil fuels than it is today. The ecological question must be placed within the framework of war and civil war, otherwise it risks being pure ideological posturing.

The other major obstacle to thinking about a new form of accumulation is the political economic strength of the global South. Since 1492, in order to produce profits, at whatever stage of technological development, capital has had the South to exploit. Technological and organizational innovations are not enough to revive profits: the exploitation of unpaid or poorly paid, servile, and slave labour is absolutely necessary to slow the fall of the rate of profit. Today, the South will no longer provide cheap or unpaid labour and free raw materials.

Capitalism cannot stand on its own (production, science, technique), as Luxemburg well knew, and not only is there no other planet to plunder, but there is also no other South to exploit.

From what we have described, *a medium- and long-term scenario emerges that will make the medium and long term disappear*: the historical continuum will be broken by wars, not only for the partitioning of the world market, but also climate wars, migratory wars, civil wars, revolts, and insurrections.

More generally, we can say that we are not in a crisis, but in a catastrophe, in the scientific sense of a state mutation. There is nothing but destruction on the horizon, and life as a whole is now in jeopardy. The situation seems to foreshadow the exhaustion of capitalism, but we should be under no illusions. Capitalism will not die its own death, but only a death inflicted by a class enemy that subjectively desires and organizes this end, because capital will put up fierce resistance to any will to scuttle it.

## Emancipation and revolution

Social movements, rather than noticing the discontinuity of the new political phase, of the new nature of conflict, seem to have fallen into it. In general, they reproduce the politics of the previous phase, while political spaces close, governmentality is replaced by policies of new fascisms, by police and judicial actions that further political, economic, and military centralizations in anticipation of a coming civil war.

Civil war still remains more or less underground because there is no opposition, no political process that even remotely resembles the communist movements of the early twentieth century or that has their organization and strength. If something like that had been produced, the civil war would have long ago become open warfare.

This situation demands that social movements practise radical ruptures: real uprisings within which they are forced to question what to do with established power. Necessity pushes them inside power dualisms in which multiplicity is confronted with the radicality of the poles.

The political and temporal breaches opened by the regime of war in the command-and-control devices of imperialism were opportunities that revolutionary moments made sure to exploit: historically, they opened up the time of revolution. But, for revolutionaries, catastrophe (change in the global order) was never the result of determinism, but emerged rather from Kairos, the rupture in history. The final stage of capital cannot be reached in reality because it is not only an economic process, but also a political one – and only another political process can decree capital's final stage.

A twentieth-century revolutionary would see in contemporary events a predictable consequence of capital's development. They would see its indispensable asymmetries, its necessary imbalances, its insatiable thirst for profit and power, but also the emergence of new possibilities – as Mao said: 'Great is the confusion under the sky, the situation is excellent.' The progress of the negative now manifests itself not only as the exploitation, domination, and destruction of the planet, but also as the outbreak of war between imperialisms. This stage usually marks a point of no return for the capitalist order, and thus could also manifest itself as revolution (or, more likely, as global civil war). At least this has been the traditional belief among revolutionaries – but not all of them. Luxemburg criticized the link between war and revolution that Lenin had established, refusing to see war as anything other than a terrible disaster. Alain Badiou identifies all the limits of the proletarian revolutions of the nineteenth and twentieth centuries in the fact that they were born in and developed with war. Have we ever seen or will we ever see a revolution that does not arise in this way? Can revolution be peaceful?

Either way, the revolutionary tradition grasped a series of continuities/discontinuities in the functioning of power and conflict that today's political movements and critical thought seem to have abandoned.

The first continuity concerned the different forms in which power is exercised: wars of subjugation, exploitation, sexual and racial domination, civil wars, and wars between states were animated by the same logic of power exercised by different means, depending on the situation. Power shifted from the world market to the local, from the micro to the macro.

The second continuity referred back to the conflict that retraced the continuum of power in the negative and interrupted it: there was to be no break between local struggles (against exploitation and domination) and global struggles (civil wars and wars between states). Revolutionaries had to act within this continuum because the strategic clash between economic-political powers, the contradictions that find no solution other than recourse to the judgement of arms, also constituted the opportunity for a possible overcoming of capitalism. Now, social struggles need to catch up to the *radicality* and *globality* of the current conflict through political-organizational activity that transcends their specificity and particularity.

The third continuity was about forms of organization: there could be no separation between the organization fighting on the local level and the one facing global issues.

These continuities were characterized by leaps, ruptures, and accelerations that, paradoxically, gave rise to discontinuities. War for Clausewitz is the continuation of politics, but evidently it is also a major discontinuity introduced by the non-peaceful means necessary for its existence.

While the exercise of power has always organized and does not cease to organize this continuity/discontinuity, the praxis and thought of the post-'68 social movements have broken with this revolutionary tradition.

Among the glories of critical thought, we can count that of revealing power, resistance, and the force of creation and subversion, where political philosophy and Marxism still saw the pre-political. Its faults include: separating the local from the global; splitting the transformation of the self, the care of the self, and of others; and the production of a new subjectivity – *which I call emancipation* – from the radical transformation of the economic and political order – *which I call revolution*. Once again, it is our poor Foucault who took it upon himself to demonstrate this misunderstanding: just as he had separated diffuse and local governmentality from the centralizations of imperialism, giving us a soft concept of contemporary power, so too did he break down the relationship between struggles 'that concern our ways of being and thinking, relations to authority, relations between the sexes, the way in which we perceive insanity or illness' and 'all projects that claim to be global or radical'.[11]

Separation implies a change in praxis and strategy: engaging in 'transformations, even partial ones' and 'thus . . . work carried out by ourselves upon ourselves as free beings', rather than fighting for the transformation of 'political power' or the 'economic system'.[12]

The construction of forms of life and processes of subjective becoming (the aesthetics of making one's life a work of art) is opposed to the subversion of the political and economic order, which thus seem to proceed on two parallel tracks. Emancipation (practices of freedom) and revolution (practices of breaking the established order, *no longer just for freedom, but for liberation*) are understood as if one process could be accomplished without the other, as if there were no relationship between the two levels. Instead, the 'uncontrolled power' exercised 'over people's bodies, their health, and their life and death', which preoccupied Foucault, has a direct relationship to imperialist centralization driven by capital, the state, and the monopoly of force.

Foucault, followed by many social movements, breaks up the historical continuity of emancipation and revolution, for good reason. Every time, revolution seems to betray emancipation, both in organization and goals. The '68 movement, in Maurice Blanchot's interpretation, operated in the same way, thus functioning as a matrix for subsequent emancipation movements: it practised rupture without giving itself 'political means for the future, without institutional power'.[13] The separation of emancipation and revolution that could be interpreted as weakness was instead its strength. Blanchot concludes, opening up to all contemporary theories of destitution, that the movement did not fail but was 'sovereignly realized'; the revolution was 'behind us'. In his own way, Deleuze went in the same direction: if revolutions always end badly, 'revolutionary becoming' does

---

11  Michel Foucault, 'What Is Enlightenment?', in *The Foucault Reader*, ed. Paul Rabinow, New York: Pantheon Books, 1984.

12  Ibid.

13  Maurice Blanchot, *Political Writings, 1953–1993*, trans. Zakir Paul, New York: Fordham University Press, 2010.

not need the revolution because it never ends, it is in constant becoming (even during war and civil wars?).

A good portion of the movements that developed after '68 consciously or unconsciously assumed the separation of emancipation and revolution as a solution to the impasses and failures of world revolution. Certainly, a repeat of socialist revolutions was neither possible nor desirable, but a new revolution was necessary because what has not disappeared is the capitalist counterrevolution that has imposed order, restoration, new fascism, civil wars, and war. The only thing decisively dismissed was the strength and tradition of the revolutionary movement, while the social movements that have taken its place are unable to organize anything equally effective and radical. As a result, power relations between classes have regressed to the pre-Russian revolution era.

The 2008 crisis opened a new political phase. While the need for a new revolution might not have emerged in the era of the '68 social movements, today there seems to be no other way out. In the current political phase, where war (actually multiple wars) has become the central political axis, our 1968 legacy is still hampering the development of class struggle.

It seems, when analysing the political ruptures that have recently taken place (starting in 2011, first in North Africa, especially Egypt, and then continuing in Chile in 2019, and Iran, but also in Peru and Algeria, as meanwhile in the North, particularly France, civil war rears its head) that the relationship between revolution and emancipation is once again posed. What '68 failed to achieve – a new form of relationship between emancipation and revolution – has once again become necessary and relevant.

Redefining the concept of revolution largely exceeds my capacity. Regarding the uprisings, insurrections, revolts in the South, and mass struggles in the North, I can make only a few preliminary remarks, forwarding hypotheses about the emancipation/revolution relationship, because a full analysis would require collective work that, for the moment, is nowhere to be found.

### Emancipatory movements

From the point of view of the insurrectional or insurgent event, there has been nothing comparable to the revolutionary era. A mass uprising shakes up established power, intensifies and radicalizes confrontation, opens a new phase of the revolutionary process, and implants a solid but momentary counterpower. What drastically changes, however, is the political subject, and thus political organization. The two processes are one and the same problem, seen from two different angles: it is no longer the working class that is driving change, but a multiplicity of social movements, subjectivities, claims, and organizational forms that demand new modes of organization and revolutions.

With the decline of the labour movement, no perspective of any movement takes precedence over any another. Despite the impossibility of reproducing any hegemony over the proletariat, over the model of the working class, each social movement thinks about the world and its transformation only from its own point of view, each claiming some central importance.

Paul Guillibert and Frédéric Monferrand, two ecological-Marxist thinkers, move easily from the centrality of the class struggle to another, making Bruno Latour's position their own: 'Ecology constitutes henceforth the main political question, on which "the meaning of history" depends, and it is from this position that socio-political antagonisms, actors and their stakes will be redefined.'[14]

Their Marxism naturally leads them to let ecology play the role that the capital/labour struggle had.

We can find similar evaluations among the multiplicity of feminist positions in Lea Melandri's viewpoint: 'Sexism is the founding act of politics and all other forms of violence, exploitation, and injustice: classism, racism, nationalism, colonialism, homolesbotransphobia, speciesism, and environmental devastation.'[15]

---

14 Paul Guillibert and Frédéric Monferrand, 'Ecology/Ontology: A Contribution to Historical Naturalism', *Dialogue and Universalism* 28, no. 3 (2018), pp. 245–51.

15 Lea Melandri, *Love and Violence: The Vexatious Factors of Civilization*, SUNY Press, 2018.

Instead, the initiator of decolonial theory puts race relations at the centre of the problem: 'The idea of "race" is surely the most effective instrument of social domination invented in the last 500 years. Dating from the very beginning of the formation of America and capitalism (at the turn of the 16th century), in the ensuing centuries it was imposed on the population of the whole planet as an aspect of European colonial domination ... Coloniality thus became the cornerstone of a Eurocentered world.'[16]

Perhaps everyone is right about the origin of domination, but what is certain, without going into the merits of the various arguments, is that capitalism, since its inception, has been able to integrate and manage these different power relations by playing them off against each other in order to reproduce and intensify its control. Just a few examples can demonstrate this strategy. The division produced by *colonial rent* and the *racism* that legitimized it separated the proletariat of the North from that of the South for centuries. After decolonization, the division was reproduced, albeit in different ways, in Western countries. Two of the poorest and most exploited strata of the French proletariat have been in revolt – those living in the *banlieues* (the racialized population) and the *gilets jaunes* (or *petits blancs*) – but they do not communicate, do not converge, do not solidarize, even though the latter benefit less and less from the colonial rent and so far have not fallen into the trap of racism that the state set for them. They remain locked in their respective worlds as if it were not the same contempt and class violence that have been directed by the state and the economic-political elites against both groups. Within the racialized struggles as well as the *gilets jaunes*, the sexual division of labour and its social functions constitutes another source of proletarian separation, this time between men and women. The virile, macho attitude of both groups constitutes, in turn, a source of misunderstanding with feminist movements. The female proletariat also has its own divisions. In Latin America, home to the strongest and most innovative feminist movements, proletarian women, the militant political vanguard

---

16 Aníbal Quijano, *Cuestiones y horizontes: De la dependencia histórico-estructural a la colonialidad/descolonialidad del poder*, CLACSO, 2014.

of the popular economy, are largely against abortion, either because of institutional religion (whether Catholic or Evangelical) or because they follow indigenous traditions.[17] And so on . . . the list would be long.

Clearly, it is not a matter of judging these differences by any yardstick of progress or regression, but of starting, realistically, from the fact that the proletariat is a multiplicity, a stratification of subjectivities that do not all present themselves at any given moment.[18]

Each of these movements (feminist, anti-racist, trade union, ecologist) expresses a perspective of its own, but also a different point of view from all the others, risking either impotence and defeat or enclosure in one's own identity, from this dispersion and difference, when a clash with the enemy actually happens (as in Chile, Tunisia, and Egypt). Based on events since 2011, different and dispersed multiplicity fails to overthrow – and cannot even undermine – the power relations that counter-revolution has imposed. While each of these movements has its *main enemy*, power has but one enemy that it easily routs as soon as the level of confrontation rises, precisely because of the enemy's deep internal divisions. Totalization is the impossible goal of power, but it can still use

---

17  Personal communication by activists and researchers intervening in the popular economy.

18  The proletariat is not homogeneous (or idealized, as in the concept of multitude). The racialized, the *gilets jaunes*, the wage earners, and the precarious workers do not live in the same space-time, although they constitute, together, the labour-force that capitalism exploits. The same thing can be said about women. The difference is not only with the white bourgeoisie. Even within the proletariat, not all women live in the same time. Here, it would be useful to dust off Ernst Bloch's concept of non-contemporaneity: 'Not all people exist in the same Now. They do so only externally, by virtue of the fact that they may all be seen today. But that does not mean that they are living at the same time with others.' The generalization that denies the spatio-temporal differences, customs, and subjectivities of entire social strata was, according to Bloch, at the origin of Marxism's failure to understand and combat Nazism. This seems to be recurring today. Many of these contradictory *non-contemporaries* are recovered and managed by the new fascisms and are probably also one cause of the failure of the Chilean referendum in September 2022. The categories of *subjectively non-contemporaneous* and *objectively non-contemporaneous* should be applied not only to the impoverished middle classes in 'an age that no longer knows the middle position', but also and especially to the proletarian strata where racism and sexism are still salient features of subjectivity.

war, civil war, repression, coups d'état, and states of emergency to achieve a provisional but real *whole* that is otherwise unattainable.

These different political movements call their point of view *revolution* ('feminist revolution', 'decolonial revolution', 'ecological revolution'). The concept of revolution has historically been attached to radical changes in economic, political, and social systems. It usually refers to a more or less violent rupture of the system as a whole. Do the two concepts of emancipation and revolution express and define the same phenomenon? Let us continue to distinguish them at our peril, to see if we may find some clarity.

Feminist or decolonial revolution seems closer to the concept of emancipation from slavery, pursued, for example, by Africans turned into slaves in the two Americas. The end of slavery meant liberation from a relationship of domination, but without shifting the set of power devices on which that system rested. Slaves became free, but were still exploited, forced into the humblest jobs or into wage labour under social conditions that were often based on racial segregation. The abolition of slavery was compatible with the reproduction of the capitalist system.

Without being immediately reducible to the emancipation of slavery, the achievements of the feminist movement have similar traits: agency, subjectivity, and self-actualization were widely extended, though always within the limits of the capitalist system. The struggles and practices of the feminist movement has failed to eliminate all the power relations to which women are subjected. Despite the freedom they may have acquired in the labour market (and in every social sphere), they still hold positions that are generally subordinate to those of men in terms of employment quality, wages, and pensions, and it is always women who suffer most from cuts in welfare and diminishing social services. In society women are still the object of direct violence that reflects the pervasiveness of femicide, sexism, and male supremacy.

In order to escape this situation, it is the set of power relations that must be attacked and radically changed. Latin American feminism understands this quite well, and has proposed the feminist strike to combine emancipation with revolution, even launching a still-embryonic revolutionary process.

In her own way, bell hooks grasped the difference between emancipation and revolution:

> Often emphasis on identity and lifestyle is appealing because it creates a false sense that one is engaged in praxis. However, praxis within any political movement that aims to have a radical transformative impact on society cannot be solely focused on creating spaces wherein would-be radicals experience safety and support. Feminist movement to end sexist oppression actively engages participants in revolutionary struggle. Struggle is rarely safe or pleasurable.[19]

The difference between emancipation and revolution could still be understood as the difference between social revolution and political revolution raised by Marx in the quote at the beginning of this chapter. The two revolutions are not to be separated, as are movements that fail to recognize war and civil war as the continuation of politics or class struggles. Such movements think that sexist and racist power relations, or cognitive capitalism, or biocapitalism of social reproduction are one thing; war and civil war are another. By denying continuity, by separating social and micropolitical revolution from political revolution, the revolutionary processes contained in the former are quickly extinguished. This is what is happening in the US, where the achievements of the 1960s social revolution (abortion, affirmative action, welfare policies for women) are being systematically dismantled because there is no resistance capable of opposing this process.

The great achievements of the twentieth century were a result of the ability to organize and develop social revolution and political revolution together. The refusal to problematize political revolution – its organization, its strategy – condemns all social movements to impotence.

This difference between emancipation and revolution can be generalized (it could be interpreted as a different way to qualify the relationship

---

19  bell hooks, *Feminist Theory: From Margin to Center*, Cambridge, MA: South End Press, 1984.

between the economic and the political – between the trade union rep and the revolutionary that was so important in twentieth-century revolutions).

Precarious labour, but also wage labour, is in a similar situation. If we take the example of workers in the informal economy (precarious, poor, and indebted – in Latin America this is called the *popular economy*), we can observe the development of processes of struggle or political/productive organization that have given them a sort of freedom and dignity (wages and income), but within the control of big capital and finance.

Again, emancipation is two-faced, each side being true. One could say that the unemployed, the inactive, migrants, and women have invented their own work and their own economy, demonstrating a great capacity for initiative and organization, and, at the same time, one could also say that the poor help to reproduce the system, because they work, consume, and pay interest on their debts (from the capitalist point of view, what could be better?). Whether we look at the phenomenon from the first point of view or the second, it is always, in any case, a matter of *poor workers* within a hypercompetitive economy subordinated to capital and finance.

But we should neither encourage such workers to become self-employed entrepreneurs, whose invented jobs provide income but for which they sacrifice autonomy and freedom, nor, on the contrary, denounce their integration into the system, their plebeian consumerism that allows capital and finance to find new sources of profit and reproduction.

It is important, rather, to recognize the outline of the struggle: the power relations between capital and this new labour. *Power is not on either side of the relationship, but in the struggle, in the conflict between the two poles*. But the relationship remains, despite the breakdown of subjugation that these movements produce, that is still asymmetrical, still largely favourable to the state-capital machine. Again, changing the subordinate status of the popular economy in relation to the financial and monopolistic economy requires higher levels of struggle and organization.

Although it no longer holds the exclusive centrality it held in the class struggles of the nineteenth and twentieth centuries, the question of *labour* remains decisive in any revolution. Wages and income affect the entire class composition. Opposition between proletarians' lives and managerial profits crystallizes around money in an explosive cocktail. Unless conflict is thought through under the new conditions of class warfare, none of the revolutions claimed by contemporary social movements will see the light of day. Unless we find a political strategy against the differentiating massification of the valorization, against its fragmentation and individualization, and against impoverishment (wage labour, precarious work, poor and indebted labour, domestic labour, servile labour), we will continue to be under the thumb of the counterrevolution.

After all, what a revolution could look like (even starting from a feminist, ecologist, or decolonial concept) in the midst of a mighty capitalist counterrevolution is difficult to grasp. If it fails to oppose stagnant wages, the destruction of welfare and its reconfiguration in favour of corporations and the wealthy, the privatization of all social services, frightening increases in poverty, limitless extensions of the retirement age, the spread of new fascism, populism, the rising tide of sexism, racism, war and civil war, can it still be called a revolution?

## Identity of production and destruction

The difference between emancipation and revolution existed in the labour movement and nineteenth- and twentieth-century political, trade union, and mutualist organizations: *practices of freedom* and the production of subjectivity constituted central points of their actions. Although it was found within hierarchical structures, militancy guaranteed a break with subservience to production and wage labour, and with subjection to the state and governmentality. It freed the individual from subordination to the laws of economics and political power, radically altering their subjectivity. Paraphrasing Marx, it can be said that the worker and the proletarian emerged from union, political, and mutualist organizations completely different from how they had entered them. They acquired new knowledge, new relationships, integrated wider networks of socialization, developed a new conception of self and of the world.

Millions of people became *free spirits* (producing themselves through themselves) through militancy, but they never deluded themselves that this freedom could be pursued and cultivated without liberation from capitalism, without revolutionizing economic and political power. They did not separate their *practices of freedom* (which profoundly changed their subjectivity), from general processes of liberation, from revolution. The local, specific, partial struggle from which this changing subjectivity emerged could not be detached from the radical and global struggles in the world market.

It is true that the global nature of the struggle and its radical character (which could go as far as war) made centralization, totalization, and hierarchy weigh on the organizations, which often ended in stifling practices of freedom and homogenizing the production of subjectivity to the model of *worker* or *professional revolutionary*, reducing them to caricatures. The relationship that the revolutionary workers' movement continually developed between local and global, between the singularity of a struggle and the generality that imposed the conflict in the world market, not only produced the revolutions of the twentieth century, but also a rise in wages and incomes and an achievement of political and social rights for all peoples of the world, albeit differentially. The result was a general advance of the world proletariat that was first violently halted and then heavily rolled back, precisely because the revolution and the threat it represented disappeared. The relationship between new emancipations and new revolutions is something that needs to be reaffirmed, albeit under different conditions, *because emancipations are incapable not only of defeating but also of merely countering the counter-revolution of capital.*

Certainly, diverse subjects – women, the racialized, ecologists – have given new meaning to practices of freedom, have enriched the shift from subjugation to the production of a new subjectivity with new content. They have certainly paid greater attention to emancipation (the realization of which cannot be postponed until after the revolution), and have invented specific devices to make the production of freedom possible, but at the risk of disengaging themselves from general confrontation. They risk becoming American-style radical movements, and falling into identity politics.

The revolutionary subject and its new forms of organization and struggle are not the only things that have radically changed since the twentieth-century revolutions. Ever since the 1970s (not only since 24 February 2022), the capital-state machine has broken any kind of class compromise, which is why war is our destiny. But, even from the point of view of social movements, every kind of mediation is breaking down. The ecological question presents unprecedented considerations because its direction is not emancipatory, but radically tragic. This movement places the question of life or death (for all humanity) at the centre of politics. It unequivocally reveals the definition of neoliberal governmentality (*make live and let die*) as absolutely false. It is equally untrue to claim that the purpose of power is to enhance life; what its devices govern is the identity of production and destruction, ensuring that the deadly forces of the market, of production and consumption, can continue undisturbed. The identity of production and destruction radically challenges socialist confidence in productive forces (and in the contemporary category of the *common*) and their socialist revolutions.

Here, the infinite dialectic of productive forces/relations of production slams up against the wall of the end of the revolutionary function (if there ever was one) of capital. Under contemporary conditions, the making of man does not prolong the power of nature, but destroys it, as it destroys itself and the environment that allowed it to exist. This is another major break with socialist revolutions, because *productive forces* are also inevitably and at the same time *destructive forces*. The ecological crisis is the manifestation of this identity that the workers' and communist movement did not contemplate in such a radical way.

It is no longer just a matter of modifying, as Marx said, the productive forces and relations of production to make them more productive (new capitalism) or of radically changing them to make them more just and free (revolution), but of conceiving them in such a way that the *destruction inherent in development does not shift from being relative to becoming absolute*, as has been happening, in an accelerated manner, for more than a century.

The identity of production and destruction that has characterized capitalism since the First World War has been accelerated by the current war. The destruction of societies, economies and their productive forces, and ecological destruction are all accumulating in an unprecedented way. This jumble of destruction projects us into a highly dangerous situation of which we have never seen the like.

## The new subject and new knowledge

The urgency to establish, construct, and organize a new continuity between emancipation and revolution powerfully emerges when conflict becomes radicalized, when our contemporary framework is traced by war and civil war. At a certain point in the struggle between classes and/or in the development of emancipation struggles that, we repeat, can initiate revolutionary processes, one is confronted with a power that is no longer just patriarchal or heterosexual power, it is no longer just racist power, it is no longer just managerial power: it is the general power of the state-capital machine that encompasses them, reorganizes them, and amplifies them. Our struggle is with the strategy of profit, power, and their destructive forces. The enemy is not mere national power, the sovereignty of any particular state. In these situations, we directly confront imperialist policies because any political ruptures – as we have seen in Egypt or Chile or Iran – risk questioning the power relations of the world market, the global organization of production and power. Both the Chilean and Egyptian uprisings were followed closely by the United States, which did not hesitate in its strategic interference.

Inside the radicalization of this battle, there comes a point of no return for both contenders, because stable forms of countervailing power, of liberated spaces or territories, cannot be consolidated except for short periods. The Zapatista solution is not generalizable and reproducible (as the Zapatistas themselves have always affirmed). At the same time, the seizure of power in two phases (first occupying the state, and then, from within it, organizing its transformation) has not been, since '68, a priority. What a puzzle!

Once this level of conflict is reached, we either advance or we retreat, win or lose – the revolutionary subject and its organization develop further, or they are blocked, regress, and fall apart! At least in the short to medium term, these are the alternatives. The Chilean insurrection, from this point of view, is exemplary: it opened up a new political phase, new power relations, and unprecedented possibilities that were quickly channelled into a constituent process. I am not in a position to judge this choice. But we can see that the decisions to be made within this level of confrontation are tragic, in the sense that they determine the situations for which we can win or lose; they define the conditions under which we can advance or must retreat.

The constituent process sparked by the Chilean uprising stirred up the participation of thousands of collectives, organizations, and individuals. The referendum's failure meant the return of the constituent process to the hands of a very few experts and the de facto closure of the process itself.[20] The next step in the Chilean class confrontation entrusted the drafting of a new constitution to the reactionary right wing, which would confirm the essentially fascist constitutional charter: the market economy.

In the global North, the French proletariat has developed an impressive sequence of struggles that highlight the conditions under which class warfare is expressed today. While the French struggles have transversal content and modes of action that objectively circulate between the *gilets jaunes*, the wage earners, the so-called barbarians of the *banlieues*,

---

20  The class enemy prepares for these moments; it is ready because it has the historical memory of class struggle, which social movements seem to lack. It knows how to act, what strategy to adopt. It seems to have read the texts of Luxemburg or Lenin: in a constituent phase, one must act quickly (wrote Luxemburg), because power shaken by insurrection does not think about the constitution of a new political regime, but only about restoring the power that the masses took away. Doing this needs time. They learned something too from Lenin: after the February Revolution, he said that the revolutionaries still had nothing in their hands – all military, economic, and political power was still in the hands of the enemy. In Chile, they used it (given enough time) to restore their order.

and the ecologists, there is a subjective gulf between these various class sections. The first processes of convergence could be seen in the battle against pension reforms and the *banlieues* revolt, but these were still very tentative. These social movements have different histories and traditions, and they live in heterogeneous times, but the new political phase and the new nature of conflict blurs into a dualism of power, regardless of the will of the opposing forces. Class composition is plural, social movements are multiple, but the forms of civil war that contemporary conflict assumes impose the obligatory passage to the two.

Ideally, the differences between various social movements should compose themselves in a *disjunctive synthesis* capable of producing harmony without erasing their differences, maintaining, on the contrary, the autonomy and independence of each component. But disjunctive synthesis is possible on one condition: there must be *at the same time* a deep enmity, a radical hostility towards the state-capital machine, otherwise one falls into a harmless and conciliatory philosophy of difference, of becoming. Without the imposition and construction of power relations in dualism, the counterrevolution will quickly organize itself (as in Chile), and, after repressing differences, will integrate a small minority and exploit the majority without any mediation, ever faithful to the will of the strategic programme of the state-capital machine and breaking the Keynesian compromise.

Multiplicity cannot prevent the confrontation of the duality, of which war and civil war are the most obvious signs of the nature of contemporary political conflict. Although class oppositions are heterogeneous, there always comes a turning point, a moment of crisis (in the medical sense of the term) in capitalism, which will decide a new distribution of power in the world market and among states – a new form of class struggle, and a different world. Those who cannot go through this dualism will inevitably be marginalized, politically dominated, and economically exploited.

Passing through the duality means building power relations and an organization that underpins and determines them. During the French strikes and struggles, the lack of organization in the use of force (force can use violence, but the two concepts do not necessarily coincide) gave police action a completely free range of the city squares. The problem of organization, and therefore subjectivity, is what has been most deeply lost from the revolutionary tradition. We think of the production of subjectivity as a problem closed in on itself, an ethical-aesthetic activity about lifestyle, or transgressive behaviour, disengaged from the problem of organization.

To cope with these levels of conflict, we need a new and specific *subject (and its organization)*, as well as *knowledge*. The subject must be capable of building organization. The subject does not pre-exist action; it is constructed within the process of conflict and as an effect of it, starting from social movements, from the multiplicity of subjectivities that compose it. Insurrections in the South, like class struggles in the North (as in France, or the US uprising after the assassination of George Floyd) are simultaneously a struggle against enemy power and a process of building a political subject. The stages of the revolutionary process are the stages of its constitution and the manifestation of its strength (or weakness).

Again, there is nothing new here. What is new is the excision of the revolutionary tradition. For example, after the rupture produced by the M15 movement in Spain in 2011, the opening of a phase of radicalization was bent to the categories of leftist populism (Podemos), which could only fail because it did not adopt and organize the independence and autonomy of class subjects from institutions, which are indispensable in constructing a revolutionary point of view. There is no political space to act within institutions, because their closure to a dialectical relationship with struggles and movements has been the central node of the strategy of counterrevolution since the 1970s. The same situation is reproduced throughout Latin America where, after electoral victories, experiments run out one after another because, as a Colombian government minister recalled, 'they won't let us govern'. Latin American governments would like to reactivate the dialectical conflict-institution relationship, but there is no political space to do so. Reformism was not the product of enlightened governments but was created by actual or threatened revolutions.

For now, we can only develop a generic argument on the relationship between different political ruptures and the process of forming a revolutionary subject. The construction of the subject is not a simple composition of heterogeneous elements, a chaining of differences (intersectionality or leftist populism). The revolutionary subject is forged on the edge of conflict; it is not directed only towards the composition of diversity (intersectionality), but also against the strategy of constituted power. It cannot exempt itself from negation, it must affirm its destructive *no* as its foundational act. It cannot avoid seeking to weaken, neutralize, and destroy enemy forces, otherwise it will emerge diminished, repressed, and undone (as has been happening regularly for the last fifty years of counterrevolution).

One of the most deleterious viewpoints introduced by critical thought (particularly political Spinozism) is the illusion of *an infinite power of being*, which would translate into an infinite praxis, or into struggles as infinity in action. The ongoing infinity of the insurrectional movement clashes with another ongoing infinity, with another infinite praxis: power and its devices of coercion. Between two powers that have an equal right to develop without limits, force decides.

Capitalism is not an infinite process of exploitation and flows that are continuously cycling and endlessly becoming, as Deleuze and Guattari seem to suggest. History is not infinitely open, as Foucault believes, implying that struggles need not be revolutionary because they impose a 'seemingly endless destabilization' of the mechanisms of power.

The same thing must be said of social movements and struggles: they do not produce endless resistance and refusal, and are not forever able to escape domination and exploitation by producing new lines of flight. To this endlessness of domination and its refusal, to the illusion of permanent destabilization, Walter Benjamin opposes singular ruptures of the historical continuum, undertaken by power and revolutionary praxis, which determine turning points, bifurcations, openings and closings of political sequences, and points of no return in power relations: 'History knows nothing of the bad infinity contained in the image of the two combatants locked in perpetual struggle. True politics is calculated in terms of events.'[21]

---

21 Walter Benjamin, *One-Way Street and Other Writings*, trans. Edmund Jephcott and Kingsley Shorter, London: Verso, 1979.

We must compare Benjamin's point of view to the naïve belief that the revolution has already happened, and that *being*, in and of itself, is revolutionary, and to the claim that there are (feminist, decolonial, ecological) revolutions going on now. What happened – and has been happening for the past fifty years – is counterrevolution: 'Even the dead will not be safe from the enemy if he wins. And this enemy has not ceased to be victorious.'[22] After '68, the enemy won again, and continues to do so. In order to avoid the trap of ontological victory (Hardt and Negri's *Multitude*) that might compensate us for political defeats, Benjamin teaches us to think not only in terms of the struggle between productive forces and relations of production, but also in terms of *winners* and *losers*.

Wars between imperialisms and the global civil war are events that *cut the infinite becoming of power relations, interrupt it, break it, and cause it to bifurcate, cause it to erupt into revolts, war, revolution or moments of conflict that reconfigure the relations of force, each time drawing a conjuncture that modifies the forces at play and their positions. Infinite becoming does not emerge from these conflicts: either a winner or a loser emerges.*

We do not manage the timing of this conflict at our pleasure; we cannot decide the time and moment of a struggle, insurrection, or revolt. They happen! And when they happen, or are produced, *one must make oneself ready, able to act within the absolute contingency of war and civil war*. Time becomes unhinged, so that conflict is subject to accelerations, to concentrations, to the emergence of possible revolutionaries in the now; it is subject to extraordinary intensities that determine sudden changes in framework – no longer the *future* of the socialist revolution, but the *present* of the making of the revolutionary subject, the present of the struggle that unfolds the negation, taking the leap from *emancipation* to *revolution*, which then becomes *revolutions. Revolution is not the purpose of an activity transferred into the future, but one that interrupts the time of domination and develops, here and now, its ends. It cannot be*

---

22 Walter Benjamin, 'On the Concept of History', trans. Dennis Redmond, 2005, available at marxists.org.

*achieved by separating ends and means, but develops from the conflict, from duality.*

When we enter the time of war and civil war, we step out of the ordinary political situation, and this is the reason why we need a knowledge of war and revolution; the knowledge of intersectionality (integrating class, race, and gender differences) is not sufficient, just as the knowledge of emancipation (producing new subjectivities, new behaviours) is insufficient. The art of revolution and a theory of revolution are necessary because the forces of revolt and the development of insurrection are blocked by a force that opposes them, that counters them, that wants to weaken them, and push them back from the positions they have conquered. The expansive dynamic of social movements is confronted with an obstacle that can divide it, divert it, but also annihilate it. The subject must be able to wield negation with the joy of affirmation, because power seeks to drive back these various social movements to their specificities, to their *identities* and *freedoms* that are compatible with the freedom of the market, consumption, and domination, neutralizing the unspeakable claim to attack the very set of devices that constitute it.

In these very moments of rupture, when time and power relations are in the balance, a new consciousness emerges. In the making of the struggle, in attacking the enemy, and in the simultaneous constitution of the subject and its organization, consciousness emerges not as awareness, an abstract understanding of power relations, but as the political necessity of working out a *tactic* and *strategy* to break the blockade of enemy forces, a way to remove the obstacle to the unfolding of the construction of the subject. The necessity of the *reflexive* moment (a different relation to the self than that of emancipation) emerges at this precise moment and its result is a double knowledge: a strategic knowledge both to beat the enemy, and for the construction of the subject that does not sacrifice emancipation to revolution. This is new, unpredictable, non-programmable knowledge that arises from conflict, in conflict.

## Many emancipations, one revolution?

I must insist on one thing: revolution is not just desirable or ethical, it is *necessary* in order to not plunge into civil war. I am not describing a wish, but what the real situation, the current conjuncture requires – what this political phase imposes on everyone. We *need* to struggle against sexism, racism, to strike or revolt, just as the Chilean, Egyptian, Iranian, and French insurgents did, or just as war needs capitalism: 'If they have clashed it is because they couldn't help clashing.'[23] Action can only take place within this framework, which has radically changed since so-called peace time. Within this necessity, a point of view or subjectivity, and a strategy appropriate to the situation emerges (or does not). For the moment, only states and imperialisms and insurgencies in the global South are responding to the requirements of the new crisis. Problems have changed from peace time as much for social movements as they have for the state-capital machinery.

Struggle in this new political phase implies a double rupture. The first concerns the rejection of subjection (the condition and status of worker, woman, or colonized). Starting from our acquired freedom (emancipation), the very dynamic of capitalism – its contradictions, its impasses – the second *obliges us* to question the system of power as a whole. Without this interrogation, the first process of rupture remains mutilated, unfinished, and constantly risks regression and reintegration, becoming either an internal difference in the development of capitalism or an impotent force.

In this chapter, we have often used and abused the word freedom. Now, the *freedom* of emancipation must become a struggle of *liberation*, in which choice, decision, and subjectification are not a matter of free will. Choice, decision, and subjectification are closely linked to the necessary temporalities of conflict – its accelerations, its intensities, and the forms of organization that these temporalities require.

Emancipation must take a qualitative leap, a break with its certainties and habits. Only under these conditions can one think of putting an end

---

23  Lenin, 'War and Revolution'.

to the coexistence of the two faces of emancipation: freedom and domination. Emancipation is not enough in itself! Emancipations involve conflict, but they are not incompatible with capitalism.

*There are many emancipations, but there will be only one revolution (from multiple to the two).* This seems to be the problem. In order to turn *emancipations* into just as many *revolutions*, it is necessary to go through *the* revolution. To create multiplicity, we must go through the dualism of power.

Can we get away with not pushing the relationship with the enemy and the conflict it implies to the limit? Without this revolution, the various emancipatory movements will not succeed in undermining the power of the counterrevolution, which will continue undaunted on its path of destruction, as the last fifty years have taught us. Failing to move in an autonomous and linear manner, from emancipation to revolution, these freedoms will always remain prisoners of the double face of emancipation.

In order to become revolutionary, we must face a series of puzzles and impossibilities: the impossibility of not going through the dualism of power and the impossibility of not overcoming it; the impossibility of totalizing and synthesizing struggles and emancipations and the impossibility of remaining in dispersion and *difference* alone; the impossibility of not revolting in defiance of power and the impossibility of merely taking it; the impossibility of organizing the transition from multiplicity to dualism and the impossibility of remaining in multiplicity alone; the impossibility of coordination and centralization and the impossibility of facing the enemy without such tools. The condition for creating the *possible* of revolution is meeting the challenge of these impossibilities. The revolution is the impossible becoming possible. Choices and decisions emerge as subjectivities, as *strategic necessities* when confronted with these impossibilities.

But the state-capital machine is also confronted with its own impossibilities: the impossibility to realize globalization and the impossibility to remain within the boundaries of the nation-state; the impossibility of becoming cosmopolitan and the impossibility of assuming a national identity. The revolutionary battle is the space-time in which these impossibilities and puzzles seek a solution.

In conditions of war or revolutionary ruptures, struggles no longer place themselves within the limits of capitalism, but objectively push beyond, whatever the insurgents may think. In any case, that is how the men of power interpret them, and they act accordingly (see the counter-revolutions in Egypt, Chile, and Iran).

Revolution is still the main question. Yet the waning of the revolutionary tradition has led to a nefarious obstacle: revolt and revolution no longer constitute two phases within the *revolutionary process*, but have become two separate realities in their own right.

In the tradition of the revolutionary movement, revolts, insurrections, and uprisings were never considered an end in themselves, as we tend think of them today. An aestheticization of revolt and a romantic exaltation of insurgency has created a separation between the subjectivity of revolt (an expression of an unusual, uncommon time, as during the carnivalesque overturning of hierarchies) and that of revolution (the expression of a conscious rationality, of a project obliged to evaluate opportunities and strategies in order to seize the propitious time – Kairos). Flashes of insurrection mark time that has come off its hinges, while revolution wisely remains within historical time. Revolt and insurrection were traditionally understood, instead, as the opening of a new phase of revolution.

The separation of emancipation and revolution also implies a break between the knowledge of the former and that of the latter. The theoretical development that accompanied the flourishing of the new movements had a richness comparable to the emergence of research and analysis about the working class in the late nineteenth and early twentieth centuries. But while revolutionaries focused almost obsessively on comprehensively understanding the workings of the capitalist system in order to combat it, these theories took no interest in the cycle of capital, the constitution of the state-capital machine, or the evolution of power relations in the world market. No theory of crisis was developed; no conception of the function of war in the development and restructuring of capital and the state was structured.

Social movements have become accustomed to conflict without revolution, manifesting the title of a book from the 1960s, *Proletari senza rivoluzione* (Proletarians without revolution), as if by fate.[24] The time of politics seems to be experienced as infinite and linear, where it is actually discontinuous, and repeatedly broken up by crises that have turned into world wars, as many as four times in the course of a single century (1914–2022). In these four watershed moments, power relations changed radically; political subjects died and others were born. One must be prepared at such moments because it is not only the collapse of capital that is at stake (and occurs with impressive regularity) but also humanity's chances for survival on this planet.

Foucault claims that the relation to self is the main form of opposition to power: there is therefore no longer any need for a theory of capital and the state, or revolution, or war – knowledge on the subjectivity, caring, and the relation to self would be sufficient.

Instead, these changes in accumulation, classes, and states matter because they reconfigure the entire situation, widening or narrowing the political space of emancipations and processes of subjectification. The First World War profoundly changed contemporary capitalism (imperialism), but also revolution. Marx still believed that revolution would start in Europe and that the danger of its repression would come from the world market. He had a point, because the French Revolution of 1848 was suppressed by the colonial army stationed in Algeria; the Spanish Civil War was also won by the colonial Spanish army stationed in Morocco and commanded by Franco. But since Lenin's time, we have seen a reversal of the situation. Revolutions have broken out on the fringes of capitalism and throughout the global South, while counterrevolutions have come from Europe. The twentieth century was the century of world revolution. The Bolsheviks were the first to understand: oppressed peoples enter the struggle and play the main role within it.

From the 1960s onward, revolution changed again, the modes of rupture and political subjects changed and definitively ended the centrality of the working class in the revolutionary process and asserted a new

---

24  Renzo Del Carria, *Proletari senza rivoluzione. Storia delle classi subalterne italiane dal 1860 al 1950*, Milan: Oriente, 1966.

multiplicity. Only fifty years after the Soviet rupture, the conditions for revolution have changed again, but cannot seem to find the subjective forces capable of realizing it. The counterrevolution that has been raging since the 1970s seems to have interrupted the continuity of the revolution that, ever since the French Revolution, had known no rest. Is this the end of the era of revolutions?

Let us refer again to Foucault, whom we will use, for the last time, as a symptom of the difficulties critical thought has had when confronted with the contemporary conjuncture of war.

The same contradictory and ambiguous attitude that Foucault had with respect to war can also be found in his relationship with revolution. Here again, we are dealing with views that are very common in critical thought: revolution, like war, is part of the past. If Foucault ended up looking to the Iranian revolution for an alternative model, not only to the revolutionary tradition, but also to European politics, he did not always think that way.

'If politics has existed since the nineteenth century, it's because there was revolution. The current one is not a variant or a sector of that one. It's politics that always situates itself in relation to revolution.'[25] This statement undermined the continuity that should have been affirmed. It would have been useful, on the contrary, to understand that both imperialism and the ancillary techniques of governmentality always relate to the revolution they defeated in the 1970s and whose return they always fear.

Instead, we can fully agree with the continuation of the text: 'The return of revolution – that is surely our problem.'[26] The return of politics can only manifest itself with the return of revolution.

Without revolution there is no politics – there is administration, there is governance (of imperialism), there is capitalism, there is war and civil war. Our problem: to regain politics, we must reinvent revolution, otherwise capitalism and its governance will inexorably evolve, as it is currently

---

25 Michel Foucault, *Foucault Live (Interviews, 1966–84)*, trans. John Johnston, ed. Sylvère Lotringer, Los Angeles: Semiotext(e) Foreign Agents Series, 1989.
26 Ibid.

doing, into new forms of fascism, war and civil war, from which, without revolution, we will still emerge defeated. Desertion and exodus, invoked from the beginning of the counterrevolution, have never actually happened.

# Index

*A Thousand Plateaus* (Deleuze and
    Guattari) 139
absolute distinct totalization 156
absolute monarchy 59
accelerationism 8
accumulation
    catastrophe point 166
    changes in 199
    by dispossession 161
    drivers of 75
    financial 142, 146
    in globalization 4
    Luxemburg's critique of 42–3
    Marx's analysis of 42–3
    primitive 100, 101, 160–1
    pursuit of 4
    through expropriation 160–1
    upward cycle, 1980s and 1990s
        97
    and waste 70
actors 5
administration 200
advertising 77
Agamben, Giorgio 102, 158–9
Algerian war 86
Alliez, Eric 80
American revolution 99
Amin, Samir 3, 37, 67–8, 160–2

anthropological change 110
*Anti-Oedipus* (Deleuze and Guattari)
    139
appropriation, wars of 154
Arab Spring 84, 179, 182
Arendt, Hannah 101
Argentina 26, 27, 86, 95, 112–14
armament oligarchy 8
arms production 7, 8
Aron, Raymond 3
Arrighi, Giovanni 6, 171–2
attacker/attacked dualism 170–1
austerity 2, 20, 79
authoritarianism 47
autonomous movement of value 134

Badiou, Alain 176
banking monopolies 57–8
Baudrillard, Jean 75, 78
Becker, Gary 23, 109n6, 114–15
being
    infinite power of 193
    revolutionary, 194
Benjamin, Walter 110, 193–4
Berlin Wall, fall of 102
Biden, Joe 6–7n1, 8n2, 36, 84
biopolitics 50, 54, 102, 103, 115, 126,
    159

# 204　Index

*The Birth of Biopolitics* (Foucault)　55, 121, 123–5, 156
Blanchot, Maurice　178
Bloch, Ernst　182n18
Bolshevism　61
Bolsonaro, Jair　90
Brancaccio, Emiliano　71
Brazil　115
Bremer, Paul　116–17
Bretton Woods negotiations　17
Brexit　32
Brown, Wendy　53
budget, balanced　107
Bukharin, Nikolai　40
Bush, George W.　26

Cacciari, Massimo　39
capital　3
　ascendant phase　52
　conceptualization　148
　contradictory double dynamic　44
　cycle of　26, 147–8
　dependence on the state　143–4
　fetishism of　135
　fictitious　69–70, 135, 137
　final stage of　40–1
　financial　40, 63, 143
　globalization and　143
　hegemony　89
　as immanent power　39, 42, 46
　industrial　145–7
　interest-producing　137
　investment flows　144–7
　and labour　1–2
　liberalization of　30
　liquidity　44
　and power　149
　pursuit of accumulation　4
　real　135
　relationship of the state to　38–41, 42–5
　as social relation　138–9
　sovereignty　72
　and state, the　147–8
　and the state political system　3–4
　tendency to financialize itself　14
　tendency to universalize itself　142
　transcendent power　39–40
　and war　96–8, 170–1
　*See also* finance capital

*Capital* (Marx)　3, 56–8, 109n6, 133–9, 161
capitalism
　acceleration of forces　8
　advent of　78
　boundless force of　64
　characteristics of new　63–5
　and civil war　101–2
　collapse of　9
　comparison with neoliberalism　49–54, 54–6
　and competition　55–6
　competitive　100–1
　and conflict　1–3, 152
　destruction phase　164
　end of　11–12
　exhaustion of　175
　Foucault's conception of　50–4
　hierarchy　5
　identity of production and destruction　188–9
　imperialism as modern form of　41
　imperialism as permanent phase of　158–62
　imperialist　3
　liberalization of　27–8
　limitation of　8–9
　monopoly　101
　national　46
　and nationalism　45–7
　neoliberal conception of　108
　and neoliberalism　5
　new contradictions　43
　not an infinite process　193
　partial views of　14
　political　147
　power relations　149
　predatory character of　173
　as production for production　51
　as production for rent　51
　proletarian separation　181–3
　subjugation of forces　149
　unbalancing force of　54
　war as regime of truth　2–3
　wills to power　150–1
capital-labour compromise, breakdown of　1–2
capital-labour struggle　23
capital/state cycle　116–17

# Index

Central Banks 140–1
central banks, accumulating dollars as reserve currency 19
centralization 56, 66, 72, 76, 149, 155, 156, 187, 197
  acceleration of 90
  China 71
  economic 56–8, 64–5, 94, 115
  executive power 86, 159
  military 60–1, 63
  neoliberalism and 70–2
  political 59–60, 63, 80, 84, 94, 115
  processes 56–8, 64
  second wave 67–70
  sovereign 160
  triple 56–8
  and war 72–4
centre–periphery polarization 161–2
chaotic destruction 174
Chile 88, 95, 98–103
Chilean uprising 84, 189, 190, 196
China 4, 169
  centralization 71
  Cultural Revolution 2, 99
  decoupling 172
  de-dollarization 30
  imperialism 43–4
  military spheres 25
  relationship with America 36–8
  rise of 6, 8n2, 31, 34, 171–3
  stakes 165
  trade surpluses 29
  US imports 28–9
  US Treasury bond investments 29–30
Chinese Communist Party 30, 172
Chinese Communist Party Congress, 2022 36
Chinese Revolution 99, 162
CIA 30, 95
circulating credit 24
civil society 78
civil war 1, 3, 6, 9, 10, 81, 95, 97, 148, 196
  American 119
  approach to 83–9
  and capitalism 101–2
  class 98
  constituent power 98–103
  contingency of 194
  Foucault's analysis 100

  government of 87
  on immigrants 88–9
  political force of 161–2
  praxis of 157
  and production 99–100
  return to the fore 163–4
  revolutionary 98–103
  rise to the forefront 94
  time of 195
  underground 175
  world 101–3
class civil war 98
class composition 191
class compromise 188
class conflict 1
class differences 88
class divisions 153–4
class formation 147
class polarizations, radicalization of 23
class relations 15, 124
class struggle 4, 39n21, 43, 52, 83, 84, 93–4, 123, 126–7, 134, 138, 186, 189, 190n20
class war 97, 113–14
Clausewitz, Carl von 4, 13, 165
Clinton, Bill 17
Cold War 3, 101
collective imperialism 37
colonial dispossession 41
colonial empires 142
colonial rent 181
coloniality 181
colonization 3, 7–8, 20, 21, 64
commodities, appearance of 111
commodity circulation 77
commodity democracy 80
commodity fetishism 134
communication patterns 38
*Communist Manifesto* (Marx) 46, 155
community 111
competition 5, 43, 55–6, 56–7, 58, 62, 65, 71
  double standard 105–6
  eliminating 74
  free and undistorted 107
  hierarchy 105–6
  and monopoly 65–7, 72, 106
competitive capitalism 100–1
competitive economy 66–7
compromise, no margin for 2

conflict
 and capitalism 1-3
 depoliticization 88-9
 dialectics of 2
 radicalized 84
 *See also* war
Congressional Research Service 30
consciousness, emergence of new 195
conscription 61
constituent power, civil war 98-103
consumer credit 24
consumer debt 69
consumer democracy 80
consumer standards 38
consumerism 185
consumption 22, 69, 70, 75, 76-9, 81-3, 110-12
continuities/discontinuities 176-7
corporate paradigm 69
corruption 115
cosmopolitanism 45
counterrevolution 2, 9, 179, 194, 200
1970s 67-70, 120-1
COVID-19 crisis 72, 102
creative destruction 174
credit 24, 57-8, 71, 110, 112
credit money 130
creditor countries 19-20
creditor's credit 24
crisis, Marx and 15
critical theory 120
critical thinking 10-11, 14, 50, 63, 177-8
Cuban Revolution 99
cultural imperialism 38
currency war 173
cyclical theory 118-20

Dardot, Pierre 15, 53, 125
death, giving of 95
debt 24, 26, 69, 75, 77, 79, 95, 185
 dispossession through 32-3
 and human capital 109-10
 neutrality 122
 and power 130
 role of public 136
 and war 130
debt reduction 20
decolonial revolution 183
decolonial thought 149, 150

decolonization 181
de-dollarization 30, 35, 173
deep war 80-1
Del Carria, Renzo 197-8
Deleuze, Gilles 3, 8, 39, 68, 100, 121, 139-41, 158-60, 161, 178-9, 193
 and power 149, 149-50, 150, 152, 153, 154, 155, 155-6, 157-8
Delphy, Christine 150
democracy 1, 7
 chimera of 88
 commodity 80
 consumer 80
 evolution of 74-83
 export of 116-17
 institutional 80, 88
 social 75, 79-80
Denmark 88-9
depoliticization 79
derivatives market 71
destruction 11
 and production 188-9
Di Cesare, Donatella 11
difference 197
differentiation 82-3
dignity 185
disjunctive synthesis 191
dispossession 41, 161
dollar, the
 accumulation as reserve currency 19
 appreciation 27
 convertibility into gold 17-18
 cycle of 173-4
 exports 26
 hegemony 33-4, 38, 95, 168, 172
 history of 130, 137
 ignoring 53
 inconvertibility 17-18, 95, 129, 136
 strength 34
dollar dependence, reducing 30, 35, 173
dollar imperialism 3, 14, 47, 51, 124, 135-6
 and 2008 financial crisis 9
 as analysis of power 148-58
 asymmetry 173
 birth of 12
 and classical imperialism 21-4
 creation and destruction of money 141
 and Europe 33
 export of political forms 75

# Index

financial capture 25–9
global vision 168
hegemony 41
history of 137
interest rates 141
internal civil war 34
legal system 106
main feature of 17
mechanisms 18–21, 53
need to destroy 49
and neoliberalism 97–8, 123
opposition 146
pillage 21
political regime 8
principles and rules of 5
relationship to war 24–31
state-capital sovereignty 104
strategic weapon of 23–4
structural function of force 58
and theory of money 129–39
transition to 15–21
and war 126, 165
dollarization 18, 119, 148
domination 150, 152–3, 176, 181, 197
dominator–dominated relationship 154–5
double regime, the 121–2
double rupture 196
dualisms, political significance of 153–4
Duménil, Gérard 21–2

ecological crisis 174, 188
ecological war 2
ecology movement 180
economic centralization 5, 56–8, 64–5, 94, 115
economic development 20
economic power 14, 55, 64, 66–7
economic science 130, 132, 137
economic theology 39n21
economic totalization 73–4
economic-military confrontation 20
economic-political powers 5
economics
  truth in 123
  and war 4
economies, heterogeneity of 138
economists, war and 24–5
Egypt 88, 189, 196

*The Eighteenth Brumaire of Louis Bonaparte* (Marx) 59–61
emancipation/revolution relationship 177–9, 183–6, 186–8, 189, 194–5, 196–201
emancipatory movements 180–6, 197
empire 158–9n22
energy crisis 8, 174
energy prices 31
Engels, F. 58, 155
enterprise society 23
entrepreneurs and entrepreneurship 23, 115, 185
equality 76
Esposito, Roberto 89, 102
euro, the 29, 31–2
Eurocentrism 101, 160
Europe 2, 3, 21, 29, 36, 37, 70, 75, 79, 96, 104, 172, 174, 199
  America's undeclared war with 31–4
  dispossession through debt 32–3
  energy prices 31
  failure of revolution in 171
  Franco-German axis 32
  Greek debt crisis 32–3
  interest rates 31
  liberalization of capital 27
  suicide 31–2
  trade outlets 32
  as US colony 7–8, 18
  war in 167–8
executive power 75, 81, 84, 86, 159
exploitation 150
expropriation 57, 117, 160–1
external markets 22
extractive oligarchy 8
extractivism 131

false consciousness 121
false/true concepts 121–3
families, indebtedness 22
Fanon, Frantz 102
fascism 1, 14, 47, 54, 81, 90, 91, 99, 114, 148, 156
Federal Reserve 26, 27, 107, 133
feminism 149, 150, 152, 180, 181–2, 183–4
Ferrari Bravo, Luciano 68
feudal society 51

feudal vocabulary, use of 33
fictitious capital 69–70, 135, 137
finance, hegemony of 64
finance capital 62, 63, 108, 137–8
  hegemony 121, 141–2
  investment flows 145–7
financial accumulation 142, 146
financial capital 40, 63, 143
financial capture 25–9
financial crises 26
  South-East Asia, 1987 27–8
financial exploitation 26, 109
financial oligarchy 8
financial system, collapse of 84
financial value, automatism of 136
financialization 3, 5, 8, 20, 44, 64, 75, 121
First World War 2–3, 11, 14, 16–17, 51, 62, 65, 80, 81, 94–5, 141, 166, 168–9, 189, 199
*The Fiscal Crisis of the State* (O'Connor) 66–7
Fisher, Irving 109
food imperialism 20–1
force
  legitimate monopoly of 60–1, 106
  modes of use 144–5
  problem of organization 191–2
  structural function of 58
Fordism 65, 66, 67, 108
foreign capital finance 22
fossil fuels 174
Foucault, Michel 3, 4, 5, 45, 67, 68, 73, 78, 87, 95, 97, 108, 164, 168, 177–8, 193, 199
  attitude to war 200
  *The Birth of Biopolitics* 55, 121, 123–5, 156
  civil war analysis 100–2
  on competition 55
  conception of capitalism 50–4
  critique of Marx 118
  critique of sovereignty 103, 104–5
  definition of power 154
  differentiation 82–3
  and human capital 109
  *Lectures on the Will to Know* 51
  on neoliberalism 120–1
  political instability 125–8
  and power 148, 149–52, 153–7
  and rationality 123–5
  reading of Nietzsche 149–51
  relation of power to truth 120–1
  shift from Marx to Weber 124–5
  *Society Must Be Defended* 126–7
  theory of human capital 114–15
fragmentation 186
France 18, 32–3, 63–4
  *gilets jaunes* [yellow vests] 2, 9, 181, 190
  Merzouk killing 85–6
  November 2015 attacks 86
  police and policing 85–7, 191–2
  revolt against pension reform 2, 9, 86, 191
  uprisings 2, 9–10, 85–7, 102, 181, 190–1, 196
Franco-German axis 7, 32
free market 17, 119–20
free spirits 186–7
freedom 75, 76, 114, 117, 178, 183, 185, 186–8, 195, 196–7
French Revolution 9, 59, 61, 77, 98–103, 99, 101
French Revolution, 1848 199
Friedman, Milton 95
Friedman, Thomas 37
functional analysis 154

G5 29
Galbraith, James 33
Gaza War 1
general equilibrium theory 132
generalized monopolies 67–8
geopolitics 63
Germany 18, 32, 32–3, 107
Giammetti, Raffaele 71
global imperialism 6
global South 36, 72, 102, 104, 111, 138, 165, 171, 196
  acceptance of capitalism 169
  American hegemony 4
  challenge to dollar hegemony 168
  civil war 161, 200
  and democracy 7, 75
  despoliation of 80
  dispossessed labour 117
  and globalization 142, 173
  growth 37

# Index

imports from 28–9
imperialism in 9
partition of 168–9
political-economic strength 173, 174
revolutions 89, 161, 199
uprisings 9
wars 84, 168
wars of liberation 168
global vision 168
globalization 9, 18, 38, 40, 42, 44, 62, 63, 156
   accumulation in 4
   ascendant phase 147
   balkanization 36–7, 172
   capital and 143
   cost 173
   destruction phase 164
   exchange in 4
   impossibility of bringing to fruition 46–7, 72–3, 74, 197
   rationality of 128
   reconfiguration 45
   space 146
   of war 94
   as world civil war 102
gold standard 17, 18
Gordon, Colin 53
governance 14, 45, 90, 97, 159, 200
governmental reason 125
governmentality 4, 6, 10, 14, 45, 47, 54, 91, 103, 115, 116–17, 118, 119, 124, 126, 127–8, 145, 149, 150, 152, 155, 157, 160, 188, 200
great acceleration, the 52
great depression (1873–95) 160
great financial crisis, 2008 2, 8, 9, 44, 88, 90, 120, 147–8, 173, 179
Greek debt crisis 32–3, 79
Greenspan, Alan 53
Guattari, Felix 8, 68, 100, 139–41, 157–8, 158–60, 161, 193
Guillibert, Paul 180

Hardt, Michael 3, 11, 42, 58, 100, 158, 194
Harvard International Relations 172
Harvey, David 161
Hayek, Friedrich 95
Hegel, G. W. F. 47
Hilferding, Rudolf 62

history 11, 193
Hobbes, Thomas 100
homeostasis 119
Hong Kong 31
hooks, bell 112n7, 114n9, 184
Hudson, Michael 16, 18
human capital 108–15
   and consumption 110–12
   anthropological change 110
   and debt 109–10
   definition 108–9
   financial exploitation 109
   the popular economy 112–14
   theory of 114–15
humanity, destiny of 39n21
'100 Orders', the 116–17

identity politics 188
ideology 14, 120–1
immanence and immanent power 39, 42, 46
immigrants, civil war on 88–9
imperialism 3, 11, 28–9, 72–3, 80
   American 4, 6, 26, 36, 43–4, 146–7, 148, 168, 172
   as analysis of power 148–58
   China 43–4
   collective 37
   colonial empires 142
   conceptualization 3–6, 38–41
   contradictions of 46
   cultural 38
   cycle of 118–20, 147–8
   double standard 103–8
   elimination of 124
   end of 65
   features of Lenin's 3
   global 6
   imperialist state-capital machine 62–5
   Lenin's analysis 14–16, 24
   linguistic 38
   as modern form of capitalism 41
   multiplicity of 146–7
   and neoliberalism 116–17
   as permanent phase of capitalism 158–62
   power of life and death 4
   predatory 3
   principles and rules of 5

imperialism (*continued*)
  regional 6
  relevance 15, 93
  return of 147–8
  Russia 43–4
  subjugation of forces 149
  subordination of neoliberalism to 54
  theoretical-political error 42–5
  Third World vision of 41
  transition to superimperialism 15–21
  United States of America 34
  way of acting 55
  zone of power 158
  zone of powerlessness 158
  *See also* dollar imperialism
*Imperialismo e classe operaia multinazionale* (Imperialism and the multinational working class) (Ferrari Bravo) 68
imperialist capitalism 3
imperialist policies 5–6
imperialist state-capital machine 62–5
impoverishment 186
imprisonment 115
indebtedness 22–3
India 20, 34, 169
individualization 77–8, 82, 186
industrial capital, investment flows 144–5
industrial war 81
inequality 154
infinite praxis 193
inflation 27, 32, 85
Institute for the Study of Long Term Economic Trends 129
institutional democracy 80, 88
insurgencies 2
insurrection 198
interclassism 111
interest rates 20, 23, 26, 27, 31, 107, 141
interest-producing capital 137
International Monetary Fund 20, 90, 159
intersectionality 195
investment banks 71
investment credit 24
investment flows 144–7
investment money 140
Iran 88
Iranian Revolution 84, 99, 196, 200
Iraq, occupation of 116–17

irrationality 128
Italy 7, 39

Japan 7, 18, 21, 29, 34, 37, 70, 75, 104
joint stock companies 69

Kalecki, Michal 22, 23, 93–4
Keynes, John Maynard 9, 17, 41n24
Keynesian compromise, the 191
Keynesianism 2, 136
Korean War 95
Koselleck, Reinhart 101

labour
  and capital 1–2
  concentration of 93–4
  disappearance of 111
  international division of 96–8
labour control 24
labour movement, decline of 180
Lacan, Jacques 75, 78
Latin American feminism 181–2, 183–4
Latour, Bruno 180
Laval, Christian 15, 53, 125
law, rule of 106
*Le Monde* (newspaper) 33–4
*Lectures on the Will to Know* (Foucault) 51
legal system 106
legislative power 75
Lenin, V. I. 3, 14–16, 20, 21, 23, 24, 25, 26, 51, 52, 62–5, 109, 149, 160, 161, 166–8, 169–71, 199
*Les Soulèvements de la Terre* (Earth Uprising) 85
Lévy, Dominique 21
Liang, Ciao 142
liberalism 53
life, management of 95
linguistic imperialism 37
liquid society 44
liquidity 26, 173
Lucarelli, Stefano 71
Lucas, Robert 122
Lula da Silva, Luiz Inácio 35
Luxemburg, Rosa 3, 16, 21, 22, 40–1, 42–3, 51, 62, 143, 174, 176

M15 movement 192
Malvinas War (1982) 27

# Index

Mao Zedong 101, 176
Maoism 34, 101, 155
market, the 54–6, 71, 137
market economy 28–9
market forces 5
Marx, Karl 3, 15, 41, 43, 51, 62–3, 69, 73, 81, 82, 108, 109, 149, 153, 155, 161, 171, 184, 199
   analysis of accumulation 42–3
   and crisis 15
   Foucault's critique of 118
   Luxemburg's critique of 42–3
   M—M' formula 135, 138
   on nationalism 46
   on political centralization 59–60
   shift from 124–5
   theory of money 131, 133–9
   and triple centralization 56–8
   and truth 122–3
Marxism 149–50, 177
   Amin's critique of Western 160–2
mass indebtedness policy 23
mass uprising 180
massification 186
mega-profits 40
Melandri, Lea 180
Meloni, Giorgia 7
Merzouk, Nahel, killing of 85–6
Mexican Revolution 99
micropolitics 149, 153
Middle Ages 110–11
military centralization 5, 60–1, 63
military expenditures 18, 23, 85
military-industrial complex 89
military-political strategy 45
Mini, Fabio 30
modernity 98–9
monetarist position 133
monetary monopoly 71–2
monetary stability 107
monetary system 20
monetization, of society 131
money 112, 139
   automatism of 136, 138–9
   control of time 131–2
   creation 140–1
   credit/debt system 130–2
   destruction 140–1
   emergence of 129–30, 131
   foundation 143–4
   history of 130–3
   influences 133
   Marxian theory of 133–9
   neutrality of 132–3, 133
   and political power 132
   as political strategy 130–1
   price of 71
   production of 130
   theories of 129–41
   true nature of 130
   virtual 130
money flows 143
   and power 139–41
Monferrand, Frédéric 180
monopoly 3, 4, 6, 22, 62–3, 65, 70–1, 89, 93–4
   banking 57–8
   and competition 65–7, 72, 106
   generalized 67–8
   Marxian theory of 131
   monetary 71–2
   sovereignty 73–4
monopoly capitalism 101
monopoly economy 66–7
monopoly rents 40
multinational corporations 146
multiplicity 151–2, 191, 197

national capitalism 46
national liberation, wars of 1
nationalism 45–7
NATO 29, 36
Nazi Germany 95–6
Nazism 95–6, 149, 156
negative, the
   positivization of 125
   rejection of 10–11
negative action 87
negative power 51, 52, 78
Negri, Antonio 3, 11, 39, 42, 58, 100, 194
neocolonialism 5
neoliberal rationality 123
neoliberal/biopolitical narrative 13–14
neoliberalism 5, 5–6, 14, 47, 87, 89, 90–1, 115, 120, 147, 148, 168
   acceleration of centralization 90
   and centralization 70–2

neoliberalism (*continued*)
  comparison with capitalism 49–54,
    54–6
  conception of capitalism 108
  conceptualization 120–3
  and dollar imperialism 97–8, 123
  double standard 103–8
  failure of 118–19
  governance 97
  governmentality 10, 116–17, 119, 188
  as ideology 120–1
  ignoring of the dollar 53
  and imperialism 116–17
  pillars 54
  positive conception of power 52–3
  rationality of 125
  regime of truth 120–1
  subordination to imperialism 54
  and war 93–6, 97–8
new political phase 171–5
*The New Way of the World: On Neoliberal Society* (Dardot and Laval) 125
*New York Times* (newspaper) 37
Nietzsche, Friedrich 120, 130–1, 148–51, 154, 158
Nixon, Richard 18
non-contemporaneity 182n18
non-political power 80
non-Western 88–9
Nord Stream 2 8, 89

O'Connor, James 66
oil prices 19, 36
oil production 36
oligarchy 8, 51, 89–91, 115
oligopolies 71
OPEC 19, 36
*operaismo* 41, 62, 65, 126
Operation Condor 95
oppression 149–50, 151–2
ordoliberalism 14, 50, 52–3, 53, 54, 70–1, 94, 95–6, 97, 107–8, 120, 121, 147, 148, 168
organization, building 191–3

Paris Commune 67, 101
participation 79
Pasolini, Pier Paulo 75, 78
peace 96–7, 117, 126, 167–8

Pentagon 19
Peru 115
petrodollars, recycling 36
Philippines, the, financial crisis, 1987 27–8
Pinochet, Augusto 95
planning 105
Poland 7, 32
Polanyi, Karl 129
polarization 47, 75, 90, 120, 155, 161–2
police and policing 85–7, 98, 191–2
political capitalism 147
political centralization 5, 59–60, 63, 80, 84, 94, 115
political difference 151
political economy 73, 104–5, 130–1
political machine, the 159
political movements, post-'68 14
political power 14, 158
political practice 83–4
political ruptures 192
political Spinozism 98, 193
political strategies 5
political theology 39n21
political totalization 73
political-economic-military strategy 130
political-military strategy 40, 84
political-organizational activity 176
politics
  definition 13
  return of 200–1
  time of 199
popular economy, the 112–13, 185
populism 47, 91, 192
positive action 87
positive power 51, 52, 78–9
positivization, of the negative 125
power 10, 149–51, 185
  and capital 149
  centralization of 69–70
  centres of 155–6
  concentration of 56
  and debt 130
  definition 154
  Deleuze and 149–50, 152, 153, 154, 155–6, 157–8
  forms 176
  Foucault and 148, 149–52, 153–7
  imperialism as analysis of 148–58

# Index

international division of 96–8
limit 155
microphysics of 153
and money flows 139–41
negative action 87
Nietzschean perspective 149–51
political 14, 158
positive action 87
productive force 155
purpose of 188
relation to truth 120–1
seizure of 189–90
state-capital machine 189
threefold centralization of 5
verticalization of 70
zone of powerlessness 157–8
power flows 145–6
power hierarchy 97
power relations 5, 35, 97, 137, 138, 149–52, 153–8, 181–3, 191, 194
practices of freedom 186–8
precarious labour 185
precarization 5
predatory imperialism 3
presidentialism 80, 83
price setting 71, 72
primitive accumulation 100, 101, 160–1
privatization 5, 186
production 11
  civil war analysis 99–100
  concentration of 93–4
  decentralization of 28
  and destruction 188–9
  socialization of 65
productive forces/relations of production 188–9
productive power 125
productivity 52, 67
profit 51–2, 64, 67, 68, 186
*Proletari senza rivoluzione* (Proletarians without revolution) (Del Carria) 198–9
proletarian revolutions, nineteenth century 59
proletarian separation 181–3
proletariat 82, 180, 181, 190
  advance of 186–8
  American 34
  conditions for existence of 100
  female 181–2
  multiplicity 182, 182n18
  power of 159n 22
psychoanalysis 114
public debt, role of 136
public opinion 170–1
public spending 22
punishments, disproportionate 87

Qiao, Liang 25–6, 28, 28–9

race relations 181
racism 181
radical ruptures 175–9
rationality 123–5, 128
Reagan, Ronald 1, 84, 159
real capital 135
recession 20
redistributive policies 5
reflexive moment, the 195
reformism 192
regional imperialism 6
relative distinct totalization 156
religion 110–11
rent 51–2, 57, 64, 108, 131
rentier economy 8
repression 125
reproduction, management of 82–3
resource distribution 45
revolt, aestheticization of 198
revolution 8–10, 94, 171, 175–9, 183, 194–5, 196–201
revolutionary becoming 178–9
revolutionary civil war, constituent power 98–103
revolutionary movements 198
revolutionary process 198
revolutionary rupture 166
revolutionary subject, the 186–8, 192–3, 194
revolutionary workers' movement 187
Roig, Alexandre 113–14
Roussellier, Nicolas 80
rupture
  double 196
  moments of rupture 195
  political 192
  radical 175–9
Russia 7, 34, 165
  imperialism 43–4

Russia (*continued*)
  oligarchy 89
  regional imperialism 6
  Russian Revolution 9, 89, 99, 166

Sandoval, Yousef 39n21
Saudi Arabia 36
Schmitt, Carl 38–9, 77–8, 81, 101, 110
Schumpeter, Joel 174
Schumpeterianism 2
Second World War 3, 16, 76, 94–5
Shanghai Cooperation Organisation (SCO) 35
'68 movement 178, 179, 194
slavery 183
Smith, Adam 104–5
social classes, definition 13
social democracy 75, 79–80
social expenditures, reduction of 85
social movements 4, 87, 88, 175–9, 180, 191, 193, 195, 196, 198–9
socialism, threat of 89
socialization 186
society
  monetization of 131
  multiplicity 151–2
*Society Must Be Defended* (Foucault) 126–7
Soros, George 27–8
South-East Asia, financial crisis, 1987 27–8
sovereign centralization 160
sovereign monetary creation 140–1
sovereign power 39–40, 143
sovereign privilege 20, 140–1
sovereign's right, the 4
sovereignty 4, 38–9, 42, 43, 60, 67, 72, 83–4, 98, 103–5, 144, 155–6, 158
Soviet Union, collapse of 3, 30, 101, 147, 167
Spain 192
Spanish Civil War 99, 199
stagnation 23, 67, 70
stasis 100
state, the
  and capital 3–4, 147–8
  definition 13
  Deleuze and 157
  demise of 98
  dependence of capital on 143–4
  legitimacy 43
  relationship to capital 38–41, 42–5
  return of 147, 164
  stakes 165
  state intervention 56, 65, 66, 72, 119–20, 142, 143–4, 146, 147–8
  state monopoly capitalism 158–62
  state mutation 175
  state of emergency 86–7
  state power, centralization of 59–60
  state relations 15
state-capital machine 11, 38–9, 39n21, 40
  American 71
  catastrophe production 166
  and centralization 65
  and class compromise 188
  and credit 24
  and economic laws 130
  form 68
  framework 141–4
  government precedes 157
  imperialist 62–5
  impossibilities 197
  limit 155
  modes of governance 90
  policy role 84
  power 189
  power relations 185
  and revolution 94
  sovereignty 119
  strategic programme 191–2
  and war 72–3
state-capital war machine 103, 143, 147
state-controlled economy 66–7
Stiegler, Barbara 53
stock ownership 71
structural-adjustment policies 79
subjectification 112
subjective becoming 178
subprime stock 108
superimperialism 16, 66–7, 95, 96–7
supply and demand, law of 67, 71
surplus value 22, 42–3
Sweezy, Paul 22, 24, 24–5, 63, 69–70, 75, 110

taxation 173
technological innovation 66
techno-scientific sovereignty 105

# Index

Thatcher, Margaret 1, 84, 116, 159
Thiel, Peter 55–6
Thucydides's Trap 172
time 131–2, 199
Tocqueville, Alexis de 76–7, 110
total war 80–1, 102, 103
totalization 72–4, 155, 156, 182–3, 187
trade unions 112, 113
transcendent power 39–40
Trilateral Commission 84
triple centralization 56–8
Tronti, Mario 39
Trotsky, Leon 62
true/false concepts 121–3
Trump, Donald 90, 114
truth 120–3

Ukraine War 1, 3, 14, 18, 31–2, 35, 71, 72, 84, 118, 163
   causes 35–6, 169–70
   and the energy crisis 174
   Germany and 107
   outbreak 167
   unbalancing force, of capitalism 54
   unequal development, logic of 41
United Kingdom 17, 27, 32, 64
United States of America
   '2022 National Defense Strategy' 37
   America First initiative 172–3
   arms production 8
   attack on the euro 29
   automobile industry 108
   balance of payments deficit 17–20, 22
   Bipartisan Innovation Act 6–7n1
   capital-state machine 14
   Chinese imports 28–9
   colonies 30–1
   creditor countries 19–20
   criminal policy 115
   debt 4
   disproportionate power of currency 17
   economic constitution 107
   economic sectors 66–7
   endless war 142
   Europe as colony of 7–8
   exports 22
   finance, insurance, and real estate industries 89–90
   financial capture 25–9
   food imperialism 20–1
   global vision 168
   hegemony 4, 7, 16–21, 163
   imperialism 4, 6, 21–4, 26, 34, 36, 43–4, 146–7, 148, 168, 172
   imports 22, 28–9
   imprisonment levels 115
   inflation 27
   interest rates 26, 27
   internal civil war 34
   legal system 106
   low-intensity civil war 119
   military bases abroad 31
   military expenditures 18, 23
   military-industrial complex 89
   monetary financial imperialism 6
   national security 19
   need to destroy 49
   the New Deal 76
   new form of colonization 7–8
   occupation of Iraq 116–17
   O'Connor's review of economy 66–7
   oil, gas, and mining lobby 89
   oligarchical lobbies 89–90
   oligarchy 8, 89–91
   overseas military operations 30–1
   polarization 34
   political-military strategy 40
   relationship with China 36–8
   revolutionary processes extinguished 184
   sovereign privilege 20
   sovereignty 72
   state-capital machine 71, 119
   state-capital sovereignty 104
   undeclared war with Europe 31–4
   as universal debtor 17–20
   view of allies 32
   wages 34
   and war 25–31
universalization 46
US Department of Defense, '2022 National Defense Strategy' 37
US Treasury bonds 19, 29–30
US–UK–East-European-countries axis 7

value chains 4, 36, 84
variable-dimension liberalism 19
Varoufakis, Yanis 33

vassal states 104
Vietnam War 95
Vietnamese Revolution 94, 99
violence 58
  industrial capital 145
  legitimate monopoly of 60–1
  structural function of 58
virtual money 130

wage flows 140
wage labour 138, 145, 185, 186
wages 5, 34, 68, 109, 111–12, 114, 186
Walmart 30
Walras, Léon 132
war 3, 34, 45
  abandonment of 123–4
  attacker/attacked dualism 170–1
  balancing function of 120
  and capital 96–8, 170–1
  as capitalism's regime of truth 2–3
  cause 6–7
  and centralization 61, 72–4
  coexistance with peace 126
  conceptualization 6–12
  consequences of 35–8
  contingency of 194
  continuities/discontinuities 176–7
  cycle of 118
  and debt 130
  deep 80–1
  dollar imperialism relationship to 24–31, 165
  economists and 24–5
  Foucault's attitude to 200
  globalization of 94
  industrial 81
  integration into the state-capital machine 94
  Lenin's analysis 15, 166–7, 167–8, 170–1
  modes of 155
  and neoliberalism 93–6, 97–8
  new political phase 171–5

  political and temporal breaches 175–9
  relationship with the economy 4, 23, 94, 96–8
  response to 13–14
  and revolution 176
  rise to the forefront 94
  role of 24–5, 65
  stakes 9, 165
  and state-capital machine 72–3
  time of 195
  total 80–1
  totalization 72–4
  understanding 165–70
'War and Revolution' (Lenin) 166–7
war debt 16–17
war/economy relationship 94, 96–8
waste 70
wealth appropriation and capture 131, 137
Weber, Max 124–5
Weil, Simone 61
Weimar Republic 96
welfare, destruction of 2
West, the
  material weakness 36
  stakes 165
  supremacy 6–7
  values 7, 169
Western civilization, end of 163–4
Western Marxism, Amin's critique of 160–2
Westphalia, Treaty of 98
wills to power 150–1
workerism 41
workers 144
World Bank 90, 159
world conflict 80–1
world market 15, 62, 138, 143, 145–7

Xi Jinping 8n2, 34

Yugoslavia 29, 31

Zapatista solution, the 189–90